Women's Poetry

Edinburgh Critical Guides to Literature
Series Editors: Martin Halliwell, University of Leicester and
Andy Mousley, De Montfort University

Published Titles:
Gothic Literature, Andrew Smith
Canadian Literature, Faye Hammill
Women's Poetry, Jo Gill
Contemporary American Drama, Annette J. Saddik
Shakespeare, Gabriel Egan

Forthcoming Titles in the Series:
Asian American Literature, Bella Adams
Children's Literature, M. O. Grenby
Eighteenth-Century Literature, Hamish Mathison
Contemporary British Fiction, Nick Bentley
Contemporary American Fiction, David Brauner
Victorian Literature, David Amigoni
Crime Fiction, Stacy Gillis
Renaissance Literature, Siobhan Keenan
Modern American Literature, Catherine Morley
Scottish Literature, Gerard Carruthers
Romantic Literature, Richard Marggraf Turley
Modernist Literature, Rachel Potter
Medieval Literature, Pamela King
Women's Fiction, Sarah Sceats

Women's Poetry

Jo Gill

Edinburgh University Press

© Jo Gill, 2007

Edinburgh University Press Ltd
22 George Square, Edinburgh

Typeset in Ehrhardt
by Servis Filmsetting Ltd, Manchester, and
printed and bound in Great Britain by
Antony Rowe Ltd, Chippenham, Wilts

A CIP record for this book is available from the British Library

ISBN 978 0 7486 2305 1 (hardback)
ISBN 978 0 7486 2306 8 (paperback)

The right of Jo Gill
to be identified as author of this work
has been asserted in accordance with
the Copyright, Designs and Patents Act 1988.

Contents

Series Preface

The study of English literature in the early twenty-first century is host to an exhilarating range of critical approaches, theories and historical perspectives. 'English' ranges from traditional modes of study such as Shakespeare and Romanticism to popular interest in national and area literatures such as the United States, Ireland and the Caribbean. The subject also spans a diverse array of genres from tragedy to cyberpunk, incorporates such hybrid fields of study as Asian American literature, Black British literature, creative writing and literary adaptations, and remains eclectic in its methodology.

Such diversity is cause for both celebration and consternation. English is varied enough to promise enrichment and enjoyment for all kinds of readers and to challenge preconceptions about what the study of literature might involve. But how are readers to navigate their way through such literary and cultural diversity? And how are students to make sense of the various literary categories and periodisations, such as modernism and the Renaissance, or the proliferating theories of literature, from feminism and Marxism to queer theory and eco-criticism? The Edinburgh Critical Guides to Literature series reflects the challenges and pluralities of English today, but at the same time it offers readers clear and accessible routes through the texts, contexts, genres, historical periods, and debates within the subject.

Martin Halliwell and Andy Mousley

Acknowledgements

Thanks are due, first and foremost, to the School of English and Creative Studies at Bath Spa University which supported this research in its early stages. Honourable mentions go to Ian Gadd, Tracey Hill, Jenni Lewis and Tim Middleton. Subsequently, colleagues in the Department of English at the University of Exeter – in particular, Margaretta Jolly and Jane Poyner – have taken up the slack while the book was completed. Participants in the 'Women and Poetry in the Twenty-First Century' conference held in Bristol in 2006 have informed and stimulated my thinking in the field. Martin Halliwell and Andrew Mousley's editorial guidance has been appreciated, as have the insights of the proposal's anonymous readers and the work of Jackie Jones and others at Edinburgh University Press. Finally, I owe a particular debt to the scholarship and friendship of Alice Entwistle.

The author and publishers are grateful to the following for permission to print extracts from poems:

Eavan Boland and Carcanet Press Limited for lines from 'The Journey' in *New Collected Poems* (2005).

Lines from 'Visions of Mexico While at a Writing Symposium in Port Townsend, Washington' from *Emplumada*, by Lorna Dee Cervantes, © 1982. Reprinted by permission of the University of Pittsburgh Press.

Lines from 'The Mirror Trade' by Zoë Skoulding (Seren, 2005). Reprinted by permission of Seren Books.

Lines from 'Epilogue' by Grace Nichols in *i is a long memoried woman* (1983) reprinted by permission of Karnak House.

Chronology

The chronology identifies key historical and literary moments; it does not provide an exhaustive list of the texts cited in this book. Additional publication dates and other contextual material is provided throughout the text and in the endnotes and list of works cited. The primary source for the material outlined below is Peter Widdowson, *The Palgrave Guide to Literature and its Contexts 1500–2000* (Basingstoke: Palgrave Macmillan, 2004).

Date	Historical events	Literary events
Late 7th *c.*– early 6th *c.*		Sappho lived and wrote poetry on the Greek island of Lesbos
BCE		
c. 43–420	Roman conquest of England	
CE		
432	St Patrick's mission to bring Christianity to Ireland	
658–80		Earliest known poem in English, *Caedmon's Hymn*
c. 750		*Beowulf*

Date	Historical events	Literary events
1066	Norman conquest of England	
c. 1304–21		Dante, *Divine Comedy*
c. 1375–1400		*Sir Gawain and the Green Knight*
1476	Caxton's first printing press	
1492	Christopher Columbus sails to the Bahamas	
1499	Amerigo Vespucci sails to South America	
1509	Henry VIII takes the English throne	
1525	Tyndale's translation of the New Testament into English	
1527	First African slaves taken to America	
1532–4	Henry VIII declares himself head of the Church in England; English Reformation begins.	
1533	Elizabeth Tudor (Elizabeth I) born	
1536–9	Dissolution of the Monasteries	
1539	First printing press in the Americas (Mexico City)	
1548–9	*Book of Common Prayer* to be used in English churches	

Date	Historical events	Literary events
1553	Mary I (Mary Tudor) takes the throne	
1554–5	Elizabeth Tudor (later Elizabeth I) imprisoned at Woodstock	Elizabeth Tudor 'Woodstock' poems
1558	Elizabeth I takes to throne on the death of Mary I	
1573		Isabella Whitney, 'The Manner of her Will'
1577	Sir Francis Drake circumnavigates the globe	
1587	Shakespeare begins acting	
1588	Translation of Bible into Welsh	
1593		Mary Sidney, *Psalms*
1603	Elizabeth I dies. James VI of Scotland (I of England) to throne; authorised (*King James*) version of the Bible	
1611		Aemilia Lanyer, *Salve Deus Rex Judaeorum*
1612	Persecution of Lancashire witches	
1620	'Pilgrim Fathers' to America in *The Mayflower*	
1620–1		Mary Wroth, *Love's Victory*
1625	James I dies; Charles I to throne	

Date	Historical events	Literary events
1640		Charles I, *Eikon Basilike*
1649	Charles I executed; Oliver Cromwell's Republic declared	
1649–60	The Interregnum	
1650		Anne Bradstreet, *The Tenth Muse*
1653		Margaret Cavendish, Duchess of Newcastle, *Poems and Fancies*
1658	Cromwell dies	
1660–1	The Restoration; Charles II to throne	
1666	Great Fire of London	Margaret Cavendish, *The Blazing World*
1667		Katherine Philips, *Collected Poems*
1702	Queen Anne to the throne	
1709–10	First English copyright act	
1713		Anne Finch, Countess of Winchilsea, *Written by a Lady*
1773		Anna Laetitia Barbauld, *Poems*
1775	American War of Independence begins	
1784		Charlotte Smith, *Elegiac Sonnets*

Date	Historical events	Literary events
1785		Ann Yearsley, *Poems, On Several Occasions*
1788		Hannah More, 'Slavery; A Poem'
1789–94	French Revolution	
1792		Mary Wollstonecraft, *A Vindication of the Rights of Woman*
1796		Anna Seward, *Llangollen Vale, with Other Poems*
1801	United Kingdom of Great Britain and Ireland formed	
1808		Felicia Hemans, *Poems*
1837	Queen Victoria to the throne	
1844		Elizabeth Barrett Browning, *Poems*
1846		Brontë sisters, *Poems by Currer, Ellis and Acton Bell*
1846–8	US war against Mexico	
c. 1847	Irish Potato Famine	
1848	Seneca Falls Women's Rights Convention	
1857		Elizabeth Barrett Browning, *Aurora Leigh*
c. 1860–5		Emily Dickinson writing

Date	Historical events	Literary events
1861–5	American Civil War; 13th Amendment abolishing slavery (1865)	
1862		Christina Rossetti, *Goblin Market*
1875	London Medical School for Women established	
1877	Jim Crow laws (US)	
1901	Queen Victoria dies; Edward VII to throne	
1914	Women's suffrage campaigns; outbreak of First World War	
1916	Easter Rising (Ireland)	Charlotte Mew, *The Farmer's Bride*
1918	End of First World War	
1921		Marianne Moore, *Poetry*
1922		Edith Sitwell, *Façade*
1924		H. D., *Heliodora*
1929	US Stock Market crash, Great Depression	Virginia Woolf, *A Room of One's Own*
1936–9	Spanish Civil War	
1939–45	Second World War	
1952	Contraceptive Pill first introduced	
1957		Stevie Smith, *Not Waving but Drowning*
1962	Cuban Missile Crisis	

Date	Historical events	Literary events
1964	US Civil Rights Act	
1965		Sylvia Plath, *Ariel* (posthumous)
1965–73	Vietnam War	
1966	US National Organization for Women established	
1978		U. A. Fanthorpe, *Side Effects*
1979		Denise Levertov, *Collected Earlier Poems 1940–1960*
1982		Medbh McGuckian, *The Flower Master*
1983		Grace Nichols, *i is a long memoried woman*
1990		Eavan Boland, *Outside History*
1991		Jackie Kay, *The Adoption Papers*
1992	South Africa grants legal equality to blacks	
1994	Church of England ordains first women priests	
1996		Anne Stevenson, *Collected Poems*
2004		Sylvia Plath, *Ariel: The Restored Edition*

Prologue

It has become something of a commonplace in critical surveys of poetry by women to announce the heterogeneity, complexity and richness of the field. Robyn Bolam's 2005 anthology, *Eliza's Babes: Four Centuries of Women's Poetry in English*, for example, 'brings together as wide a variety of female voices as possible to give readers a better understanding of the range and diversity of poetry in English through these centuries'.[1] Jane Dowson notes, with reference to her 1996 anthology, *Women's Poetry in the 1930s*, that 'editors of anthologies of women's poetry, myself included [. . .] tend to claim "diversity" as the outstanding feature of their contents'.[2] However, Dowson proceeds to recognise the need to define and classify the object of study in order to make any meaningful assessment of it. This is a view with which I concur; it is important to nuance or qualify any claim to diversity.

If poetry by women is disparate and heterogeneous, on what grounds do we study it as a distinct strand within the larger poetic genre? More pressingly, perhaps, how would we justify the focus of a book such as this Edinburgh Critical Guide? In other words, if all that can be said about poetry by women is that it is various, why do students study it, publishers publish it and critics write about it as a coherent body of work? It is difficult, on the one hand, to claim diversity as one of the hallmarks of women's poetry and, on the other, to point to some kind of homogeneity or sameness as its characteristic feature. If we make the former claim, it proves almost impossible to find any meaningful or lasting points of connection across and between distinct periods, modes, poets and texts. The risk of such a broad approach is that we are left unable to say anything, unable to suggest any points of influence, comparison or significance. This arguably does a disservice to the shifting currents, cross-currents and counter-currents which a close reading of poetry by women over successive generations and across different cultures clearly brings to light. On the other hand, to opt for asserting that there is some kind of essential unity of theme, form, voice, language or concern at the heart of women's writing generates even more problems. Such an approach implies an unmediated relationship between female experience and its representation. It also risks ignoring the specific historical, cultural and ideological circumstances in which individual women's poetry has been produced and read.

According to Vicki Bertram:

> Unless used within a specific context, 'women's poetry' implies a uniformity that is derogatory and inaccurate [. . .] its shortcomings now outweigh its usefulness: not only does it collapse differences between women, it also encourages comparison of women poets with men poets, as though there is some fundamental opposition between them.[3]

And although to a large extent I share Bertram's misgivings about the use of the catch-all term 'women's poetry' (in preference to the rather more nuanced 'women and poetry'), I also justify using it in the 'specific context' of this book and as a recognisable and necessary shorthand for a complex nexus of issues, qualifications, reservations and concerns. This volume seeks to recognise heterogeneity and to remain alert to the multiplicity of contexts, experiences and forms evidenced in women's poetry. It looks for areas of common ground which, however narrow and meandering, are shared by women's poetry of different periods, cultures and modes. The starting point of this study (Chapter 1) is the suggestion that such common ground might be found in the self-reflexivity or self-consciousness evidenced in women's poetry. It is here, I suggest, that we see unity within diversity.

In terms of methodology, each of the following seven themed chapters nominates a number of different poets through whose work and reception relevant issues and arguments are examined. The book rejects a chronological approach in favour of one which picks up thematic and stylistic concerns across different periods and which places disparate poets in productive proximity. Nevertheless, it does give detailed consideration throughout to questions of historical and cultural context, asking, for example, about the reception of women poets in their own time and about their relationship to larger literary movements such as Romanticism and modernism. In the introduction to her 1975 anthology, *Salt and Bitter and Good: Three Centuries of English and American Women Poets*, Cora Kaplan poses the question of 'what it has meant, over some 300 years, to be a woman and a poet'.[4] My own book continues this line of enquiry.

The book begins with a discussion of self-reflexivity, then moves on to consider poetry and performance (Chapter 2), private, embodied and public voices (Chapters 3 to 5), poetry and place (Chapter 6) and finally, experimentation and form. A closing section offers guidance on study skills and recommends useful resources. A number of key poets appear in successive chapters of the book, thus allowing continuity across different themes and permitting an exploration of the ways in which certain poets have addressed a variety of issues. Other poets feature less frequently, and in association with specific arguments where their work suggests or exemplifies particular points. Every chapter provides lengthy close analyses of a small number of poems, coupled with briefer readings of and commentaries on a wider selection of texts.

The selection of poems has been guided by a number of factors. With an audience of students and interested general readers in mind, I have tried to reflect the current 'canon' of poetry by women – that is, to offer readers some new ways of thinking about poets and texts which are fairly widely collected, anthologised, read and studied. However, I have also striven to offer some new, unexpected and stimulating work – poetry which has not yet made it into the mainstream. The intention has been to provide ideas, readings, perspectives and questions which will serve as a starting point for the reader's own exploration of the field. Finally, I have endeavoured to look beyond the horizons of the dominant 'lyric' mode of poetry (more on which in Chapter 3) within whose confines the apparent 'diversity' of women's poetry has often been identified. Marjorie Perloff has said that 'the equation of poetry with the lyric is almost axiomatic in contemporary criticism', and I share her reservations about the adequacy of this to a full appreciation of the variety and innovation in recent work.[5] To fully address the richness of poetry by women, we need to look at a range of poetries from myth and fairytale forms to elegy, verse fiction, 'slam' and performance poetry, and the radically innovative 'Language' poetry of the present day. I have attempted to reflect some of these broader stages in my selection here.

Marianne Moore famously declared that 'omissions are not accidents'.[6] Fleur Adcock rather more contentiously invoked this saying in defence of her own editorial policy in *The Faber Book of Twentieth-Century Women's Poetry* (1987). In the spirit of the rejection, or at least rethinking, of binary models implicit throughout this book, I wish to say that omissions are neither accidental nor deliberate. They are, rather, inevitable. One of the aims of this book is to discuss a full range of poetry by women. Given the enormity of the field it is, of course, unthinkable that one might cover any more than a small proportion of the material available. I have therefore chosen to offer a sampling – of texts, periods, genres, poets, voices and forms. Primarily, although not exclusively, the focus is on poetry written in English by British and American poets, and I regret that for reasons of space it has not been possible to range more widely. Nevertheless, I hope that many of the ideas and perspectives suggested here will be relevant to a range of other contexts. *Women's Poetry* aims to proffer some useful ways of thinking about poetry by women and some initial readings in the hope that these will engender each reader's own thoughts, questions, ideas and interpretations of their favoured poets and texts.

NOTES

1. Robyn Bolam, *Eliza's Babes: Four Centuries of Women's Poetry in English, c. 1500–1900* (Newcastle: Bloodaxe, 2005), p. 20.

2. Jane Dowson, ' "Older Sisters are Very Sobering Things": Contemporary Women Poets and the Female Affiliation Complex', *Feminist Review*, 62 (1999), 6–20, 13.
3. Vicki Bertram, *Gendering Poetry: Contemporary Women and Men Poets* (London: Pandora, 2005), p. 20.
4. Cora Kaplan, *Salt and Bitter and Good: Three Centuries of English and American Women Poets* (New York and London: Paddington Press, 1975), p. 11.
5. Marjorie Perloff, *The Dance of the Intellect: Studies in the Poetry of the Pound Tradition* (Cambridge: Cambridge University Press, 1985), p. 159.
6. Quoted in Bonnie Costello, *Marianne Moore: Imaginary Possessions* (Cambridge, MA and London: Harvard University Press, 1981), p. 12. Fleur Adcock (ed.), *The Faber Book of Twentieth-Century Women's Poetry* (London: Faber and Faber, 1987).

Introduction

The aim in this book is to draw on the insights of recent feminist scholarship, but not to be restricted to this perspective or to a body of work which might be defined as 'feminist' in any historically specific way. The 'Women's Poetry' of the title is not, then, necessarily or always a synonym for feminist poetry; instead, it encapsulates a whole range of concerns and interests – about women as poets, women as readers, women as speakers and addressees, and women as objects and subjects of the text.

A FEMINIST FRAMEWORK

The term 'feminist' is raised here, and it is important at this point to outline something of the history, the permutations, the potential and the limitations of the term when used in the context of literary studies. Throughout the twentieth century, successive waves of feminist criticism have offered a range of different ways of thinking about women – as subjects and objects, as producers and consumers of the literary text. In brief, in the 1960s and 1970s, renewed attention (renewed because it revisits the concerns of Enlightenment, *fin de siècle* and modernist movements) was placed on the representation of women in literature and their exclusion, as writers, from the literary canon. Key figures in this early period included Mary Ellmann's *Thinking about Women* (1968) and Kate Millett's *Sexual*

Politics (1969). From this grew a hugely influential group of studies which emphasised the role of the woman as writer, as a spokesperson for the experience of her gender, and as a potential force of resistance against patriarchal culture. Chief among the proponents of this 'gynocritical' approach were Sandra M. Gilbert and Susan Gubar with their *Madwoman in the Attic: The Woman Writer and the Nineteenth-Century Literary Imagination* and *Shakespeare's Sisters: Feminist Essays on Women Poets* (both 1979), Elaine Showalter's 1977 book, *A Literature of their Own: British Women Novelists from Brontë to Lessing*, and Ellen Moers with *Literary Women* (1976).

A new 'French feminist' criticism emerged from this point onwards. This perspective (or rather set of philosophies and practices) merges poststructuralist and psychoanalytic thought with a new attentiveness to language – specifically the language of the body. Hélène Cixous, Luce Irigaray and Julia Kristeva are, as we shall see later, the key figures in this field. More recently, a move away from a notion of a female-specific criticism to a broader notion of 'gender studies' (which is also aligned in a number of respects with 'queer theory') has come to the fore. Queer theory puts sexuality or sexual orientation centre stage. It arises in part as a response to the marginalisation of sexuality in some of the groundbreaking books about women's writing cited above (and in that way its marginalisation from the new or 'counter' canon of women's writing established by Gilbert and Gubar, Moers et al.) and in part as a consequence of a broader contemporary rethinking of the nature of identity or subjectivity as a construction. From this point of view, subjectivity – our sense of personal identity or the position in and from which we experience, think and speak – is not fixed and innate. Rather, subjectivity is generated and shaped by a range of factors – by language, by ideology, by unconscious processes, by our particular circumstances in place and time. Queer theory challenges the firmness of many of the distinctions which conventional critical theory, including feminist theory, takes for granted – distinctions between man and woman, gay and straight, for instance – and it questions the hierarchy implicit in these distinctions. Drawing on poststructuralist thought, it recognises that the meaning of any of these terms is dependent upon and contains traces of the other (so, to recognise the signification of straight, we must implicitly also recognise the traces of queerness which sustain it). Such an approach (characterised by the work of, for example, Judith Butler and Jeffrey Weeks) is interested in reading the provisionality and aporia of language as it grapples to represent sexual identity. Another current theme in literary studies is the recognition of the impossibility of separating out gender studies from broader discourses of subjectivity, language and power – hence a new body of work which thinks in terms of postcolonialism (Gayatri Chakravorty Spivak) or postmodernism (Patricia Waugh, Linda Hutcheon).[1]

CRITICAL PERSPECTIVES

One of the issues which arises when undertaking a survey of the kind proposed in this book relates to the challenges associated with suggesting connections across periods of time and vast cultural differences. Can we make any meaningful association between, say, Aemilia Lanyer's appropriation of the voice of the wife of Pilate in the 1611 poem 'Salve Deus Rex Judaeorum' or Charlotte Brontë's mid-nineteenth-century poem 'Pilate's Wife's Dream' and Carol Ann Duffy's even more recent annexing of the story in 'Pilate's Wife' (1999)? One answer is that although, of course, there are huge differences between each poet's literary, cultural and indeed spiritual context, all begin to some, albeit varying, extent from the position of the outsider or 'other' whose relationship to the dominant patriarchal culture (and thus to its stories and its modes of representation) is always defined by the dominant group. These women poets' understanding and acceptance or manipulation of their position may vary from period to period, from culture to culture and, most importantly, from individual to individual. Nevertheless, it is this sense of writing from a position outside or beyond the mainstream which, arguably, all share.

I do not wish necessarily to speak in terms of centre and margins in this context, or to define women's poetry in terms of its ex-centricity (its externality in relation to the central circle), even though such a case has been persuasively argued of late (for example by Alice Entwistle). Such a perspective, although fruitful in some cases such as in relation to some of the modernist poets discussed later, risks occluding the complexity of women's experience and cultural production. Even in relation to modernism, to speak of the centre and the margins is to suggest a singularity of cultural expression which belies the multiple, overlapping, concentric circles in which women poets perhaps operate. It may be more useful, as the contemporary Chicana critic and writer Gloria Anzaldúa has proposed, to think not in terms of in/out, or centre and margins, but in terms of liminal, border positions.[2] The borderlands, for Anzaldúa, are a 'place of contradictions' but a place which, nevertheless, has compensations not least in the stimulus this position offers to the articulation of a new consciousness, a new perspective. As Chapter 6 shows, Anzaldúa's argument provides a useful lens through which to think about a range of borderland identities.

A further difficulty in entering into this field – of developing a perspective on these poets which does justice to its diversity, its stylistic and chronological spread, and its varied reception – relates to the risk of substituting one set of binaries (women vs. men, good vs. bad) for another – that of 'genius' vs. 'minor'. What are we looking for when we study a range of poetry by women, such as that proposed in this book? What kinds of criteria are we applying? What are the grounds on which we assess the relative merits of different poets' work? Louise Bernikow's introduction to her 1974 anthology, *The World Split Open: Women Poets 1552–1950*, concedes that she has lowered the bar in admitting for publication work which has political interest but not necessarily clear aesthetic quality: 'the poems that sometimes don't quite make it on purely aesthetic grounds, whatever those grounds are'.[3] For some writers, the goal of a feminist criticism might be precisely to evaluate the good, the bad and the indifferent – to bring women poets forward for judgement. As Carol Rumens has said: 'What matters is to make audible the range of different voices, partly in the interests of historical accuracy, but not least so that female genius, when its next time comes, has a natural order in which to take its place.'[4] One of the questions which this book will ask, however, is whether we should try to escape these kinds of hierarchies altogether.

ANTHOLOGIES

As this indicates, anthologies of poetry play an important role in canon formation and in the development of audience 'taste'. Joanna Russ, Jeni Couzyn and, more recently, Vicki Bertram have provided statistical evidence of the marginalisation of women poets in many anthologies of poetry. What difference has it made to the presentation, contextualisation and reception of poetry by women – to its validation and accessibility – if anthologists have tended to be male? Is it the case, as Cora Kaplan suggests, that poetry by women has less frequently been anthologised 'because of subjects that do not appeal to male anthologists'?[5] This is a tempting argument, but it merits some scrutiny. Should we think about women's poetry primarily in terms of its subject matter or content? Is there not much, as the rest of this book will demonstrate, about the style and voice and structure – the aesthetics and poetics – of women's poetry which deserves attention, over and above its ostensible 'subjects'? Even if we do want to put content above form, is it the case that poetry by women can be identified and evaluated on the grounds of female-specific (and therefore culturally demeaned) 'subjects', and what 'subjects' would these be? Where, say, Samuel Taylor Coleridge writes lyrically and eloquently of the parent's bond with the infant child in 'Frost at Midnight', or where Douglas Dunn writes of his grief at the loss of a loved one in *Elegies*, or where Allen Ginsberg writes about the sexual body, or Shakespeare about love and desire, can we be sure that it is 'feminine' subject matter that debars women from the anthologies? (Or conversely, should we argue, as Elizabeth Gregory does in an essay on John Berryman and Allen Ginsberg among others, that it is precisely the novelty and daring of the male appropriation of concerns which are culturally defined as 'feminine' that marks the validity and success of their work?)[6] The discussion of Romantic poetry in Chapter 5 indicates how important it is to be discriminating in any consideration of gender and genre. Helen Carr urges caution in this context:

> Men certainly predominate in prestigious anthologies or on
> library shelves, but I am less sure whether the gender associ-
> ations that cling to the concept of poetry, making the writing

of it seem a legitimate and appropriate activity for one gender or the other, are so monolithically male. What about the idea of poetry as soft and unmanly?[7]

It is not only male anthologists who have eschewed certain kinds of women's writing. Fleur Adcock makes a particular point of excluding Anne Sexton, for example, from *The Faber Book of 20th Century Women's Poetry* on the grounds that her work seems now 'excessively derivative (first from Lowell, then from Plath) and repellently self-indulgent'.[8] Plath, too, is to be treated with care: 'Plath has been innocently responsible for a mob of more or less feeble imitators.'[9] As Chapter 1 explains, this exemplifies a suspicion about the readers of women's poetry which continues to thrive.

It would be a simplification, then, to conclude that women poets have been excluded from male-edited anthologies largely because of what they write about. Instead, we might think about the structural or institutional barriers (in terms of education, participation in elite circles of publication, promotion and reviewing, and so on) which might count against women writers' full and equal participation. It is necessary to think, too, about the different forms which anthologies might take and about the politics of anthologisation. One argument about anthologies (and specifically about anthologies of women's poetry) is that they place women in a ghetto. It is on such grounds that Laura Riding and Elizabeth Bishop, among others, have refused to permit the publication of their work in this format. Deryn Rees-Jones's *Modern Women Poets* does include some of Riding's work with an editorial note explaining the change in policy of the Riding literary estate in this regard:

Until July 2005, the Laura (Riding) Jackson Board of Literary Management maintained the author's own policy of refusing permission for the inclusion of her work in women-only compilations. In now granting permission, the Board asks us to record Laura (Riding) Jackson's view and policy (1986): 'I regard the treatment of literary work as falling into a special category of women's writing as an offence against literature as of human generalness, and an offence against the human identity of women. I refuse every request made of me to contribute to, participate in, such a trivialising of the issue of literature, and oppose this categorisation in public commentary, as I can'.[10]

In some contexts it is a source of concern that women poets have not been admitted into mainstream (most often male) anthologies and instead have been relegated to what is, by implication, an inferior female version. In other contexts, women poets and readers have valued the space and visibility afforded by a female-only literary environment and, as in the anthologies used in this book (and referenced in the 'Student Resources' section later), have relished the range of poetries made available there.

READERS AND WRITERS

I referred earlier to the role of the woman as reader. Hitherto, much of the critical attention paid to women's poetry has concentrated on the role and reception of the woman writer. The place of the woman as reader, and more generally of the reading process, in the generation and reception of meaning has only recently merited concentrated scrutiny. Interestingly, it is in relation to this issue that two divergent but nevertheless fruitful methodologies – methodologies which shape the study of women's poetry in the broadest conception of the field – come into focus. The first of these is a historicist or cultural materialist study of the historical and cultural circumstances in which girls and women have read poetry. The second is a relatively recent understanding, informed by poststructuralist theories, of the ways in which poetry might be perceived as a form of discourse. From this perspective, the meaning of the poem is not the property of the poet, is not fixed and determinate. Rather, its meanings are generated and shared in the discursive relationship between text (note, not poet) and reader. For Antony Easthope, who has written persuasively in this field: 'No such object, a poem with a single fixed or univocal meaning, exists. A poem constantly changes its meanings as it is read and re-read.' What this means is that 'the meaning of a text is always produced in a process of reading'.[11] This new way of thinking about poetry, a perspective which informs much of this book, is interested in the ways in which, as Alison Mark says, poetry works 'through the power of poetic artifice to manipulate syntax so as to allow many readings, many naturalisations, narrativisations, and often with little or no certainty of which is to be "preferred"; for there is no ultimate authority. There are only readers – who are also writers.'[12]

An examination of the history of women as readers reveals a possible explanation for their apparent marginalisation as writers. Alberto Manguel's 1997 book, *A History of Reading*, indicates that 'most women throughout the fourteenth century – indeed throughout most of the middle ages – were educated only as far as was useful to a man's household'.[13] Women's access to books, as Virginia Woolf was so dramatically and eloquently to explain in the opening pages of her 1928 book, *A Room of One's Own*, was restricted – even prohibited: 'Here I was actually at the door which leads into the library itself,' she explains:

> I must have opened it, for instantly there issued like a guardian angel barring the way with a flutter of black gown instead of white wings, a deprecating, silvery, kindly gentleman, who regretted in a low voice as he waved me back that ladies are only admitted to the library if accompanied by a Fellow of the College or furnished with a letter of introduction.[14]

Woolf's simile of the dark angel tacitly anticipates some modern poets' use of the same ambiguous image as metaphor for the muse, inspiration, temptation and despair. Woolf's account confirms a point that Alberto Manguel goes on to make and which women poets exemplify: 'From early days, women readers found ways of subverting the material that society placed on their shelves.'[15] Thus Woolf's black-clad angel comes to symbolise forces of chaos, evil and despair instead of the enlightened, rational thought that the image ostensibly connotes.

From Manguel, too, we learn of the apparently paradoxical importance which early Christian cultures ascribed to nurse and mother figures as nurturers of children's reading habits: 'The image of the teaching mother-figure was as important in Christian iconography as the female student was rare in depictions of the classroom.'[16] Women's reading practices, arguably like their writing practices, have tended to be kept under strict surveillance. The decision to read and the context in which reading takes place (such that reading instructional books for children is perceived to be good, while reading for pleasure is regarded as bad) are both subject to cultural scrutiny. So too is the choice of reading matter and even, as Janet Badia has recently and convincingly shown, the ways in which the woman reader chooses to interpret the text. Badia argues that readers of Sylvia Plath's novel, *The Bell Jar*, are disparaged by reviewers and critics and are stereotyped and parodied in a range of popular cultural forms, from the film *10 Things I Hate about You* to the cartoon series *The Fall Guy*. According to Badia, the view of such critics is that Plath's readers have 'been reading [. . .] all wrong, or, if not wrong, then for all the wrong reasons. The corollary of this argument requires Plath to be rescued from her readers and from certain reading practices that might diminish the importance of her work.'[17] Jacqueline Pearson has shown that similar debates surfaced during the Enlightenment when 'in the age's literary discourses, misreading tended to be gendered as feminine'.[18]

Such debates return us to important and challenging questions about the relationship between reader and text. A basic tenet of feminist readings of poetry of the 1970s and 1980s was that in the lyric poetry of the second-wave feminist movement, the woman reader might find the expression or representation of an experience with which she could identify and from which she could gain the advantages of inspiration, solidarity or instruction. In the introduction to the 1983 anthology, *In the Pink*, for example (a collection which brings together a selection of poems originally performed by a trio of women, Anna Carteret, Frances Viner and Sue Jones-Davies, as part of a touring show and on public television), the performers/editors situate their selection very firmly in the context of contemporary political movements. They yoke their selection with a hitherto repressed female energy ('This book is about that power in women, expressed in our poetry'), and they assert: '*In the Pink*'s reception, and the spate of letters we received after it was broadcast, showed that we had tapped a source of feeling common to thousands of women.'[19]

This confidence in the collective solidarity of women readers, and in the nurturing, encouraging or reassuring nature of the reading experience, is one which we might wish to query. The supposed dynamic, although conceivably resonant in specific periods and contexts, does not necessarily or fully explain the connection between women's poetry and its readers in earlier historical contexts, and it would be a mistake to transpose the mechanisms which may have pertained in one time to those of another. Moreover, the reading model which seems to fit lyric poetry (with its apparent expressive-realist 'I' and direct communication with an attentive reader) does not necessarily translate to other forms – to Renaissance sonnets or earlier oral ballads with their own sets of conventions. It does not fit, either, with the non-referential 'Language'-based poetics of some current practitioners. Most worryingly, a reading model which posits a straightforward and affirmatory relationship between reader, poem and poet risks undervaluing the aesthetic qualities of the poetic text, the constructed nature of experience, and the performative potential of the speaking 'I' (a concept which will be explored in more detail in Chapter 2). For the feminist critic, such a model risks conceding – even colluding with – an antithetical critical perspective which would see all women's poetry as the inadvertent expression of private, personal experience. It is on these grounds that poetry by women has, over the years, been disparaged. If we claim identification with the personal, authentic and sympathetic voice as the hallmark of women's poetry, do we not undermine our own attempts to assert the breadth, diversity and authority of women's writing?

In any case, the poetic text, however personal, direct and authentic it may seem to be, might be an elaborate (and impressive) work of artifice. American poet Anne Sexton's 'For Johnny Pole on the Forgotten Beach' (1960) seems to speak of personal and traumatic experience and to invite readerly identification on that basis. However, as Sexton was to explain after a critic had sympathised in print about the wartime loss of the brother figure invented in the text:

> Well, there's enough fiction so that it's total confusion if one were to . . . I remember Ralph Mills talking about my dead brother who I've written about. And I met Ralph and I said [. . .] 'Ralph, I had no brother, but then didn't we all have

brothers who died in that war?' Which was the Second World
War, which is a long, a few wars ago. But didn't we all,
somehow, have brothers? But I write *my* brother, and of course
he believes it. I mean, why not? [. . .] I should say 'excuse me,
folks, but no brother,' but that would kind of ruin the poem,
so . . .[20]

This is not to say that it is wrong to read and identify with the poem
in any personal or experiential way. Rather, it is to say that this is
not the only or ideal way of reading it, and that alternative readings
(for example, those which situate the poem's imagined scenario in
the real context of contemporary American unease about the
Second World War or the Korean conflict) might uncover a whole
sequence of alternative and rewarding interpretations. It is the rich-
ness of reading possibilities which women's poetry invites and
which this book seeks to elucidate.

Thus far we have focused on the condition of women as readers.
It is equally important not to overlook the circumstances in which
women poets, historically, have struggled to be permitted to put pen
to paper. Looking at the Romantic period, for instance, Anna
Seward is said to have been forbidden to write by her parents who,
devastated by the death of her sister (see her 1799 Sonnet LXXXI),
required that she devote herself to caring for them.[21] In the same
period Felicia Hemans was abandoned by her husband and left to
support her sons. The pressure to make a living from fast and fre-
quent poetic production arguably explains what to some readers has
seemed a frustrating inability fully to develop and perfect her work.
Another contemporary, L. E. L. (Letitia Elizabeth Landon), author
of 'Home' (1824) and 'Lines of Life' (1829), had begun writing as
a child and bribed her brother to listen to her drafts. When her
father's business failed, she was forced to make money as best she
could, perhaps sacrificing the authority and integrity of her voice in
order to make a living. Germaine Greer summarises the situation
thus:

The story of Letitia Landon is the story of the exploitation and
destruction of an extremely talented but uneducated young
middle-class woman at the hands of the London literary

establishment of the 1820s and 1830s [. . .] Her story illustrates in a concise and appalling way the complex of causes that have excluded women from a full participation in literary culture. If the truth were that women were simply denied access to print and the literary establishment, there would be no problem to solve; the problem that confronts the student of women's creativity is not that there is no poetry by women, but that there is so much bad poetry by women.[22]

Greer's point is a contentious one which needs some unpicking. Before accepting her claims, we need to define what is meant by 'bad' poetry and to ask what the effect has been, historically, of male-dominated standards of 'good' and 'bad', of 'creativity' and 'talent'. It is necessary to ask whether the poetry that is read is necessarily representative of the poetry which has been written. It is possible that a hidden body of poetry by women, which has been denied a public platform for a range of reasons from booksellers' hostility to authorial reticence, has been lost to us such that the surviving poetry gives a misleading impression of the nature and quality of the rest. Nevertheless, Greer's point is persuasive. Denied the opportunity fully and freely to develop their art, women poets may not always have worked to their true potential. To quote from stanzas two, three and four of L. E. L.'s 'Lines of Life':

> I never knew the time my heart
>   Look'd freely from my brow;
> It once was check'd by timidness,
>   'T is caught by caution now.
>
> I live among the cold, the false,
>   And I must seem like them;
> And such I am, for I am false
>   As those I most condemn.
>
> I teach my lip its sweetest smile,
>   My tongue its softest tone;
> I borrow others' likeness, till
>   Almost I lose my own.[23]

The prohibition which colours the woman writer's experience is encapsulated in the succession of negative qualifiers and metaphors of restraint: 'never', 'check'd', 'caught'. The speaker herself is caught between the 'lines': a word which signifies the barriers which constrain her and, paradoxically, the language which offers the only possible – if figurative – means of escape.

ANDROGYNY

There are many women poets in this book who, as Chapter 1 will explain, reflect – consciously or otherwise – on what it means to be a woman and a poet. They do this both within the poetry (in the seventeenth-century New England poet Anne Bradstreet's 'The Author to her Book', for example) and in commentaries on their work such as the Irish poet Eavan Boland's recent *Object Lessons*.[24] There is, though, an equally valid tradition of women poets who refuse to concede the significance of gender in discussions of their work. Contemporary Welsh writer Sheenagh Pugh, for example, insists that 'if there is such a thing as a poetry which is limited to part of humanity, I think there is a simpler name for it than women's poetry [. . .] I think the word in question is mediocre.'[25] Another contemporary poet, Anne Stevenson, insists that the best poetry will not 'be written by a culture, a gender, a race, a nation, a political party or a creative writing group'.[26]

Margaret Atwood's 'Introduction' to the *Paris Review* anthology of interviews with women writers summarises some of the problematic issues connected with the idea of androgyny: 'Virginia Woolf may have been right about the androgynous nature of the artist [Atwood's allusion is to Woolf's argument in Chapter 6 of *A Room of One's Own* that the writer must be 'woman-manly or man-womanly'], but she was right also about the differences in social situation these androgynous artists are certain to encounter.' Atwood goes on to say that the book of interviews, instead of being titled 'Women Writers at Work', should be known as 'Writers who are Women'.[27] In an essay on Emily Dickinson, Cynthia Griffin Wolff asserts that 'Emily Dickinson was a great poet who happened to be a woman.'[28] And although the point is, I think, to privilege the poetry over the gender – and to be fair to Wolff her larger argument is about the surprises, the wit and the richness in Dickinson's work – there are some problems with embracing such a view. To say that she just 'happened to be a woman' is to suggest that gender is irrelevant, that it is immaterial to the production and the reception of poetry. The present book proposes that gender is relevant, that it does have a bearing. Even the act of denying gender's importance is itself implicitly a way of confirming its stranglehold. It is, after all, only women who are required to address questions such as these and to distance themselves from, or to disavow, their sex. One might also say, adopting a position deriving from recent psychoanalytic and French feminist theory, that sexual difference is so completely embodied in language that it is logically impossible to stand outside it.

The 'flight into androgyny' as Elaine Showalter calls it, or the appeal to a consciousness and mode of expression free of 'the gender of things' in the words of Sexton's 'Consorting with Angels', has its attractions.[29] The kind of studied gender neutrality one finds in, say, the twentieth-century American poet Elizabeth Bishop is born in part of the desire to be judged independently of the reader's perceptions of one's gender. It is not that gender is unimportant; surely it is that it should not precede (and thereby in many cultures prejudice) the reading of the poem. Lorrie Goldensohn suggests that in Bishop's case, 'The whole thrust of her early public experience seems to have been to avoid being ghettoized as a woman.' She goes on to quote Bishop from an interview: 'Most of my life I've been lucky with reviews. But at the very end they often say "The best poetry by a woman in this decade, or year, or month." Well, what's that worth? You know? But you get used to it.'[30] Her contemporary Denise Levertov's work is damned with faint praise in a recent anthology of poets' prose. The editors tell us that she became 'involved with the Objectivist and Black Mountain schools, effectively becoming the strongest woman poet of a group including Robert Creeley and Duncan'.[31] In circumstances such as these, to be free of gender imperatives and expectations must seem like a form of liberation. However, this is arguably an impossible position to achieve given the bonds between sex (biological) and gender (cultural) in society. To attempt to achieve androgyny is itself, arguably, a denial of the real contradictions of female experience. Cora Kaplan suggests of Elizabeth Barrett Browning's *Aurora Leigh* (1857) that 'Aurora rejects androgyny as a mask or aspiration for women writers.'[32] In Elaine Showalter's terms, 'The notion that women should transcend any awkwardly unorthodox desire to write about being women comes from timidity and not strength.'[33] This is not to say that women poets' mission in life should be to foreground and right/write this experience (nor is it to say that experience is homogeneous and shared), but rather to suggest the impossibility of their ignoring these conditions.

NOTES

1. For useful summaries of the field, see *The Feminist Reader: Essays in Gender and the Politics of Literary Criticism*, ed. Catherine Belsey and Jane Moore (Basingstoke: Macmillan, 1989) and Toril Moi, *Sexual/Textual Politics: Feminist Literary Theory* (London: Methuen, 1985).
2. Gloria Anzaldúa, *Borderlands/La Frontera: The New Mestiza*, 2nd edn, intro. Sonia Saldívar-Hull (San Francisco, CA: Aunt Lute Books, 1999), p. 19.
3. Louise Bernikow (ed.), *The World Split Open: Women Poets 1552–1950* (London: Women's Press, 1979), p. xxi.
4. Quoted in Jane Dowson, *Women, Modernism and British Poetry, 1910–1930: Resisting Femininity* (Aldershot: Ashgate, 2002), p. 251.
5. Kaplan, *Salt*, p. 11.
6. Elizabeth Gregory, 'Confessing the Body: Plath, Sexton, Berryman, Lowell, Ginsberg and the gendered poetics of the "real"', in *Modern Confessional Writing: New Critical Essays*, ed. Jo Gill (London: Routledge, 2006), pp. 33–49.
7. Helen Carr, 'Poetic Licence', in *Contemporary Women's Poetry: Reading/Writing/Practice*, ed. Alison Mark and Deryn Rees-Jones (Basingstoke: Macmillan, 2000), pp. 76–100, p. 77.
8. Adcock, *Faber Book*, p. 13.
9. For more on the influence of Sylvia Plath on subsequent American and British poets, see Linda Wagner-Martin, 'Plath

and Contemporary American Poetry' and Alice Entwistle, 'Plath and Contemporary British Poetry', both in *The Cambridge Companion to Sylvia Plath*, ed. Jo Gill (Cambridge: Cambridge University Press, 2006), pp. 52–62; pp. 63–70.

10. Deryn Rees-Jones, *Modern Women Poets* (Tarset: Bloodaxe, 2005), p. 414.

11. Antony Easthope, *Poetry as Discourse* (London and New York: Methuen, 1983), pp. 5–6, 7.

12. Alison Mark, 'Writing about Writing about Writing (About Writing)', in Mark and Rees-Jones, *Contemporary*, pp. 64–75, p. 65.

13. Alberto Manguel, *A History of Reading* (London: Flamingo, 1997), p. 218.

14. Virginia Woolf, *A Room of One's Own* (Harmondsworth: Penguin, [1928] 1945), p. 9.

15. Manguel, *History*, p. 228.

16. Ibid. p. 72.

17. Janet Badia, '*The Bell Jar* and other Prose', in Gill, *Cambridge Companion*, pp. 124–38, p. 131.

18. Jacqueline Pearson, *Women's Reading in Britain: 1750–1835* (Cambridge: Cambridge University Press, 1999), p. 5.

19. The Raving Beauties (eds), *In the Pink* (London: Women's Press, 1983), pp. 11–12.

20. Anne Sexton, interview with William Heyen and Al Poulin, reprinted in *No Evil Star: Selected Essays, Interviews and Prose – Anne Sexton*, ed. Steven E. Colburn (Ann Arbor: University of Michigan Press, 1985), pp. 130–57, p. 136.

21. Germaine Greer, *Slip-Shod Sibyls: Recognition, Rejection and the Woman Poet* (Harmondsworth: Penguin, 1996), pp. 58–9.

22. Ibid. p. 259. For more on women poets in the Romantic period, see *British Women Poets of the Romantic Era*, ed. Paula R. Feldman (Baltimore, MD: Johns Hopkins University Press, 1997).

23. L. E. L. (Letitia Landon), 'Lines of Life', in *The New Oxford Book of Romantic Period Verse*, ed. Jerome J. McGann (Oxford: Oxford University Press, 1994), pp. 733–6.

24. Eavan Boland, *Object Lessons: The Life of the Woman and the Poet in Our Time* (Manchester: Carcanet, 2006).

25. Sheenagh Pugh, 'Symposium: Is there a Women's Poetry?', *Poetry Wales*, 23: 1 (n.d.), 30–1, p. 31.

26. Anne Stevenson, 'A Few Words for the New Century', in *Strong Words: Modern Poets on Modern Poetry*, ed. W. N. Herbert and Matthew Hollis (Newcastle: Bloodaxe, 2000), pp. 181–3, p. 183.

27. Margaret Atwood, 'Introduction', in *Women Writers at Work: The Paris Review Interviews*, ed. George Plimpton (Harmondsworth: Penguin, 1998), pp. ix–xviii, p. xiii; Woolf, *A Room of One's Own*, p. 102.

28. Cynthia Griffin Wolff, 'Emily Dickinson', in *The Columbia History of American Poetry: From the Puritans to our Time*, ed. Jay Parini and Brett C. Millier (New York: MJF Books, 1993), pp. 121–47, p. 127.

29. Elaine Showalter, *A Literature of Their Own: British Women Novelists from Brontë to Lessing*, 2nd edn (London: Virago, 1982), p. 263; Anne Sexton, *The Complete Poems* (Boston: Houghton Mifflin, 1981), p. 111.

30. Lorrie Goldensohn, *Elizabeth Bishop: The Biography of a Poetry* (New York: Columbia University Press, 1992), p. 63.

31. Herbert and Hollis, *Strong Words*, p. 102.

32. Cora Kaplan, 'Introduction', in Elizabeth Barrett Browning, *Aurora Leigh and other Poems* (London: Women's Press, 1978), pp. 5–36, p. 33.

33. Showalter, *A Literature of Their Own*, p. 290.

CHAPTER I

Self-Reflexivity

In the preface to Alison Mark and Deryn Rees-Jones's collection of essays *Contemporary Women's Poetry: Reading/Writing/Practice* (2000), Isobel Armstrong notes that 'what it means to write as a female lyric poet, explored problematically rather than polemically, is the concern of poets and critics alike'.[1] This comment serves as a starting point for this chapter's reflection on a key issue uniting the work of women poets of many periods and cultures, that is, the evident self-consciousness of the writing. The point, it is important to stress, is not that women poets are characteristically self-obsessed or unable to see beyond the limits of their own work. The point is that the poems themselves reflect on their own 'processes of production and reception'. They are committed to enquiring about their own authority, their own status, their own place in a cultural context which has, historically, tended to find them aberrant.[2] Across many different periods, and in many different forms, women poets have demonstrated an acute self-awareness about their work. Jane Stevenson and Peter Davidson, for example, identify this as one of the major concerns of early modern women's poetry: '[an] important theme [. . .] is women's writing itself'.[3]

This self-consciousness emerges in a number of ways. It can be seen in poems which contemplate creativity or inspiration, or which reflect on the poet's own daring in entering into this hitherto masculine field (see, for example, Mary Barber's 1734 'Conclusion of a Letter to the Rev. Mr C –'.). It emerges in poems about the relationship, which may be nurturing, combative or inspiring, with other women writers' work, with audience, or with form. This is, as Cora Kaplan puts it in the introduction to Elizabeth Barrett Browning's *Aurora Leigh*, 'that most difficult venture for women, writing about women writing'.[4] The discussion which follows takes each of these dimensions – poetic daring, poetic inspiration, poetic relationships and poetic form – in turn and asks what women poets have made of these concerns. In closing, the work of contemporary critic Linda Hutcheon is proposed as a way of theorising the self-reflexivity (or textual narcissism) which emerges in the writing of a number of these poets.

POETIC DARING

By and large emerging into cultures which have restricted women's access to an education, and thus to a voice, women who did write – privately or for publication – were subverting all kinds of expectations in so doing. It is this consciousness of their own daring which underlines much of their work. As Greer describes the historical scene:

> The flying-pig or dancing-dog syndrome is the chain of mis-understanding and misrepresentation that is set off by the assumption that a woman active in the arts is performing some arduous and unnatural contortion of her personality. Dr Johnson explained that women preachers are like dogs walking on their hind legs; we are so surprised to find it being done at all that we do not expect it to be done well. Many of the women who dared to write verse were astonished at their own daring and as expectant of applause as the dancing dog. They were also as likely to crash as the flying pig.[5]

Atwood draws the same analogy in her introduction to the *Paris Review* book of interviews with women writers: 'There is still a sort of trained-dog fascination with the idea of women writers – not that the thing is done well, but that it is done at all, by a creature that is not supposed to possess such capabilities.'[6]

Mary Barber's 1734 poem 'Conclusion of a Letter' delivers a passionate defence of a woman's right to write, and to read. This is a poem about writing as a woman, or about writing as a woman in a culture which disapproves of such a project. Barber's choice of the form of the epistle or letter permits her to bring multiple voices (subject, addressee, other people such as the speaker's son, 'Con') into interesting proximity. Jane Dowson, among others, has pointed to the use of 'various personae' in women's poetic monologues and dialogues as a way of 'draw[ing] attention to the processes of representation'.[7] Barber's poem does this. It opens with the first-person address of the subject 'I', who here apostrophises an unknown reader; we then move to her own self-reported speech. Embedded in this are the comments and accusations of others about the very process of writing which she is here so visibly performing. Thereafter, we have intimate address from mother to son as the speaker gives 'Con' advice about choosing a wife. There are multiple voices here but not necessarily multiple identities; the point is that the subject assumes and articulates different roles, different perspectives. The strategy works to encourage the full play of irony. This irony is generated by the gap between, and thus uncertainty about, what the speaker says in the letter and what she really thinks.

More importantly, Barber's use of shifting voices and indeterminate 'I's is dialogic in Bakhtin's sense of the term as 'a dynamic of more than one voice'. Jane Dowson and Alice Entwistle explain that the use of such a 'dynamic', or 'dialogic indeterminacy', functions as

> a critique of mythical or idealised female representations [. . .] Multivocality particularly suits women poets because it emphasises the social origins and contexts of language [. . .] Textually, voices may seem to have equal status but the author can stage-manage their dramatic effects; she may challenge readers' preconceptions, direct their sympathies or collude with an implicitly female audience.[8]

Dowson and Entwistle trace this technique in the work of modern women poets from Charlotte Mew and Anna Wickham to Carol Ann Duffy. Barber's use of hidden voices in dialogue, particularly when mediated, as here, through the first-person speaker, functions both to expose those contradictory voices and to demonstrate how deeply internalised their reservations are.

The poem opens: "'Tis time to conclude; for I make it a rule / To leave off all writing, when Con. comes from school.' This vignette dramatises a much larger set of conflicts. It exposes a battle between those who disapprove of women's literacy (including, 'Con', the son, who is representative of the next generation of patriarchs, and the 'Rev. Mr C' of the title, representing the old guard) and those who persist in displaying it, here surreptitiously but to considerable satiric effect. Barber's poem subverts expectations, transgressing its own opening prohibition against writing. It gives us the misogynist law which prevents women from writing poetry (explicitly voiced by the son, merely presumed by the Rev.) but then quite consciously disobeys it. The rest of the poem, after that opening prohibition (the expectation or 'rule' that she should 'leave off' writing) represents a deliberate flouting of the law. It displays a deep self-consciousness about the conditions in which women of the period came to write and, by belittling the views of the dominant males, laments women's lack of educational opportunities: ' "He thinks it a crime in a woman to read." ' It exposes women's vulnerability to male-dominated social conventions: ' "I pity poor Barber, his wife's so romantic: / A letter in rhyme! – Why the woman is frantic!" ' Mary Barber takes a brave stance. She refuses to distance herself from the story she tells and explicitly names herself ('poor' Barber's wife) as the person mocked, disparaged and accused of insanity: ' "This reading the poets has quite turned her head!" '

The allusion to insanity is a telling one, and leads Barber to stage and thereafter to satirise the contemporary (and indeed persistent) conflation of women, poetry and forms of sickness or contagion. The speaker quotes her imagined interlocutor:

> 'There's nothing I dread like a verse-writing wife:
> Defend me, ye powers, from that fatal curse,
> Which must heighten the plagues of *for better for worse*!'

As Jacqueline Pearson has shown, during the Enlightenment, 'while men's reading was shown to facilitate intellectual development, women's tended to be located in the female body, represented as a physical not an intellectual act. Consequently it was believed to have a direct effect not only on female morals but also on the female body.'[9] Similar rhetoric, and a similar confusion of women, poetry and disease, have emerged in relation to more recent women's poetry. Of Sexton's work, for example, poet Louise Bogan complained, 'one poem [. . .] made me positively ill'.[10]

Barber's poem is notable for its appropriation of a tone which is simultaneously conciliatory and satirical, beguiling and critical. She knows who her enemy is, and her use of different layers of dialogue, different voices and different addressees, allows her to deliver a fatal blow. The tone is reminiscent of Woolf's *A Room of One's Own*, which also has to tread lightly, has to appear not to take itself too seriously, and has to mollify its potentially hostile target audience (I use the word 'target' advisedly). Aemilia Lanyer's 1611 poem *Salve Deus Rex Judaeorum* also makes strategic concessions to conventional views of women's authorial unworthiness, describing 'my weak distempered brain and feeble spirits, / which all unlearned have adventured this'.[11] However, this is done primarily to register the speaker's spiritual, rather than gendered, unworthiness (the point is that she feels herself to be unworthy of writing about Christ) and, in any case, has the effect of confounding such views and affirming this woman's right to a voice.

Returning to Barber's 'Conclusion of a Letter', in the second half of the poem, the speaker adopts a far more placatory tone. She offers her son the benefits of her 'wisdom': wisdom which is evidently the product of her own 'reading' and 'learning'. Arguably this is a tactical concession, confirming the role and responsibility of the educated woman in shaping the minds and virtue of future generations. Barber's poem performs in a similar way to the work of later Enlightenment writers, aligning female poetics with moral improvement and against degeneracy. In the words of Jacqueline Pearson, women writers 'found it useful to legitimise their own access to literacy and provide comforting self-images for the female reader, whose activity is presented not as a time-wasting self-indulgence but as the result of, indeed identical to, virtue'.[12]

It is in the study of books, the poem concludes, that true happiness lies. Thus the poem defends and exemplifies the rightness of its position. In the form of an open letter, it offers both a public and a self validation. What is especially interesting about this poem is its self-conscious audacity in broaching so skilfully and persuasively the very criticism which would deny its possibility. It enters into debates about the education of girls which, as Manguel says, have been 'hotly debated' since the medieval period, and although it assimilates the opponent's perspective at crucial points, it does this finally for its own rhetorical purposes.[13]

POETIC INSPIRATION

Two modern poems, both written by poets who were born in the United States but who made their adult homes in England, describe the process of receiving poetic inspiration as – to quote Sylvia Plath's 'Black Rook in Rainy Weather' (1960) – the prolonged 'wait for the angel, / For that rare, random descent'.[14]

Ruth Fainlight's poem 'The Other' (1973) opens on a note of anxious qualification and uncertainty: 'Whatever I find if I search will be wrong.'[15] It is unclear, as yet, wherein the potential error lies. Should we emphasise the word 'I' in this line (is the line suggesting that it is the speaker, the 'I', who is at fault?) or should we emphasise the verb 'search' (is it the act of searching which is the mistake?)? By the end of the stanza, we see that it may be both. In order to find inspiration, or attract the muse, the speaker must sit passively and wait until it finds her. I say 'passively', but the poem is ambiguous in this respect. Passivity, which is so often indicted as a characteristic of women's poetry and ascribed to women's role as the acquiescent, silent object of the male poet's scrutiny, is here re-envisioned, or inverted. It becomes a demanding choice which, paradoxically, must be worked at. The 'sternest trial of all', as line two has it, is an aesthetic strategy not a default position. Fainlight's poem, like Plath's 'Black Rook in Rainy Weather', sees the maintenance of this cultivated receptivity as the 'longest task'. The necessary seduction of the muse by the speaker is a game of tactics demanding great skill and courage, and it is only by successfully performing passivity that the muse might be won over.

Visitation by this muse/other is represented in both poems in terms of pregnancy and childbirth. This is connoted by the 'miracle' or 'accident' with which Plath's poem opens and by the long, pregnant delay in both poems. The emphatically domestic setting of Plath's poem (with the 'kitchen table or chair') and the gruelling labour of Fainlight's ('And this will be my longest task: to attend, / To open myself') also imply the conditions of labour, childbirth and maternity. Both convey the demanding, visceral and painful nature of the anticipated encounter. In Plath's poem the rook/muse will 'seize my senses, haul / my eyelids up'; in Fainlight's, it pushes 'against the grain of my ardent nature . . . painful / And strong as a birth in which there is no pause'.[16]

In 'The Other' and 'Black Rook', the seduction or entrapment of the muse (the 'wild awkward child' and 'forgotten sister' in Fainlight, the 'rock', 'angel' in Plath) signifies only the beginning of something: 'I begin / To understand' in the closing words of Fainlight; 'the wait's begun again' as Plath insists. Finding inspiration, then, is just the first of several steps. Only Fainlight's poem explicitly genders this encounter. Plath's is studied in its neutrality; the rook is 'it' throughout, and with the exception of the allusion to the domestic sphere in stanza four, there is nothing to suggest the gender of either speaker or muse. 'The Other', though, with its opening allusion to a 'child', to childbirth and to the femininity of the muse ('let her come closer, a wary smile on her face', 'her faint reedy voice' in stanza three), makes it very clear that the productive bond which this speaker desires is one between female subject and female muse. This speaker seeks the transmission of a message from the past which she will understand in the present and carry with her into the future. In this context, there is a significant shift to the future tense in the final two lines of the poem where the speaker avows that she 'shall' learn her 'own secret at last from the words of her song'. The implication is that there is a female poetic inheritance, or a sisterhood, from which successive generations of poets can learn a long-awaited lesson and a language. Fainlight's confidence in the inspirational and nurturing qualities of a female poetic tradition is, as we will see below in the context of Amy Lowell's work, not necessarily shared.

In other poems, the process of inspiration is less receptive and rather more purposive but no less ambivalent for that. The title and epigraph to Sharon Olds's 2004 selected poems, *Strike Sparks*, is

taken from a slightly earlier poem, 'I Go Back to May 1937'. The
title of the poem inscribes at one and the same time the deliberate
steps the speaker takes in figuratively revisiting – or going back to –
the past, and the rather more passive and inevitable sense in which,
regardless of one's own actions, one's roots go back to some past
moment of origin. Like Plath and Fainlight before her, Olds sets lit-
erary creativity in the context of biological productivity and in
terms of a specific cultural and ideological formation (heterosexual
family life). This is here shown to be riddled with violence, oppres-
sion and fear, hence the use of similes and metaphors of blood,
'glinting' weapons, 'sword tips', 'hurt', 'suffer' and 'die'. The
speaker/daughter imagines, or fantasises, being able to pre-empt
and thus head off her own moment of genesis, her own conception.
Only then, the poem suggests, might she avoid the otherwise
inevitable bloodshed of her own subsequent experience. The logical
consequence of the fulfilment of such a fantasy would, of course, be
her own annihilation. A similar trope is used in Sexton's 1974 poem
'End, Middle, Beginning'.[17]

At the last moment in Olds's 'I Go Back', we see that eros (or the
Freudian life instinct) rises and asserts itself: 'I want to live.'[18]
Living, for the speaker, is inescapably wrapped up with writing
about it. The sparks of inspiration which are so fundamental to her
existence are implicitly also sparks of conflict – volatile and dan-
gerous but none the less necessary for that. The poem recalls the
1937 courtship of the speaker's parents and likens them to two
paper dolls (the 'paper' suggests their vulnerability to being
destroyed by the speaker's poetic energies). The speaker describes
how she wishes to bring them together, bashing them against each
other like two 'chips of flint' in order both to punish them and to
generate her own poetic inspiration. The images (of flints and
sparks) are elemental, suggesting the primordial nature of this
process, as though in an attempt to 'Strike sparks from them, I say
/ Do what you are going to do, and I will tell about it'.[19] The allu-
sions conjure up images of the childhood game 'scissors, paper,
stone', while the paper (metonymically the textualisation of the
scene in this very poem) represents the daughter's claim to the last
word. In Plath's 1960 poem 'Hardcastle Crags', the speaker/poet
strides out along a 'steely street' with her feet, described as

'flint–like', striking echoes as they go.[20] In 'Hardcastle Crags', though, the environment quenches the sparks of her creativity, which can only be protected by her retreat in the final stanza out of the open and back to the safety of home.

POETIC RELATIONSHIPS

Jane Dowson has suggested that women poets display 'an ambivalence towards one another's reputation, status and creativity'.[21] While Dowson has a point, her comment makes what is arguably often an intertextual relationship (in other words, a familiarity with the writing, not the writer) into something rather more personal than it necessarily is. Nevertheless, Dowson is right in suggesting that the relationships of successive generations of women poets with their foremothers are not always positive and emulative ones with prior models as likely to set up barriers as to lead the way. In the poems discussed in this section, the poetic text is used by women writers as a space or medium in which they can 'write back to' (explore, develop, modify or critique) earlier works. American poet Amy Lowell's 'The Sisters' (1925), for example, explicitly contemplates the poetry of earlier generations of women writers and implicitly asks what it offers to writers of the current age.

In 'The Sisters', as Dowson explains, the speaker (who is not necessarily Amy Lowell, but a constructed voice; the point is an important one) 'imagines meeting [. . .] three different kinds of predecessor, with whom she cannot identify'. In the words of the poem: 'Taking us by and large, we're a queer lot / We women who write poetry.'[22] There is considerable wit and irony here with the opening line, 'Taking us by and large', parodying the critical propensity to lump all women poets together or to fail to discriminate between their different voices. In addition, by its use of the collective 'we', the poem mocks any kind of assumed homogeneity or essential unity of identity and perspective; who, the question is begged, are 'we'? What makes women, the poem asks, 'scribble down, man-wise, / The fragments of ourselves?' Lowell mocks a critical consensus which sees women writers (Nathaniel Hawthorne's 'damned mob of scribbling women') as seeking to emulate men or become 'man-wise', but which also regards them as inevitably exposing somatic 'fragments of ourselves'. The voice of the poet ventriloquises, and thereby mocks, the kinds of questions typically levelled at women poets. It exposes not a lack of faith in the traditions of female poetry, but contempt for orthodox expectations of it.

'The Sisters' exhibits an irony and a self-consciousness which transform it into much more than a discussion of the adequacy of specific role models. It is not the weakness of her predecessors that Lowell's speaker describes, but the diversity of different positions that she celebrates:

> Strange trio of my sisters, most diverse
> And how extraordinarily unlike
> Each is to me, and which way shall I go?

The poem is confident in its invocation of, and identification with, the witch-like identity ('strange trio of sisters') typically assigned to women writers and thus implicit in their silencing. As Woolf notes in *A Room of One's Own*, when 'one reads of a witch being ducked, of a woman possessed by devils, of a wise woman selling herbs [. . .] I think we are on the track of a lost novelist, a suppressed poet'. Looking back to the imaginary life story of the sister, Judith, she has invented for Shakespeare, Woolf goes on: 'Any woman born with a great gift in the sixteenth century would certainly have gone crazed, shot herself, or ended her days in some lonely cottage outside the village, half witch, half wizard, feared and mocked at.'[23] In Lowell's poem, the figure of the wild woman, witch and outsider is proudly claimed and thus validated.

What Lowell's speaker learns from the strange triumvirate of 'sisters' is her own agency, her capacity to go her own way ('which way shall I go?'). She does not have to be like them – 'I cannot write like them' – just as they do not have to be like each other. She is writing here, as much as anything, against the perception that, as a woman, she should find in an earlier generation of female poets a model to emulate. The closing lines of the poem, 'No, you have not seemed strange to me, but near, / Frightfully near and rather terrifying', might be read as evidence of the perceived dominance of earlier traditions and of the desire to escape their grasp. Alternatively, it might be read as an acknowledgment of the inspirational power of the women writers of the past who continue to instruct and to strike awe in their successors.

Lowell's resistance to, or at least problematisation of, any assumed bonding or identification between women poets is salutary. One of the mainstays of the second wave of feminism, which has so shaped the reception of poetry by women in the second half of the twentieth century, is the notion of sisterhood. The assumed affinity of and identification between women as poets, readers and female subjects (or what Nancy K. Miller has described as 'the textual bonding between women as reading and writing subjects') has fostered an expectation, in some quarters at least, that women will naturally relate to, empathise with, and support each other both personally and in their writing.[24] Lowell shows that the relationship between different poets and, more importantly, between different poets' work, is far more complex than this suggests.

The ambivalence in Lowell's poem replicates that expressed by some women poets in connection with the spectre of the ancient Greek poet Sappho. In what Susan Gubar has called the 'swerve from Sappho', a number of women writers from Amy Lowell at the end of the poem discussed above, through Gertrude Stein and Muriel Rukeyser to Carolyn Kizer, have displayed misgivings about the model: 'Their swerve from Sappho seems less a fear of being obliterated by her power as literary foremother [. . .] than a fear that Sappho was herself enmeshed in contradictions that threatened to stunt their own creative development.'[25] We cannot assume that there is a bond of sisterhood which will transcend the multiple differences between women and between texts. As Betsy Erkkila says of the friendship between Emily Dickinson and her friend and sister-in-law Susan Gilbert Dickinson, their relationship represents 'a site of dissension, contingency, and ongoing struggle rather than a separate space of some untroubled and essentially cooperative accord among women'.[26]

As this suggests, it is impossible to think about the question of 'influence' in poetry by women without recognising the importance of the figure of Sappho. Ellen Greene succinctly explains that 'As the earliest surviving woman writer in the West, Sappho stands at

the beginning of Western literary history [. . .] Sappho has exerted
an intense and lasting presence in the Western imagination.'[27] The
figure, or more properly perhaps the myth or icon, of Sappho
emerges again and again in poetry both by women and by men.[28]
The real Sappho is thought to have lived from the end of the
seventh through to the beginning of the sixth centuries BCE on
what is now known as the Greek island of Lesbos. Her work has
been preserved largely in fragments and/or by reputation (that is,
its detail and its qualities have been reported or quoted by succes-
sive readers and writers). Its cultural significance far outweighs the
body of extant work. In the Greek tradition, as Pamela Gordon
explains, Sappho came to be regarded as the lone female figure
among the nine great lyric poets. Elsewhere, she was regarded as
the tenth muse – an appellation which was subsequently to be used
of the seventeenth-century New England poet Anne Bradstreet
on the publication of her *The Tenth Muse Lately Sprung up in
America*. In turn, Katherine Philips was widely known as 'the
English Sappho'.[29]

Fragments of Sappho's poetry which survive into the present
day reveal a number of striking and still resonant qualities: the
apparent intimacy of tone, the complex and evocative imagery, and
the expression of what appears to be same sex desire. To quote
Gordon again:

> Many scholars believe that Sappho's fragments do indeed
> view desire from a distinctly female angle. Some have claimed
> that Sappho presents an erotics of reciprocity and mutuality
> that stands in stark contrast to other archaic poets' themes of
> masculine pursuit and feminine submission.[30]

However, as always in thinking about women poets from periods
and cultures different from the reader's, Gordon urges caution: 'If
one wants to take Sappho as a model for desire among women, it is
best to read with an acute awareness of the distance and difference
between her world and one's own.'[31] Modern critics have noted the
degree of confidence, wit and bravado in Sappho's work – particu-
larly as regards her engagement with an otherwise predominantly
masculine set of concerns and effects. Of late, scholarship on

Sappho – like that on more recent women poets – has considered her influence on subsequent women poets (on H. D. or Amy Lowell, for instance), and has debated whether her work should be read as a private, intimate discourse or as a social and ritualised form. It has also discussed her use of an embodied female language and asked whether Sappho's poetics should be read as accepting of, or resistant to, dominant contemporary norms.

Eavan Boland's 'The Journey' (1987) reflects on the resonance of Sappho in the present day. It speaks both to and about Sappho (or, metonymically, the influence of a female poetic tradition) and to and about a feminist literary criticism which is here gently rebuked and resisted.[32] The speaker in 'The Journey' operates, from the outset, in two different registers. First, she uses a formal, rhetorical, intellectually sophisticated and culturally knowing register (signified by the poem's epigraph drawn from Virgil's *Aeneid*, book VI). Second, she adopts the language of the domestic, everyday and intimate: ' "there has never" ', lines one and two report, ' "been a poem to an antibiotic" '. The quotidian and personal are conveyed partly by the direct address, reported here, and partly by the apparently mundane subject matter; the point is the contrast between the sublime and the ostensibly ridiculous.

The speaker in 'The Journey' parodies the set of conventions which dominate the English verse tradition, the 'odes on / the flower of the raw sloe for fever'. This, it is implied, is a tradition which is male dominated and therefore out of touch with the everyday concerns or the lives (and the deaths) of the women the poem commemorates:

> somewhere a poet is wasting
> his sweet uncluttered metres on the obvious
> emblem instead of the real thing.

Then, in a moment of near-Keatsian negative capability (hence the 'loosening and sweetening heaviness'), the speaker leaves behind the everyday world, an unsatisfying melange of messy rooms, unread books and unfinished drinks, and follows Sappho down into the underworld. Sappho's influence is instinctive and wordless. The poem posits a union based on an apparently charged moment of mutual recognition and trust, speaker with poet, woman with woman:

> I would have known her anywhere
> and I would have gone with her anywhere
> and she came wordlessly
> and without a word I went with her.

The point is both to connote a difference between the blustering male poet of stanzas two and three who is devaluing the currency of language by overuse, and to anticipate the silenced voices of the women who the speaker proceeds to find.

As they reach their destination in the underworld, Sappho shows the speaker the suffering shadows of women and children, victims of diseases in the years before the invention of antibiotics. The startling image puts the (male-dominated) poetic tradition to shame. The 'obvious // emblem' of lines eight and nine has occluded the 'real thing', failing to register the 'horror' of the lived experience of the overlooked women and children. In a doubly loaded message, though, Sappho reminds the speaker of her own responsibility to see the ordinary dailiness of women's lives, of her own obligation to see below and beyond the superficial point at which a modern, feminist perspective might pause: ' "be careful" ', Sappho admonishes her, ' "Do not define these women by their work" ' (stanza fifteen). Responsibility is a key theme in the poem. What the speaker takes from her encounter with Sappho is a desire to bear witness, to give voice to the silent. This desire acknowledges, while proceeding to critique, a feminist tradition which would advocate such a move: ' "let me be" ', the speaker pleads, ' "Let me at least be their witness." '[33] But Sappho refuses this desire; it is enough, it seems, for the speaker to learn from what she has seen and thereby to learn something about her own status as woman and poet. She should not automatically assume the right or responsibility to speak for others; that, in itself, is a form of colonisation. As Sappho explains in the antepenultimate stanza:

> 'I have brought you here so you will know forever
> the silences in which are our beginnings,
> In which we have an origin like water.'

In a final and supreme paradox, though, the poem precisely articulates that which Sappho has urged the speaker to leave silent. It is in telling us of that injunction not to speak that these women's stories are brought to light.

'The Journey' makes extensive use of repetition, in part for emphasis and in part as a way of registering the barely credible horror of the scene to which the subject is party. She must enunciate carefully, deliberately, repetitively in order, first, to etch the scene on her own mind and, second, to represent it faithfully to her audience. In stanzas nine and ten, for example, 'down' is repeated in the first line. Significantly, this is without the commas one would expect in such a clause, thereby signifying the remorselessness of the descent. The word 'down' is then carried over into the next stanza to convey its depth. So, too, 'always' and 'went on' are used several times to invoke the length and persistence of the journey. The assonance and sibilance slow the lines down giving a sense of strange dislocation, conjuring a dreamlike world devoid of conventional markers of time or space:

> down down down without so much as
> ever touching down but always, always
> with a sense of mulch beneath us,
> the way of stairs winding down to a river
>
> and as we went on the light went on
> failing and I looked sideways to be certain

The enjambment suggests one way of reading the initial line of the phrase, and then confounds it in the second. Hence we think we are hearing that 'the light went on', but we find, in fact, that the opposite is the case: it 'went on / failing'. We, like the speaker, become disorientated. This technique is used to particular effect in stanza twenty, where the speaker seems at first to be asking to be left alone 'let me be', but in fact is asking to be allowed to act as witness 'let me be / let me at least be their witness'. Here as throughout the poem, the 'I' (or 'me' or 'my') is emphatically delivered, confirming against all logic or reason the speaker's presence in this scene. It is as though she needs to convince herself that this really happened and thereafter to persuade us of her experience: 'I stood fixed. I could not reach or speak to them.'

POETIC FORM

Self-consciousness about form, language, tone and poetic conventions figures frequently, albeit sometimes implicitly, in poetry by women. It is the relationship with language, particularly but not exclusively in the twentieth century, that most preoccupies women poets. This is, of course, not only a female concern. T. S. Eliot's 'East Coker', for example, agonises about 'the intolerable wrestle / With words and meanings'.[34] Nevertheless, we might say that women poets, writing in a language which in its very history and structure seems to marginalise female subjectivity, feel most acutely the disjunction between experience and its representation. Successive generations of poets – from Chicana poets such as Cherríe Moraga to the Welsh poet Gillian Clarke – who are working in the language of a coloniser, a language which has historically been implicated in exploitation and violence, take this as their specific, if paradoxical, concern. I say 'paradoxical' because in many respects there is a reversal of authority here such that the racial or gendered 'other' hitherto placed in the position of object is now reversing the roles and assuming the position of subject. Poetry by women emerging from oral traditions (for example, from the Gaelic inheritance which Jeni Couzyn describes in her introduction to *The Bloodaxe Book of Contemporary Women Poets*, or from a Native American culture explored by, for example, Joy Harjo) stands in a particularly fraught relationship to both the authority attendant on the use of written language and to its material and physical properties.

The work of the contemporary Welsh poet Gillian Clarke offers a valuable example. She writes primarily in English but always with an ear to the cadences and conventions of the Welsh language. As she explains: 'There's an extra loss for a Welsh poet writing in English, and that is the longing for Welsh, for the secret language, mother tongue of all the stories, of all the centuries of speech and song.'[35] 'Border', for example, (a poem, incidentally, which anticipates some of the themes looked at in more depth in Chapter 6) dwells on forms of and barriers to communication. The certainties of identity, authority and discourse are unsettled by a primary uncertainty about alternative registers of language – the Welsh of the native speakers and the English of the alien incomers. In a contradictory and unsettling move, it is the native language which is rendered inoperable by the incomprehension of the immigrant – yet colonising – other. The speaker, as stanza one of 'Border' explains, is deprived of her own language and thus feels herself to be a foreigner in her own land.

The poem opens with an indeterminate 'it'. In refusing to define the referent of this 'it', 'Border' paves the way for a sequence of similarly slippery, elusive and fragile terms ('crumbles', 'slips', 'fade' and 'blur'). These are all verb forms and the effect of their use is to emphasise the fluidity, transience and vulnerability of the language, and by extension of the culture, that the poem laments. Language here is violent. Its loss is felt viscerally, on the body. In the final stanza the shopkeeper's inability or refusal to hear the speaker's Welsh tongue is experienced as a kind of punishment: 'I am slapped / by her hard "What!" '.[36]

Gwyneth Lewis, also a contemporary Welsh poet, draws similar analogies. For her, though, speaking Welsh in shops is a form of resistance – a code of alterity which is used to strategic and subversive effect:

> It's very tempting to treat a minority language as a personal code, which can be used to exclude other people. For this reason Welsh, like Navajo, has been used to transmit secret messages in wartime. It's very handy in shops with snotty assistants.[37]

In both Clarke and Lewis, it is in the everyday spaces of women's lives – in shops and schools and the home – that these tussles with language are played out. In Lewis's poem 'Welsh Espionage No 5', she pictures a little girl learning English from her father. This education is literally acquired on the body – it is in the process of naming her body parts, of translating them from the familiar Welsh into the new language of English, that she absorbs the vocabulary of the other. As the poem opens: 'Welsh was the mother tongue,

English was his. / He taught her the body by fetishist quiz.' This is more than language acquisition alone though: this poem enters the contested ground between two cultures, between the dominant English of the outside world (the symbolic order of language, transmitted by the male) and the dominated Welsh of the home (associated with the mother and, by extension, with the semiotic order).

In contemporary Irish poet Nuala Ní Dhomhnaill's 'Ceist na Teangan' (translated from the Irish by Paul Muldoon as 'The Language Issue'), the speaker addresses the complexities of translation from one language into another – and thus implicitly of all forms of linguistic exchange. The poem draws on the Hebrew story of the infant Moses, whose mother set him afloat in a basket on the River Nile in order to protect him from being killed by the Pharaoh (Exodus 1: 2). Thus it invokes a context which is characterised by hostility (Hebrews vs. Egyptians and, by implication, Irish vs. English) and tackled by subtle, but nevertheless dangerous, means. Ní Dhomhnaill uses the ancient story as a metaphor for her own attempt to make the language survive, placing her own 'hope on the water / in this little boat / of the language'.[38] She, like Moses's mother, wishes for a safe passage for her writing, but recognises that once cast adrift its destination remains uncertain. The poem demonstrates how intimately language is tied up with forms of power. The critical reception of the book in which this poem was first published, *Pharaoh's Daughter* (1990), further exemplifies the point. As Ní Dhomhnaill explains:

> A few years ago a number of poets, mostly as it happens male, collaborated in a book of translation of my work . . . Immediately the critics hailed me in terms of being a kind of Muse. Now let us get one thing quite clear. I was not their Muse: they were my translators.[39]

For women poets, language is arguably always experienced as strange, as alien and as other – this is not only an issue for women poets, such as those discussed above, who straddle different languages and cultures. The nineteenth-century American poet Emily Dickinson's 'Poem 427' ('I'll clutch – and clutch') takes its own poetic processes as its primary focus.[40] The poem exemplifies the at times tortuous route by which the subject comes into language and the poem comes into being. The curious mixture of future and present-tense action suggests the immediacy of the creative process that the poem is simultaneously anticipating, experiencing and describing.

'I'll clutch – and clutch – ', the poem opens, demonstrating the desperation and the persistence with which the speaker strives to grasp at poetic inspiration or the right word:

> I'll clutch – and clutch –
> Next – One – Might be the golden touch –
> Could take it –
> Diamonds – Wait –

The repetition and the dashes show just how fraught and how uncertain this moment is. The act of writing poetry is like skating on ice, hence subsequent metaphors of stars, diamonds and other white, glassy, crystalline surfaces. However smooth and kinetic the movement, at any moment it might end in disaster. Success seems always beyond the speaker's grasp – each moment might, or might not, bring 'the golden touch'. The use of present and future-tense forms illustrates both how close (it is here and now) and how far (it is in the future and cannot yet be grasped) poetic inspiration, or the right word, is.

Frequent caesurae, dashes and monosyllabic clauses ('wait', 'make', 'count') cause the poem to stop and start, recording and performing a creative ritual. The larger shape of the poem describes while it enacts its own coming into being. The opening line of stanza one describes the moment of inspiration, which must be seized or clutched while it lasts. Stanza two describes the next step ('I'll string you – in fine necklace') using a metaphor which invokes the act of arranging and stringing together precious words into lines of poetry. Stanza three ('I'll show you') conveys the public exposure of the poem, or its dissemination to an audience. Finally, the poem reflects on the legacy which it will provide:

> And – when I die –
> In meek array – display you –
> Still to show – how rich I go –

Language in this poem is a precious thing (hence 'diamonds'), made more precious still by being worked on, strung together and arranged into decorative ('necklace', 'tiaras'), symbolic ('diadem') or functional objects ('Wear you on Hem – ' and 'mend my old One'). The poem describes and embodies the complex procedure by which the speaker seeks first to possess ('clutch') and then to control (to 'count – hoard') a language which proves finally able to possess and control her: 'Count – Hoard – then lose – / And doubt that you are mine – '. 'Poem 427' gestures finally to the speaker's fear of annihilation by the language which she has striven so hard to manipulate:

> Still to show – how rich I go –
> Lest Skies impeach a wealth so wonderful –
> And banish me –

Because she has turned the elements of language (metaphorically stars and diamonds) into a whole even more beautiful than its parts, the speaker fears punishment.

Dickinson's poem raises a crucial issue in current literary debates, one which strikes at the heart of the shift in the recent study of poetry by women outlined in the Introduction. A fundamental issue for twentieth-century and contemporary literary studies is the nature of language, its relation to the subject and to the world. The debates about language are not, of course, relevant only to the study of writing by women. However, the nature of some recent perspectives on women's poetry, with their assumptions about the referentiality of language, its expressiveness, its function as a mere conduit or vehicle for subjective experience (for example, Diana Scott's view in the introduction to her anthology of nineteenth and twentieth-century women's poetry that it 'communicates [. . .] experience with perfect clarity' and thus 'may empower us to recreate the experience for ourselves') do make these matters particularly germane in the context of this book.[41] Is language an instrument or tool which poets can simply pick up and apply? Is it, as the turn-of-the-century Swiss linguist Ferdinand de Saussure has so influentially argued, a system or structure which precedes and thus dominates the subject: 'language is not a function of the speaker; it is a product that is passively assimilated by the individual'?[42] How do ideas deriving from postcolonial theories about language and otherness help us to read the work of some women poets? Is there something, as French feminist thinkers such as Hélène Cixous, Luce Irigaray and Julia Kristeva would suggest, about the ways in which women assume a gendered identity which places them in a peculiar relationship with the symbolic language which dominates literary (indeed all) modern cultures? As Chapter 4 will ask, is there a unique kind of language, a semiotic language or language of the body, to which women poets are particularly attuned?

A THEORY OF SELF-REFLEXIVITY

How might one theorise the self-reflexivity identified here as a feature of the work of a number of women poets? One fruitful avenue is by way of what Linda Hutcheon has called, in a slightly different context, textual narcissism. The narcissistic text is one which works 'to make readers aware of both its production and reception as [a] cultural product'. It 'call[s] attention to authority structures in such a way as to subvert' them. It functions either overtly or covertly to mirror its own creative processes and – equally importantly – the processes at stake in its own reading. In this way it draws the attention of readers to their own responsibility for the generation of meaning.[43]

This narcissistic process is rendered particularly visible in women poets' use of metaphors of mirrors, glass and other reflective surfaces. There is, of course, a long tradition of thinking about the literary text in terms of its relationships with mirrors and catoptrics (or mirroring processes). Most famously, perhaps, M. H. Abrams's *The Mirror and the Lamp* proposes a theory of literature which is predicated on the distinction between art as reflection and art as projection, or art as imitative and art as expressive. Abrams describes 'two common and antithetic metaphors of mind, one comparing the mind to a reflector of external objects, the other to a radiant projector which makes a contribution to the object it perceives'.[44] The distinction is analogous to the differences between the classical realist and Romantic literary traditions, or the 'world-imitative' and 'artist-orientated' as Linda Hutcheon puts it.[45]

More recently, Hutcheon has posited mirroring, reflection and other narcissistic processes as fundamental to avant-garde and post-modernist writing. Although her interest is primarily in fiction, Hutcheon also offers valuable insights into women's poetry. She sees textual narcissism as part of a postmodern questioning and exposure of hitherto accepted givens – about the nature and origins of authority, about language, subjectivity, referentiality, and about the cultural and discursive contexts in which meanings are generated and read.[46] Two key elements of Hutcheon's argument are helpful in theorising self-reflexivity in women's poetry. The first is the primacy of the relationship between the text and its reading; it is the 'interactive powers involved in the production and reception of texts' which narcissistic narrative (and women's self-reflexive poetry) 'makes visible'.[47] The second, and this may at first seem paradoxical, is the emphasis which Hutcheon places on the textual nature of this narcissism. Narcissism is otherwise a difficult and in some respects a dangerous term for women poets to embrace. It has so often been used as an accusation or a form of disparagement that one might expect practitioners to go to great lengths to avoid it. However, before throwing our hands up in horror, we should take note of Hutcheon's clear admonition that her use of the term 'narcissistic' is 'meant to be critically neutral' for 'it is the narrative text and not the author' that is being described in this way.[48] This at one and the same time allows us to recuperate the term as a valuable way of thinking about the 'textual self-consciousness' of women's poetry, and it sustains the point made throughout the present book about the importance of distinguishing between poet and speaker, biography and textualisation.

Jean Delumeau arguably understates the case when he comments that 'the mirror was and is particularly ambiguous for women'.[49] This is a point which both Simone de Beauvoir and Virginia Woolf have explored in their own writing.[50] Associated since the Middle Ages with feminine sins of pride, lust and envy, the mirror appears in art, in fairy stories and in literature throughout the ages as an emblem and reminder of woman's alleged self-love and potential for corruption. Jan Montefiore traces the relationship between women and the mirror in the poetry of this tradition:

The love poem as it appears in the Western tradition of poetry represented by Petrarch and Sidney is characteristically spoken by a male poet celebrating the beauty and virtue of an unattainable woman who is at once the object of his desire, the cause of his poetry and the mirror which defines his identity.[51]

The mirror functions in Western culture both as a means of self-monitoring or self-surveillance and as a constant reminder of the feminine ideal to which women must conform. For Sabine Melchior-Bonnet, author of *The Mirror: A History*, 'The authority of the reflection is imposed primarily upon women who, at least at a certain stage of cultural development, construct themselves under the gaze of the other.'[52] For French critic and theorist Jacques Lacan, it is only through successful negotiation of the mirror stage that the aspiring infant subject can leave the realm of the imaginary and enter the symbolic order of language (a journey that is invoked in Sexton's poem 'The Double Image', discussed below).[53]

We can see from all this how very important the motif of the mirror is for women poets as they negotiate their cultural place. Mary Elizabeth Coleridge's poem 'The Other Side of a Mirror' exploits the uncanniness of the mirror in its representation of the image of the woman, caught within the confines of its frame. Here the process of mirroring cruelly reflects back to the woman her own oppression and her own silencing. Looking for a sense of self, she can see only her own voiceless despair. The mirror – because it cannot 'speak' – paradoxically both reveals and confirms her own silence:

> Her lips were open – not a sound
> Came though the parted lines of red,
> Whate'er it was, the hideous wound
> In silence and secret bled.[54]

The truth which the mirror reveals to the woman is the truth of the mature female body.

Sexton's long and widely anthologized poem 'The Double Image' (1960) takes a succession of mirrors, self-portraits and other reflective surfaces (including the double images or dual portraits of the title) as its central metaphors. Although ostensibly a confessional poem about the complex relationships between three generations of women – the elderly and dying mother, the psychologically unstable adult daughter (the main speaker) and the vulnerable infant granddaughter – the poem might also be read as a contemplation and confession of its own creative processes. The dying mother commissions her own self-portrait and then a 'matching' one of her mentally-ill daughter in a vain (I use the word 'vain' in both senses of the word) attempt to protect and preserve both of them.[55]

Linda Hutcheon suggests that textual narcissism might be used in either 'overt' or 'covert' ways (in overt narcissism, 'self-consciousness and self-reflection are clearly evident, usually explicitly thematized'; in the covert form 'this process would be structuralized, internalized').[56] Both of these strategies are evident in 'The Double Image' where mirrors function at the visible level, and mirroring operates beneath the surface. It is the covert level which is, perhaps, most interesting. The subject 'I', the addressee 'you' and the others ('she' and 'they') stand in a finely balanced and mutually reliant role akin to that of a mirror, an object and its reflection. The text itself assumes the characteristics of a mirror with the arrangement of its seven sections representing a near-perfect symmetry of action. In the first three sections the infant daughter and then the speaker leave home while the central (fourth) section hangs in the balance, denoting a liminal moment of uncertainty or indecision. Symmetry is restored in the closing three sections wherein first the speaker and then the child return. The opening and closing sections of dense syllabic verse contain the fullness of the poem; establishing first the terms of the debate, and then its resolution. Like an object and its reflection, they are drawn together by the central hermetic mirror, or the concise, self-contained, central section.

The closing stanza of the poem offers an important additional reading of the 'double image' of its title. The speaker finally acknowledges to her infant daughter that 'I needed you'. The child has replaced the speaker's mother in that it is she – the infant child – who has bestowed (gender) identity on the speaker. The infant child makes good the failure of the speaker's mother:

> I, who was never quite sure
> about being a girl, needed another
> life, another image to remind me.

The 'image' is that of the daughter, produced literally and figura-tively by the speaker in order to confirm her own identity. Hence, the speaker's final admission: 'And this was my worst guilt; you could not cure / nor soothe it. I made you to find me.' This is a com-pelling conclusion. However, the real interest lies in the confession not that the speaker made the daughter (biologically) but that she has constructed her in the poem (textually). These final lines confirm my reading of the poem as textually narcissistic, for the ultimate referent of 'the double image' is the poem itself. The 'worst guilt' to which the speaker refers pertains to her fabrication and manipulation of the mother/daughter relationship in order to construct this very poem and thereby to create or found (and emphatically not to reflect) her singular identity as poet: 'to find me'.

Zoë Skoulding's recent collection *The Mirror Trade* (2004) fea-tures poems of flux and change – geographical, historical and per-ceptual. There are poems here which trace movement from one place to another on trains ('Trans-Siberian, 1927'), in taxis ('Taxi Driver, Delhi') and across bridges ('Brittania Bridge', 'The Bridge'). There are elegies ('Binocular') and poems which trace the passing of time and of generations ('Letter to my Grandfather'). And there are poems of shifting, turning, fluctuating perspectives: 'light as slender trees / spattered with gold' in the words of the poem 'Klimt's Buchenwald'.[57]

Centring all of this are metaphors – and whole poems – about mirrors and mirroring processes. As we have seen, Hutcheon dis-tinguishes between overt and covert forms of textual narcissism; both are evident here. In 'At the Dressing Table', for example, rather like in Sylvia Plath's 1963 poem 'Mirror' or Sharon Olds's 'The Spouses Waking Up in the Hotel Mirror' (1999), it is the mirror which speaks, placing terrible demands on the human viewer who gazes into it. 'At the Dressing Table' reveals a self-conscious confusion of subject and object such that the object (the mirror) becomes the speaking subject while the conventional subject (the viewer) becomes the mirror's object, or the thing which is being looked at. In this way, to refer back to Hutcheon, the poem thematises, reflects, and thereby implicitly critiques readerly expectations about identity, speaking position, subjectivity and authority.

So, too, the title poem 'The Mirror Trade' is ostensibly about the manufacture of mirrors (Skoulding's own note to the poem gives us a little background: 'The secrets of the Venetian mirror industry [. . .] were once closely guarded on the island of Murano'). But it is also implicitly a reflection on and of the poetic process.[58] Like Plath's 'Black Rook in Rainy Weather' and Fainlight's 'The Other', discussed earlier, the poem opens with an allusion to that vital pre-creative moment which must be seized before the making (of poem or mirror) begins: 'Air shines. / We snare it in our glass.' Thereafter the poem records the mirror's (and its own) genesis in 'furnaces and transubstantiations / quicksilver and tin amalgams'. Such images reflect the productive combination of magical, alchemical and abstract processes fundamental to the creation of mirror and poem alike.

Crucially, both mirror and poem are dependent on their 'other' – the observer/viewer/reader – in order to consolidate and confirm their own meaning. 'The Mirror Trade' speaks in the plural (we, our, us) throughout in order to exemplify and confirm the discursive process (the necessary relationship between subject and object, text and reader, mirror and viewer) by which meaning is produced. More importantly, it reflects in its final stanza on the way in which meaning is shared:

> As we load mirrors, ships
> bleed pictures of more ships
> which lap the warehouse steps; we send out
> pieces of ourselves which bear no trace of us.[59]

In the case of this poem, it is fragments of text which are dispersed. Free of their moment of creation, they set off alone – no longer, if they ever were, to be identified with the experience, intentions or interpretations of the maker. This insight is in keeping with the reticent, elliptical nature of the rest of the poems in this collection and in keeping with some of the experimental poetry we will look at in the final chapter.

A number of other poems distort the conventions associated with the mirror. These reveal not the female subject/viewer but the figure of a man. This reflection of a male 'other' curiously determines the female speaker's identity; it is in relation to this 'other' that a subordinate 'self' is constructed. The *fin de siècle* poet Anna Wickham was born in London in 1884, brought up in Australia, but lived most of her adult life back in England. Her poem 'The Mirror' conveys a moral tale about self-knowledge and self-correction. In this macabre poem, the speaker confides her initial selfishness in refusing 'on the eve of Christmas day' to help a poor beggar man. The beggar perishes outside in the cold, but then uncannily returns and assumes the place of the speaker's reflection or double: ''Twas then a wonder came to pass / *He* waited in the looking-glass.' The closing lines of the poem confirm the indivisibility of self and other, object and reflection: 'I am thyself.'[60]

Two more recent poems by American poet Louise Glück also experiment with the gender dynamics of the mirroring process. The first of these, 'The Mirror', startles with its opening reversal of our expectations about the gender of the subject and object of the gaze. Here, it transpires, the female speaker assumes the position of the viewing subject while the man is the passive object, caught in the gaze: 'Watching you in the mirror I wonder / what it is like to be so beautiful'. Objectified in this way, the man resists in the only way such a stereotyped world view leaves open to him, by aggressively asserting his latent power: 'you can turn against yourself / with greater violence'. He wrests back control and agency in order to break the female viewer's hold.[61] Glück's 'Mirror Image', too, is notable for its depiction of a female observer and a male object. Here the speaker looks to the mirror to find an image of herself and sees instead her ageing father. Again, the man dominates the space, crowding out the daughter's potential for self-realisation with all of the despair of his own life – a life which 'contained nothing' and thus absorbs the possibility of reflection. Like Mary Coleridge's 'The Other Side of the Mirror', discussed earlier, the image silences the female viewer.

CONCLUSION

When Isobel Armstrong suggests, in the quotation cited at the beginning of this chapter, that female poets problematise rather than proselytise their situation, it becomes evident that the self-consciousness or self-reflexivity outlined here should be seen as a positive feature. It represents a purposive, thoughtful and productive means of engagement rather than a limiting and limited statement of position. Poetry by women, then, is engaged in a constant process of self-assessment or self-scrutiny; it is constantly asking questions about its own place in poetic traditions, or cultural contexts, or poetic forms.

SUMMARY OF KEY POINTS

- One of the issues which is shared by women's poetry across generations and cultures is the self-reflexivity of the writing.
- Poetry by women problematises its own relation to the muse and to poetic inspiration more generally. It presents a range of perspectives on its relationship to the dominant canon and to the work of female predecessors.
- In some cases, poetry by women displays a critical self-consciousness about the language and forms available to it.
- This self-reflexivity is particularly visible in a range of poems about mirrors and mirroring processes.

NOTES

1. Mark and Rees-Jones, *Contemporary*, p. xv.
2. Linda Hutcheon, *Narcissistic Narrative: The Metafictional Paradox* (London and New York: Methuen, 1984).
3. Jane Stevenson and Peter Davidson (eds), *Early Modern Women Poets: An Anthology* (Oxford: Oxford University Press, 2001), p. xl.
4. Barrett Browning, *Aurora Leigh*, p. 35.
5. Greer, *Slip-Shod Sibyls*, p. xxi.

6. Plimpton, *Women Writers*, p. xvi.

7. Dowson, *Women, Modernism*, p. 174.

8. Jane Dowson and Alice Entwistle, *A History of Twentieth-Century British Women's Poetry* (Cambridge: Cambridge University Press, 2005), p. 212.

9. Pearson, *Women's Reading*, p. 4.

10. Louise Bogan, *What the Woman Lived: Selected Letters of Louise Bogan 1920–1970*, ed. Ruth Limmer (New York: Harcourt Brace Jovanovich, 1973), p. 375.

11. Reprinted in Marion Wynne-Davies (ed.), *Women Poets of the Renaissance* (London: Dent, 1998), pp. 99–103 (p. 102).

12. Pearson, *Women's Reading*, p. 7.

13. Manguel, *History*, p. 73.

14. Sylvia Plath, 'Black Rook in Rainy Weather', in *Collected Poems*, ed. Ted Hughes (London: Faber and Faber, 1981), p. 56.

15. Ruth Fainlight, 'The Other', in *The Bloodaxe Book of Contemporary Women Poets: Eleven British Writers*, ed. Jeni Couzyn (Newcastle: Bloodaxe, 1985), p. 135.

16. See Tracy Brain, *The Other Sylvia Plath* (Harlow: Longman, 2001), p. 79, n. 49 for a comparison of the American and British terms rook, crow and raven.

17. Sexton, *Complete*, p. 534.

18. See Sigmund Freud, 'Beyond the Pleasure Principle', in *The Freud Reader*, ed. Peter Gay (London: Vintage, [1920] 1995), pp. 594–626.

19. Sharon Olds, *Strike Sparks: Selected Poems, 1980–2002* (New York: Knopf, 2004), p. 44.

20. Plath, *Collected*, p. 62.

21. Dowson, ' "Older Sisters" ', p. 9.

22. Dowson, *Women, Modernism*, pp. 7–8; Amy Lowell, 'The Sisters', in Kaplan, *Salt*, pp. 210–13.

23. Woolf, *A Room of One's Own*, pp. 50, 51.

24. Nancy K. Miller, *Getting Personal: Feminist Occasions and Other Autobiographical Acts* (New York and London: Routledge, 1991), p. 125.

25. Susan Gubar, 'Sapphistries', in *Re-Reading Sappho: Reception and Transmission*, ed. Ellen Greene (Berkeley: University of California Press, 1996), pp. 199–217 (pp. 214–15).

26. Quoted in Karen Jackson Ford, *Gender and the Poetics of Excess: Moments of Brocade* (Jackson: University Press of Mississippi, 1997), p. 38.

27. Ellen Greene, 'Introduction', in *Reading Sappho: Contemporary Approaches*, ed. Ellen Greene (Berkeley: University of California Press, 1996), pp. 1–8 (p. 1).

28. In one case, an edition of Christina Rossetti's poems edited by her brother, Sappho emerges as a mere trace. According to Louise Bernikow, William Rossetti expunged poems entitled 'Sappho' and 'What Sappho would have said, had her leap cured instead of killing her' (Bernikow, *The World*, p. 5).

29. Donna Landry, *The Muses of Resistance: Laboring-Class Women's Poetry in Britain, 1739–1796* (Cambridge: Cambridge University Press, 1990), p. 86.

30. *Sappho: Poems and Fragments*, trans. Stanley Lombardo, intro. Pamela Gordon (Indianapolis, IN: Hacket Publishing Company, 2002), p. xx.

31. Ibid. pp. xxii–xxiii.

32. Reprinted in *The New Poetry*, ed. Michael Hulse, David Kennedy and David Morley (Newcastle: Bloodaxe, 1993), pp. 49–51.

33. See Adrienne Rich, *On Lies, Secrets and Silence: Selected Prose 1966–1978* (London: Virago, 1980); Tillie Olsen, *Silences* (London: Virago, 1980); Joanna Russ, *How to Suppress Women's Writing* (London: Women's Press, 1984).

34. T. S. Eliot, *Four Quartets* (London: Faber and Faber, 1959), p. 26.

35. Gillian Clarke, quoted in Rees-Jones, *Modern*, p. 191.

36. Gillian Clarke, 'Border', in Rees-Jones, *Modern*, p. 191.

37. Gwyneth Lewis, 'First Person', *The Guardian*, 'Family' section, 18 November 2006, p. 3. Interestingly, Lewis was raised speaking Welsh and writes bilingually. Clarke is not a native Welsh speaker and does not currently write in Welsh.

38. Nuala Ní Dhomhnaill, 'Ceist na Teangan' (trans. Paul Muldoon, 'The Language Issue'), in Hulse et al., *The New Poetry*, pp. 170–1.

39. Quoted in Lucy Collins, 'Contemporary Irish Poetry', in *A Companion to Twentieth-Century Poetry*, ed. Neil Roberts (Oxford: Blackwell, 2001), pp. 585–95 (p. 592).

40. Emily Dickinson, *The Complete Poems* (London: Faber and Faber, 1970), p. 204. In manuscript, Dickinson's dashes vary in size and direction, but they are usually reproduced typographically as 'en rules' (dashes with a space on either side). See also Susan Howe, 'These Flames and Generosities of the Heart: Emily Dickinson and the Illogic of Sumptuary Values', in *Artifice and Indeterminacy: An Anthology of New Poetics*, ed. Christopher Beach (Tuscaloosa and London: University of Alabama Press, 1998), pp. 319–41.

41. Diana Scott, 'Introduction', in *Bread and Roses: Women's Poetry of the 19th and 20th Centuries* (London: Virago, 1982), pp. 1–28 (p. 1).

42. Ferdinand de Saussure, 'Course in General Linguistics', in *Literary Theory: An Anthology*, ed. Julie Rivkin and Michael Ryan (Oxford: Blackwell, 1998), pp. 76–90 (p. 76).

43. Hutcheon, *Narcissistic*, pp. xiii, xvi, 23.

44. M. H. Abrams, *The Mirror and the Lamp: Romantic Theory and the Critical Tradition* (Oxford: Oxford University Press, 1971), p. ii.

45. Linda Hutcheon, *The Politics of Postmodernism* (London and New York: Routledge, 1989), p. 6.

46. Hutcheon, *Narcissistic*, pp. xvi, xiii, xv.

47. Ibid. p. xv.

48. Ibid. p. 1.

49. Jean Delumeau, 'Preface', in Sabine Melchior-Bonnet, *The Mirror: A History*, trans. Katharine H. Jewett (New York and London: Routledge, 2001), p. xi.

50. Simone de Beauvoir, *The Second Sex* (Harmondsworth: Penguin, [1949] 1983), p. 642ff.; Woolf, *A Room of One's Own*, p. 37.

51. Jan Montefiore, *Feminism and Poetry: Language, Experience, Identity in Women's Writing*, 3rd edn (London: Pandora, 2004), p. 96.

52. Melchior-Bonnet, *The Mirror*, p. 271.

53. Jacques Lacan, 'The Mirror Stage as Formative of the Function of the I as Revealed in Psychoanalytic Experience', in *Ecrits: A Selection*, trans. Alan Sheridan (London: Routledge, 1989), p. 2.

54. Mary Elizabeth Coleridge, 'The Other Side of a Mirror', in *Nineteenth-Century Women Poets: An Oxford Anthology*, ed. Isobel Armstrong, Joseph Bristow and Cath Sharrock (Oxford: Clarendon Press, 1996), p. 756.

55. In his essay on 'The Uncanny', Freud cites Otto Rank's work on the contradictory role of the double as a 'preservation against extinction' and as 'the uncanny harbinger of death'. See 'The Uncanny', in *The Standard Edition of the Works of Sigmund Freud*, vol. 17, ed. James Strachey (London: Hogarth Press, 1953), pp. 219–52 (p. 235).

56. Hutcheon, *Narcissistic*, p. 23.

57. Zoë Skoulding, *The Mirror Trade* (Bridgend: Seren, 2004), p. 46.

58. Ibid. p. 70.

59. Ibid. p. 11.

60. Anna Wickham, 'The Mirror', in *The Writings of Anna Wickham: Free Woman and Poet*, ed. R. D. Smith (London: Virago, 1984), p. 268.

61. Louise Glück, 'The Mirror' and 'Mirror Image', in *The First Five Books of Poems* (Manchester: Carcanet, 1997), pp. 121, 254.

CHAPTER 2

Performance

In a recent essay, poet Selima Hill recalls a dream in which she is on stage, about to read her own work, when a doctor 'thrust his fingers down my throat and pulled out miles and miles of long slimy tubes like spaghetti'.[1] The image is uncannily like those used by Anne Sexton, who refers to her own work in poems, interviews, essays and letters as a form of 'blood-letting', self-immolation or self-sacrifice.[2] It recalls, too, Elizabeth Bishop's account of undertaking poetry readings and being '*sick* for days ahead of time' [her emphasis] and hence giving up poetry readings for twenty-six years.[3] The strongly visceral nature of these images is striking. What do they say about the relationship between women's poetry and their biological existence? (This question will be addressed in detail in Chapter 4.) In tandem with this rhetoric of poetry reading as a form of ritualised sacrifice or self-display, we find many examples of women poets likening the public display (and even the private writing) of their work to a form of striptease or prostitution. For Sexton, poetry readings are 'a one-night stand', and for Medbh McGuckian, 'by writing the poem you're becoming a whore. You're selling your soul which is worse than any prostitution.'[4]

What, this chapter asks, do these comments and reservations have to say about the performance of women's poetry? The term 'performance' is used to connote both the theoretical or conceptual sense of the way in which the woman poet might perform a particular identity (by what Judith Butler calls 'a stylised repetition of acts'), and the more literal sense of the way in which poetry is delivered in public readings on the stage.[5] Butler's sense of the term has been highly influential in contemporary gender and queer studies. It proposes that sexual, gender and indeed many other forms of identity are, in fact, forms of construction. More properly, they are imitations, impressions or approximations. They are constructed versions of an identity which, itself, has no original. 'There is no gender identity behind the expressions of gender,' Butler argues. Thus 'identity is performatively constituted by the very "expressions" that are said to be its results'.[6] In other words, we make gender rather than express or reflect it. She goes on to explain that 'acts, gestures, and desire produce the effect of an internal core or substance' which is entirely illusory; 'gender parody [drag, for instance] reveals that the original identity after which gender fashions itself is an imitation without an origin'.[7] Thus, what we take to be gender is not a fixed or stable category; rather, it is an imitative practice or set of practices. Gender, from this point of view, is 'not expressive but performative'.[8] For many contemporary critics and readers, Butler's argument makes a valuable contribution to debates about subjectivity, gender and sexual identity. It says something about the instability of gender and about the irrelevance of hitherto accepted ideas about essential male or female experiences and behaviours. To an important extent, then, Butler offers a complex challenge both to a patriarchal order based on determinate sexual difference and to a feminist critique which has, itself, often been based on a sense of fundamental and fixed female identity.

Nevertheless, the theory does have some limitations in terms of its applicability to the analysis of the poetic text. Deryn Rees-Jones in her critical study *Consorting with Angels* (2005) offers a useful distinction between gender performativity ('acts which constitute the self') and performance of gender ('an idea of identity as "interior essence" which can be expressed'). As Rees-Jones proceeds to argue, and as the poems discussed below confirm, 'performance of the poem, and performativity of the self, specifically a gendered self, must be read as part of a complex matrix between poet, text and speech, which is mediated through culture, intention, expression, language and the often prescriptive ideas of the woman poet and her role'.[9] Both terms are germane to the discussion which follows, but it will nevertheless be helpful to bear in mind a distinction between conscious modes of performance or self-display and the kinds of unconscious practices of gender constitution and performativity that Butler has in mind. To reiterate, 'performance' presumes a prior original (the object of the imitation), whereas 'performative' disputes the existence of a source or origin.

Amy Lowell's poem 'Patterns' is worthy of consideration in this context. It opens by establishing an aesthetics of order or a set of structures and constraints in which the subject 'I' must put herself on display:

> I walk down the patterned garden paths
> In my stiff, brocaded gown.
> With my powdered hair and jewelled fan,
> I too am a rare
> Pattern.

The subject seems to be playing or performing femininity. To borrow from Butler, the subject's 'words, acts, gestures, and desire produce the effect of an internal core or substance, but produce this *on the surface* of the body'. This is '*performative* in the sense that the essence or identity that they otherwise purport to express are *fabrications*' [Butler's italics].[10]

As the poem proceeds, there is a striking dissociation of the speaker and subject or, more properly, of the subject of the enunciation (the person doing the describing) and the subject of the enounced (the person being described). The female speaker views herself as though from the outside, as though watching her own performance:

> Just a plate of current fashion,
> Tripping by in high-heeled, ribboned shoes.
> Not a softness anywhere about me,
> Only whalebone and brocade.

Thus she both performs femininity and refuses it. She refuses the performance itself by dissociating herself from it and by exposing its constructedness, its illusoriness, its dependence for its effects on a skeleton of 'whalebone and brocade'. And she refuses femininity by undermining its conventions, hence 'not a softness anywhere about me'.

The 'Patterns' of the poem's title is in some respects misleading, for what the poem explores above all are the forces of instability and disorder. 'Patterns' are illusory, constructing stability where none exists. The poem closes with news of the death of the speaker's fiancé in the First World War. Written in 1915 in the throes of the catastrophic failure of hitherto accepted social patterns, structures and hierarchies, the poem exposes the fragility of the old order – of gender, place, time and faith – and reveals the artifice this culture has constructed in order to mask this chasm. Most tellingly, it is the necessity for the female speaker/subject to lament the death of the male lover/object which so dangerously inverts all expectations of the natural order in poetry as in life. The greatest transgression here is that it is the woman mourning the loss of her love object. To quote the critic Northrop Frye, 'The most logical person to lament the death of Adonis is Venus, though she seldom does so in literature.'[11] Lowell's 'Patterns' provides one of those rare occasions.

SELF-EXPOSURE

In the comments from Sexton, Bishop and McGuckian cited above, it is significant that the act of being, and being seen to be, a female poet is regarded as aberrant and abhorrent, as immoral, improper and deserving of punishment. The strategies which women poets have employed in addressing this predicament have varied from frank confrontation to evasion or, in the case of Mary Barber discussed in the previous chapter, an attempt at mollification. They include exaggerated, rhetorical poses, the better to invite and thus expose or undermine judgement, and the assumption of various forms of camouflage, costume or mask. At times, for example, in the work of Helen Farish and Carol Ann Duffy, the face of authenticity and self-revelation is, itself, a form of subterfuge.

Lowell's 1914 poem 'The Captured Goddess', like two later poems, Sexton's 'Her Kind' and Plath's 'Witch Burning', features a transcendent and spectacular female subject who escapes constraint and in so doing literally and figuratively illuminates the conditions of that containment.[12] The title of the poem is more enigmatic than may at first appear, particularly when read in the context of the first few stanzas. At first the word 'captured' suggests a sight only momentarily glimpsed. The transience and preciousness of the image is invoked by the constant fluctuating movement of the scene; the 'rotating chimney pots', the 'shiver of amethyst' and flickering colours. At this point 'captured' conveys, too, the very process being enacted in this poem of capturing an impression, scene, or likeness on the page. The final and perhaps most disturbing interpretation of the word 'captured' is, of course, the sense of imprisonment, containment and punishment.

Before this moment of crisis, though, the goddess puts on a dazzling display, an act which offers a metaphor for the performativity of the female poet. Like in other Lowell poems ('Opal', for instance) the multicoloured hues in the poem such as the 'lustre of crimson', the 'saffrons, rubies', 'yellows' and 'indigo-blue', while deeply evocative in their own right, are also connotative of the qualities of white light when split by a prism or crystal into its component parts. What we see of the goddess is a richly coloured surface display. What lies beneath this spectacular surface is a pure light which in Platonic thought is symbolic of insight, knowledge and understanding. Cathryn Vasseleu explains that, as far back as Plato's allegory of the cave (from his *Republic*), 'the nature of light and existence are deeply entwined in the history of Western thought. Fundamental to this tradition is an image of light as an invisible medium that opens up a knowable world.'[13] In Lowell's 'The Captured Goddess', unlike in the Plath and Sexton poems discussed later, the first-person speaker does not voice the role of the transcendent goddess/witch. Instead she speaks from the position of observer (although as we will see shortly, there is some transposition of perspectives such that the distinction between the two becomes unclear). In this sense, it is the subject 'I' who functions as a prism; it is through her observation of the goddess (object) that the goddess's latent luminescence is split into the spectrum of colour. Again, the poem reads as a commentary on its own processes. In this context, we might note the repeated allusions to veils and lustres, to opaque, clouded, filmy shades. The effect is twofold. First, it conveys the uncertainty of vision. It is as though this is such a rare sight that the speaker is unsure what she sees. Second, it implies a certain constraint, containment or restriction on the first-person speaker, as well as on the goddess. Both are captured and the positions of subject and object become interchangeable; the visions or horizons of both are, metaphorically at least, curtailed.

One of the factors which contributes to the imprisonment, and finally the annihilation, of the goddess is the pressure of the 'market-place' (stanza five). The poem speaks of an anxiety among women poets about being put on public display. The anxiety is about their work being exposed, fingered, measured or assayed, particularly by the men who hold economic power. 'Men chaffered for her,' as Lowell's poem puts it:

> They bargained in silver and gold,
> In copper, in wheat,
> And called their bids across the market-place.

The verb 'chaffered' means to sell or haggle, but more importantly to traffic, a term which connotes the sexual exploitation of women. Appalled by this spectacle, the speaker of the poem is forced into retreat and thus a new form of entrapment:

> Hiding my face I fled,
> And the grey wind hissed behind me,
> Along the narrow streets.

The retreating subject in abandoning the tormented goddess ('The Goddess wept,' the one-line penultimate stanza tells us) shares her abjection and her shame. The flamboyant self-display which had once seemed such an attraction ('I cared not where she led me') has come down to this; the hidden rhyme of 'led' and 'fled' emphasises the shared change in fortunes, the shared vulnerability and punishment.

Two later poems by acquaintances and contemporaries, Sexton and Plath, also use the figure of the siren, witch or goddess to convey some of the anxieties implicit in the assumption of the role of female poet and in the performance (the public articulation on paper or on stage) of the work. Both Sexton's 'Her Kind' and Plath's 'Witch Burning' were written in 1959, and both open with the witch/woman writer (the first-person speaker of the poem) hovering – literally and figuratively – on the margins of society.[14] Sexton's speaker imagines herself 'haunting the black air' and flying over the 'plain houses'. Plath's determines to 'fly through the candle's mouth like a singeless moth'. Both settings are emphatically domestic, realised in metaphors of 'caves' and 'cellars' (Sexton and Plath respectively), of cooking ('skillets' and 'potlids'), and of housekeeping ('closets', 'jars' and 'shelves'). Michèle Roberts's slightly later poem 'The Sibyl's Song' uses similar motifs. Her first-person speaker, too, lives as a kind of monstrous outsider, entering into a generative relationship with the muse/other: 'she whose winged breath / wrestles with mud and / shapes it to pots and houses'.[15]

Plath's and Sexton's speakers figure themselves as the cook or provider, as the person charged with satisfying the emotional needs of an avaricious audience. Sexton's speaker 'fixed the supper for the worms and the elves: / whining, rearranging the disalligned'. Plath's speaker offers her body to feed her audience. In an early exemplification of the process which we see in her later 'Lady Lazarus' (1962), she sacrifices herself for their gratification. This is a metaphor which is developed in later poems by both poets where the emotional self-exposure of confessional writing is reduced to mere entertainment and the subject herself becomes fodder for the audience.

The first-person speakers of 'Her Kind' and 'Witch Burning' reveal a sense of dislocation or self-alienation, seeing themselves as though from the outside and identifying themselves as misfits.[16] Sexton's speaker is a 'lonely thing, twelve-fingered, out of mind', she is 'not a woman quite'.[17] Similarly, Plath's subject 'inhabit[s] / The wax image of myself, a doll's body'. The next and final poem in the sequence ('Poem for a Birthday') from which 'Witch Burning' comes develops this synecdoche. 'The Stones' features multiple images of dislocated organs and limbs ('the stomach', the 'mouth-hole', the 'ear', the 'pink torso', 'any limb'). Here, as in numerous Sexton poems ('Consorting with Angels' or 'Live' with its 'sawed off body'), autotomy (the casting off of parts of the body) is fundamental to the performance. The female poet's body is dis-located, splayed, dissected for examination by her audience. In both poems it is the fingers and the mouth as metonyms of the process of writing/speaking the poem which are displaced and thus empha-sised. 'Her Kind', as we have seen, represents a 'twelve-fingered' uber-creative subject; 'The Stones' similarly closes with a synec-dochic representation of the writing/confessing woman, with 'ten fingers shap[ing] a bowl for shadows'.

At the heart of 'Witch Burning' and of 'Her Kind' are images of fire and of the witch woman's sacrifice or immolation. In Michèle Roberts's 'The Sibyl's Song', too, the speaker recognises that she will be punished for her generative power: 'I shall burn for this,' she says. Yet she remains defiant. The immolation is itself the ultimate creative act: 'I will sing high in the fire / my body her torch: oh let / the fierce goddess come'.[18] Sexton's 'Her Kind' closes with the subject defiantly approaching the pyre, waving her 'nude arms' at her tormentors:

> where your wheels still bite my thigh
> and my ribs crack where your wheels wind.
> A woman like that is not ashamed to die.
> I have been her kind.

Plath's poem echoes this in tone, language and imagery. Sexton's vision of torture (the 'wheels wind') re-emerges in stanza two of Plath's poem, where 'the smoke wheels from the beak of this empty jar'. Plath's speaker, like Sexton's, sacrifices her body ('hand and ankles' in Plath, 'arms' and 'ribs' in Sexton) to the flames. There are the same rhymes and half-rhymes ('beak' / 'crack'; 'thigh' / 'bright'/ 'bite' / 'light') and, crucially, the same – latently sexual – image of the bright flames encroaching up the woman/witch's thighs: 'My ankles brighten. Brightness ascends my thighs. / I am lost, I am lost, in the robes of all this light.' Again, like in Lowell's 'Captured Goddess', this is a spectacular display, but in every case a spectacular display of female failure, punishment or despair.

In an earlier period, Emily Brontë's 1837 poem 'Alone I Sat' opens with a lone speaker who, struck by the sublime but fading view she sees before her, feels herself suddenly overwhelmed by the desire to convey this in words. More importantly, she is oppressed by the impossibility of doing it justice: 'I could not speak the feeling.' Her powerlessness and abjection are realised in metonyms of silenced voices ('sing') and ineffective writing ('fingers'). In the final stanza:

> But now when I had hoped to sing,
> My fingers strike a tuneless string;
> And still the burden of the strain
> Is 'Strive no more; 'tis all in vain'.[19]

Charlotte Mew's 1916 poem 'Fame' conveys a sense of the intensity, claustrophobia and fear attendant on the speaker's self-presentation as a poet. The social spaces of literary life in which the poet is required to perform (the 'over-heated house', the 'crowd', the 'painted faces') are juxtaposed with the freedom and solitude promised by an idealised natural world: 'the folded glory of the gorse, the sweet-briar air'. The poem dramatises the tension between these two different scenes. The social life pulls her in one direction while the natural world compels and repels in turn. Out of inspiration, as the final lines of the poem show, may come sterility and despair (the aborted lamb, or 'moon's dropped child', in the lines which follow are a dreadful metaphor for the female poet's creative aspirations):

> Just now, I think I found it in a field, under a fence –
> A frail, dead, new-born lamb, ghostly and pitiful and
> white,
> A blot upon the night,
> The moon's dropped child![20]

In 1850, American author Edgar Allen Poe avowed that the 'most poetical' thing in the world was the death of a beautiful woman. He went on to say that 'the lips best suited for such a topic are those of a bereaved lover'. Poems such as those discussed above which enact the immolation of the female subject/speaker are radical in their appropriation of this story and the power to tell it, and are thereby instrumental in its repudiation. Cynthia Griffin Wolff suggests that

some of Emily Dickinson's poems function in a similarly transgressive way: 'Dickinson was able to fashion some of her most masterful poems in response to this challenge – poems in which the
speaker (often explicitly gendered female) has already died.'[21]

THEATRICS

Laura Severin has written persuasively about the many strategies
which women poets have adopted in performing their work.
Referring to the poetry of Mew, Stevie Smith and Jackie Kay,
amongst others, Severin points to an alternative tradition within
modern British women's poetry of appropriating and juxtaposing a
range of different forms – music, art and staged performances (or
what she calls 'lift[ing] poetry off the page'). Women poets do this,
she argues, to 'create an awareness of the way in which culture produces social categories, such as woman'. This is a 'first step towards
dismantling them'.[22] Performance from this point of view destabilises or distorts conventional sign systems. Here, on the stage, is
a woman's body and what we attend to is a woman's speaking voice.
This contravenes a print orthodoxy, specifically one which derives
from lyric tradition and which would see the woman as silent object
(reaching its nadir in Poe's 'most poetical' object) not as voicing
subject.

Edith Sitwell's work is particularly noteworthy in this context.
Her poem *Façade*, written to be accompanied by the music of the
young composer William Walton, was first performed and published in 1922. This performance was complicated, though, by its
being delivered from behind a curtain through a megaphone-like
device called a 'sengerphone'.[23] The effect of this is that, rather like
Lowell in 'Patterns' cited above, Sitwell both performs and denies
(and thereby critiques) her female identity. She offers it up and displaces it from view. As Rees-Jones argues, 'The performances of the
Façade poems did not adhere to a stable repertoire. Within the performance, the disembodied female voice [. . .] is constantly working
alongside the music, and does indeed become the music.'[24] This is
transgressive in a multitude of ways, causing a rethinking of definitions of poetry, performance, even of gender itself.

Looking again at the exaggerated and uncomfortable femininity presented in 'Patterns' for an analogy with performative elements in Sitwell's work, we might focus on the latter's renowned use of costume as part of her self-presentation. From this point of view, to quote Rees-Jones again, Sitwell's 'strategy of dress' (a highly stylised and self-consciously feminised mode of display which is also a form of masquerade or disguise) indicates that her own 'construction of herself as a woman poet might, in these terms, be seen as a kind of drag act'. This unsettles notions of femininity by performing it 'in terms of the transvestite's promise of a revelation of the something which it is not'.[25]

For Mew and for Anna Wickham, writing at the fin de siècle, 'performance added another expressive dimension' to their work, allowing the 'twentieth-century woman to further deconstruct the lyric's restrictive gender roles'.[26] It is not only gender roles that are destabilised, though. Sexuality is also at stake. As we have seen, one of the key elements in Butler's argument is that it is sexual and not simply gender identity that is performatively produced. Mew and Wickham take as one of their subjects a hitherto occluded lesbian sexuality. They speak of this most effectively when ventriloquising or performing the voice of another. Thus, they enact the separation of subject from speaker which orthodox expectations of lyric poetry (particularly poetry by women) typically conflate. In Mew's 'The Fete', for example, or Wickham's 'Queen's Song on Saint Valentine's Day' or 'Song of Ophelia the Survivor', the appropriation of alternative voices and roles permits the poet to register desire while simultaneously removing herself from it.[27]

More radically still, Christina Rossetti's 1862 poem 'Winter – My Secret' (collected as 'My Secret' in Isobel Armstrong et al., *Nineteenth-Century Women Poets*) implies a self-protective process of self-division. The female subject both is visible and hides herself from view. This concealment is a form of defence and a strategic subterfuge affording a certain kind of liberation: 'I tell my secret? No indeed, not I.' The imagined dialogue in the poem affords the speaker the opportunity to mount a robust defence of her position: 'I wear my mask for warmth,' she says, before asking why anyone would show 'His nose to Russian snows / To be pecked at by every wind that blows.'[28]

Stevie Smith's poetry performs in a different way again. In readings, she is said to have displayed the persona of little girl or ingénue (Jeni Couzyn says that 'she played the part of the eccentric nervous spinster because it gave her a form in which to be courageous').[29] In her poetry, too, the apparently whimsical surfaces mask a far more complex and profound set of concerns. The short poem 'Piggy to Joey', for example, although so slight on a first glance, is rendered more profound on each subsequent reading, particularly when read alongside the pen and ink sketch which accompanied it on its original publication. Smith frequently chose to illustrate her work in this way, and as Rees-Jones and Severin have shown, the illustrations function sometimes to distract, sometimes to contradict, but always to complicate the narrative of the poems.[30]

'Piggy to Joey' is printed alongside an image of a long-haired woman, notable both for her inappropriately – given the context of the poem – jaunty hat and for her shapely and well-defined breasts. Casting her eyes downwards, she appears to be lamenting her commission of the mistake the poem describes. The text itself, though, only reveals the story in stages. The opening line 'Piggy to Joey' might, at first, be thought to denote dialogue (this is 'Piggy', perhaps a pet-name in a relationship, speaking to 'Joey'). But it transpires that this is not the dominant meaning. Instead, the poem reads as a first-person confession that the woman (one presumes from the illustration that the speaker and Piggy are one and the same, although this may not necessarily be the case) has been 'piggy' or unpleasant to her lover, Joey. Even in this context, the word 'Piggy' – so glib, so colloquial – undermines the seriousness of its effects. As the irrevocable loss of the lover shows ('Will he come back again? / Oh no, no, no'), to be 'piggy' is a serious error.[31]

ROLE-PLAY

Margaret Cavendish, the Duchess of Newcastle, was born in 1623, married the Marquess of Newcastle in exile in Europe in 1645, and returned to England on the Restoration of Charles II in 1660. Eccentric, daring, intellectually curious (she was fascinated by the ideas of thinkers such as Descartes and Hobbes and by new scientific discoveries), she had no children of her own but plentiful resources including the support of her husband.[32] For Woolf in *A Room of One's Own*, what Cavendish lacked was the formal framework within which to turn this potential to account: 'What could bind, tame, or civilize for human use that wild, generous, untutored intelligence?' According to Woolf, nobody took Cavendish seriously: 'No one checked her. No one taught her [. . .] at court they jeered at her.'[33] Samuel Pepys reports the curiosity and excitement caused by her occasional visits to London, saying that her journey by coach was accompanied by '100 boys and girls running looking upon her'.[34] Cavendish, for Pepys, was 'a mad, conceited, ridiculous woman'.[35]

It would be a mistake, though, to see Cavendish's public performance or self-display as inadvertent and risible. Instead, we might read what Anna Battigelli calls her 'self-fashioning' as a kind of protective mask: 'Her eccentric fashions, her theatrical manners, her odd self-portraits – each of these gestures is calculated to engage people while keeping them at a comfortable distance.'[36] Moreover, there is a political dimension to this. Cavendish's masquerades are a form of gender subversion as well as a rhetorical and provocative affirmation of the Royalist cause: 'She choreographed her public appearances so as to appear in the role of the female cavalier, sometimes donning men's clothes or the cavalier hat or resorting to masculine gestures.'[37] According to Emma L. E. Rees, Cavendish's spectacular self-display was a strategic move which allowed her to continue to speak as she liked: 'By focusing attention on the image, the appearance, Cavendish kept censorial attention away from the content – her publications.'[38] The real spectacle, of course, is not the costumed progression around London; it is the figure of the unashamed writing woman. Cavendish's books, *Poems and Fancies* and *Philosophical Fancies* (1653), were both published under her own name at a time when this was extremely uncommon. Kate Lilley's summation of Cavendish's role arguably speaks for successive generations of women poets: 'Cavendish used the interdicted practices of writing and publishing to challenge the negative consequences for women of patriarchal codes of femininity, delighting in the subversive potential of generic and intellectual hybridization.'[39]

Cavendish's short poem 'The Clasp' (c. 1653) is bold and sweeping in its claim to a certain kind of poetics.[40] The poem is confident in its opening demands, daringly asserting the rights of the first-person speaker to freedom of expression and to the authority that goes with it (hence 'noble'): 'Give me a free and noble style.' It reveals the discontinuity between apparent wildness and the man-nered decorum of conventional form. However, what appears to be wild, untutored and undisciplined has a structure and aesthetics of its own. It dares more in finding its own way than in subordinating itself to convention: 'though it runs about it cares not where, / It shows more courage than it doth of fear.' The poem establishes a series of binaries (free/curbed, courage/fear, nature/art, imagina-tion/pedantry), but what is interesting, and speaks particularly to the gendered subtext, is two things. First is the way in which Cavendish refuses or unsettles these apparent poles. At one and the same time she seems both to validate and to eschew the wildness of her work, work which, although 'wild', perhaps only 'shows' or pre-sents in this way. The latter construction indicates that beneath the wildness of the surface lie controlled depths. In other words, she both suggests, and refuses to offer, an apology for her 'uncurbed' ways. Second is the way in which the poem openly and brazenly embraces 'nature', rendering it artful and strategic rather than inadvertent and irrelevant.

In this breaking of the binaries or the 'clasp' of the poem's title (signifying perhaps the clasp of a piece of jewellery or, as Robyn Bolam suggests, the 'metal fastening of a book cover' or an 'embrace'), the poem rejects containment and restriction.[41] Instead, it stakes a claim to an idiosyncratic, unfettered or, at the very least, self-fettered poetic style. There is a doubleness or duplicity in 'The Clasp', a feature which Isobel Armstrong has noted as a character-istic of later nineteenth-century women's poetry: 'The simpler the surface of the poem, the more likely it is that a second or more difficult poem will exist beneath it.'[42] Thus, we might conclude that the poem performs its own sleight of hand, delivering an impres-sion which masks something rather different beneath.

There are multiple forms of displacement and denial in Cavendish's work, and although, as we have seen, she performs the social and cultural role of poet, she also plays the part of poet's wife, of modest, coy, subordinate attendant: 'A poet I am neither born nor bred; / But to a witty poet marrièd.' Even here there is a crucial indeterminacy in the syntax. From one perspective, the opening line disavows the identity 'poet' (I am neither born nor bred a poet). From another entirely opposite point of view, this line rather craftily asserts the role: 'A poet I am' who, although neither born nor bred to that part, has nevertheless learnt how to play it by emulating the practice of the husband. The 'I' here is both the subject and the object of the poem (the person speaking and the person who is being spoken about), and this tactic contributes to the unsettling uncertainty about who, precisely, this 'I' represents.

This is, perhaps, a speculative reading of these opening lines, but it nevertheless anticipates the movement of the rest of the text, which performs, while simultaneously undermining, the role of poet manqué. Germaine Greer describes such false modesty thus:

> In the seventeenth century the great ladies who confessed to an itch for rhyming were careful to present the product of their labour in an offhand manner, although they may have taken great pains with it. Gentlemen who penned verses had also to affect to set no store by them; publication, even in manuscript but above all in print, brought about loss of caste, in that intimate feelings were made common. The ladies whose thoughts became public were in worse trouble for their writings exposed their ignorance and their self-delusion.[43]

Another of Cavendish's poems, 'The Poetess's Hasty Resolution', performs a similar volte-face.[44] Here the speaker permits herself a little critical distance on her own character and behaviour, describing and judging herself as though from the outside. Certainly she is presenting to us an image or caricature of the (foolish) self she would like us to see: 'Reading my verses, I liked them so well, / Self-love did make my judgment to rebel.' What the speaker had planned was to construct a 'pyramid of fame'. The use of the past tense in the first part of the poem, shifting to the present tense in the final four lines, is important in establishing the apparent distance between the 'old' and 'new' selves. This distance, however, proves to be chimerical. The term 'pyramid' in line six is significant, perhaps unwittingly suggesting a monument to, or mausoleum for, a fame which must by implication be dead. Moreover, as Ann Rosalind Jones has pointed out, ' "Fame", in English, comes from the Greek root *phanei*, to speak and to be spoken about. The two were linked through prohibition in the ideologies aimed at women in early modern Europe.'[45]

The speaker is enacting her own humiliation, and it is her guile-lessness in so doing which entices the reader's sympathy and atten-tion: 'Thinking them [her poems] no good, I thought more to write, / Considering not how others them would like.' We should, of course, take caution that if she can fool herself so easily, how simple it must be for her to fool her readers. The poem has the force of a confession. Like many confessions, it requires the beneficent forgiveness of its other in order to reach completion.[46] The speaker confesses her pride and self-love, her vain ambition, her refusal to listen to 'reason', and her ultimate repentance. The process of con-fessing to a tolerant auditor (this is the reader's role in this drama) restores equilibrium and, incredibly and flamboyantly enough, ensures the restoration of the speaker's spirits. In a final theatrical note, the speaker reveals that she has learnt little from her moment of soul-searching and has abandoned none of her original plans. Her literary ambitions remain, still clamouring for the praise which she so hopes her poem deserves (a goal which this poem, paradox-ically, helps to achieve): 'Take pity, and my drooping spirits raise, / Wipe off my tears with handkerchiefs of praise.'

SLAM POETRY

The theatrical and spectacular nature of poetry identified and exploited by the poets discussed thus far in this chapter is crys-tallised and even magnified in contemporary performance, slam, 'open mike/mic' and Dub poetry. Emerging in the United States, the United Kingdom and the Caribbean in the latter years of the twentieth century, live performance of this kind arguably has long and, importantly, multiple roots. For some, as Kalamu ya Salaam argues, 'What could be more afrocentric than an emphasis on poetry's performative aspects growing out of the oral and aural tradition?'[47] In other contexts, specifically in European traditions, performance poetry emerges from vernacular and folk cultures, often historically aligned with the dissenting voices of the eighteenth and nineteenth centuries.

In Jean 'Binta' Breeze's poetry, it is often the musicality of the line which strikes the reader. Breeze, who was born in Jamaica and lives now in the UK and the Caribbean, links the development of Dub poetry with that of reggae music: 'I speak and think in Jamaican and English, with my poems it just depends . . . Every poem is different, they each decide their own music.'[48] 'The Wife of Bath Speaks in Brixton Market' (2000) displays a complex multilayering of voices, discourses and contexts including the biblical idiom and Chaucerian intertext. It also proffers a voice which bridges lyric and performed modes. While clearly a voice which addresses an assumed audience, it is also the voice of contemplation and self-enquiry more familiar in lyric forms. It mixes the contemplative and the comic, the spiritual and the scatological, asking why women have been born with 'private parts so sweet' if their only purpose is to 'piss' or 'tell man apart from woman / das wat you tink?' Here as in a number of other poems, Breeze assumes a challenging voice – that of the female outsider/madwoman – and in entering the hitherto male-dominated 'Dub' scene, she performs a transgressive role. C. L. Innes explains:

> The title poem of [Breeze's] first volume and record, *Riddym Ravings and Other Poems*, takes as its persona a 'mad' woman whose voice and plight and commentary question received notions of sanity and the politics that debase women. Through the use of a variety of women's voices and contexts, Binta Breeze's poetry challenges the usual voices and stances of a masculine dub and performance poetry tradition.[49]

The attractions of performance poetry might seem particularly compelling for women. If we take it to be a descendant of a vernacular tradition which Tom Paulin defines as follows: 'springy, irreverent, chanting, quartzy, often tender and intimate, vernacular voice speaks for an alternative community that is mostly powerless and invisible', we might conclude that the vibrant spaciousness of the form gives women opportunities perhaps denied to them by the orthodoxies and mechanics of a print culture.[50] Nevertheless, there is a risk that performance of this kind might trap the woman poet. By placing the gendered body so visibly on view, the relationship between reader and text might be diverted, obstructed or corrupted. Moreover, women poets may find themselves marginalised on this new scene just as they have been in orthodox circles. And even if women poets do make a name for themselves in this alternative poetic mode, if the mode itself is marginalised or disparaged, their cultural capital in the mainstream sees little improvement.

As this implies, the critical response to performance and slam poetry has been mixed. The form has been valorised by some as a truly democratic, popularising, energising new mode or as a way of 're-establish[ing] the audience' for poetry.[51] Similarly, Jeffrey McDaniel insists that 'if there's one lesson the academy might learn from slam, it's that the audience matters'.[52] Others have taken exception to precisely this popularising, demotic tone, seeing performance poetry as a novelty which is interesting enough in its own right but has little lasting or viable connection with the mainstream. After all, audience matters to many print poets, too. Meta DuEwa Jones explains that it is the audience-centric and theatrical nature of slam poetry where 'showmanship, charisma, and theatricality of performance seems [*sic*] to count just as much as the artistic merits of the poems presented – that has fuelled critical scepticism over whether the "poems" performed within a slam environment count as literature'.[53]

Certainly, slam or performance poetry might work to overthrow some of the conventions and expectations associated with more conventional print (for which, often, read lyric) forms. By making poetry visible, dramatic, entertaining and above all publicly shared, performance poetry overturns many of the conventions associated with the private, introspective, lyric mode. Paradoxically, though, as we will see in the next chapter, there may be more common ground than is usually thought between the lyric mode and performance work (as Northrop Frye suggests, the lyric form itself might be defined as 'poems to be chanted').[54] There are a number of features of contemporary performance poetry which are worthy of note. These include the deployment of emphatic repetition and rhyme, of short, often staccato lines and of oral devices such as onomatopoeia and alliteration. So, too, use is made of repetitions and refrains in order to consolidate a point or to allow the listener to catch up. Silence is also important. This is used to particular and dramatic effect in slam and performance work, although one might argue that it is also implicit in the structure of print poetry. There is often a strong narrative thread in performance poetry which leads the audience to some point of revelation or closure. Apostrophe (direct address) is used as a means of ensuring audience participation. Another characteristic is the political context. By claiming a voice and a space, performance poets – particularly women – refuse to be silenced and excluded, and they work to awaken, to provoke and to inspire their audience.

CONCLUSION

There are disadvantages for women's poetry of an emphasis on the spectacular and performative nature of their work. One negative consequence is that it leads to its marginalisation and belittling. From the eighteenth century, when, as Greer points out of Mary Leapor, women poets were 'being merchandized as freaks of nature, the greater the novelty the greater the acclaim,' have women poets seen much progression?[55] Donna Landry contextualises Leapor's reception thus:

> That Mary Leapor, a gardener's daughter and a domestic servant, should have her work published at all, even posthumously, may still seem to us in the late twentieth century little short of miraculous. That too tells us something about the appeal of the unlikely, the curious, the peculiarly marginal, in this period of expanding literary markets.[56]

One riposte to the unease which these comments suggest is that in the case of Sitwell, Smith, Sexton, Cavendish and others, it is the women poets themselves who are very consciously manipulating their performances, the roles they play, the voices and identities they choose to project. This is part of a strategic, and again a self-reflexive, examination of vital questions about subjectivity, authority and language. It is a strategy in which women position themselves centre stage as subjects rather than accepting the place of marginalised objects. Another response is to suggest that it is femininity itself which is being exposed as freakish. Mary Russo describes 'the construction of femaleness as a stunt'. From this point of view, women poets (indeed women per se) always already 'speak' simply by virtue of their gender. In the poems discussed in this chapter, though, women subvert this apparent truism. By performing a kind of hyper-femininity, by exaggerating for public display the role of female and poet, they undermine some of the orthodoxies associated with it. To quote Russo again: 'To put on femininity with a vengeance suggests the power of taking it off.'[57] All this having been said, for some poets, for example Adrienne Rich, there is some power in poetry which entirely cuts through any residue of spectacle or performance: 'The reading of a poem, a poetry reading, is not a spectacle, nor can it be passively received. It's an exchange of electrical currents through language.'[58]

SUMMARY OF KEY POINTS

- Many women poets – in their poetry and in interviews, letters and commentaries – express unease about the spectacular or theatrical nature of their work. This ambivalence emerges in a number of poems by women which exercise the role of witch/madwoman.
- Recent theories of performativity and gender, principally the work of Judith Butler, suggest one way of reading the constructed nature of the female role. Work by women poets exaggerates and thus exposes the artifice of femininity.
- Contemporary Slam and performance poetry may offer opportunities for women to work in a new dimension apparently free of the conventions of the past. However, there is more crossover between aural and print forms of poetry than may, at first, be apparent, and there is a risk of the continued marginalisation of women.

NOTES

1. Selima Hill, 'God's Velvet Cushions', in Mark and Rees-Jones, *Contemporary*, pp. 26–30 (p. 28).

2. Anne Sexton, unpublished letter to Mrs F. Peter Scigliano 7 February 1963, Harry Ransom Humanities Research Center, University of Texas at Austin.

3. 'Elizabeth Bishop' [interview with Elizabeth Spires], in Plimpton, *Women Writers*, pp. 181–207 (p. 193).

4. Anne Sexton, *A Self-Portrait in Letters* (Boston, MA: Houghton Mifflin, 1977), p. 304; McGuckian quoted in Deryn Rees-Jones, *Consorting with Angels: Essays on Modern Women Poets* (Newcastle: Bloodaxe, 2005), p. 186.

5. Judith Butler, *Gender Trouble: Feminism and the Subversion of Identity* (New York and London: Routledge, 1990), p. 140.

6. Ibid. p. 25.

7. Ibid. pp. 136, 138.

8. Ibid. p. 141.

9. Rees-Jones, *Consorting*, pp. 12, 13.

10. Butler, *Gender Trouble*, p. 136.

11. Northrop Frye, *Anatomy of Criticism: Four Essays* (Princeton, NJ: Princeton University Press, 1957), p. 297.

12. Amy Lowell, 'The Captured Goddess', in *The Norton Anthology of American Literature: Volume Two* (5th edn), ed. Nina Baym et al. (New York: Norton, 1998), p. 1085.

13. Cathryn Vasseleu, *Textures of Light: Vision and Touch in Irigaray, Levinas and Merleau-Ponty* (London: Routledge, 1998), p. 3.

14. For more on the origins of these poems, see Diane Middlebrook, *Anne Sexton: A Biography* (London: Virago, 1991), pp. 113–14, and Sylvia Plath, *The Journals of Sylvia Plath*, ed. Karen V. Kukil (London: Faber and Faber, 2000), p. 523. For a longer comparison of the two, see Jo Gill, *Anne Sexton's Confessional Poetics* (Gainesville, FL: University Press of Florida, 2007).

15. Michèle Roberts, 'The Sibyl's Song', in Scott, *Bread and Roses*, p. 205.

16. See Laura Mulvey on the woman's 'to-be-looked-at-ness' in 'Visual Pleasure and Narrative Cinema', *Screen*, 16: 3 (1975), 6–18 (17).

17. Robert Lowell uses similar rhetoric in his description of the self-transformation which he identifies in Plath's *Ariel*: 'Sylvia Plath becomes herself, becomes something imaginary, newly,

wildly, and subtly created – hardly a person at all, or a woman.'
'Sylvia Plath's Ariel', in *Robert Lowell: Collected Prose*, ed.
Robert Giroux (London: Faber and Faber, 1987), pp. 122–5
(p. 122).

18. Michèle Roberts, 'The Sibyl's Song', in Scott, *Bread and Roses*,
p. 205.

19. Emily Brontë, 'Alone I Sat', in *Five Late Romantic Poets*, ed.
James Reeves (London: Heinemann, 1974), p. 113.

20. Charlotte Mew, 'Fame', in *Charlotte Mew: Collected Poems and
Selected Prose*, ed. Val Warner (Manchester: Carcanet, 1997),
p. 3. For more on the biographical context to this and other
Mew poems, see Penelope Fitzgerald, *Charlotte Mew and her
Friends* (London: Harvill, 1992).

21. Wolff, 'Emily Dickinson', p. 133.

22. Laura Severin, *Poetry off the Page: Twentieth-Century British
Women Poets in Performance* (Aldershot: Ashgate, 2004), p. 4.

23. Rees-Jones, *Consorting*, pp. 41–2.

24. Ibid. p. 44.

25. Ibid. p. 48.

26. Severin, *Poetry off the Page*, p. 17.

27. Charlotte Mew, *The Farmer's Bride*, ed. Deborah Parsons
(Cheltenham: The Cyder Press, 2000), p. 9; Wickham, *The
Writings of Anna Wickham*, pp. 263, 277.

28. Christina Rossetti, 'My Secret', in Armstrong et al.,
Nineteenth-Century, p. 522. For more on the biographical
context to this and other Rossetti poems, see Kathleen Jones,
Learning not to be First: The Life of Christina Rossetti (Moreton-
in-Marsh: The Windrush Press, 1991).

29. Couzyn, *Contemporary Women Poets*, p. 35.

30. See Laura Severin, *Stevie Smith's Resistant Antics* (Madison:
University of Wisconsin Press, 1997) and Rees-Jones, *Consorting*,
pp. 70–92. See also Frances Spalding, *Stevie Smith: A Critical
Biography* (London: Faber and Faber, 1988).

31. Stevie Smith, 'Piggy to Joey', in *The Penguin Book of Poetry
from Britain and Ireland since 1945*, ed. Simon Armitage and
Robert Crawford (Harmondsworth: Viking, 1998), p. 22.

32. Anna Battigelli, *Margaret Cavendish and the Exiles of the Mind*
(Lexington, KY: University Press of Kentucky, 1998), p. 1.

33. Woolf, *A Room of One's Own*, p. 62.
34. Quoted in Battigelli, *Margaret Cavendish*, p. 5.
35. Quoted in Emma L. E. Rees, *Margaret Cavendish: Gender, Genre, Exile* (Manchester: Manchester University Press, 2003), p. 5.
36. Battigelli, *Margaret Cavendish*, p. 7.
37. Ibid. p. 5.
38. Rees, *Margaret Cavendish*, p. 4.
39. Margaret Cavendish, *The Blazing World and Other Writings*, ed. Kate Lilley (Harmondsworth: Penguin, 1994), p. xiv.
40. Cavendish, 'The Clasp', in Bolam, *Eliza's Babes*, p. 72.
41. Ibid. p. 72.
42. Isobel Armstrong, *Victorian Poetry: Poetry, Poetics and Politics* (London: Routledge, 1996), p. 324.
43. Greer, *Slip-Shod Sibyls*, p. 41.
44. Cavendish, 'The Poetess's Hasty Resolution', in *The Norton Anthology of English Literature: Volume One*, 7th edn, ed. M. H. Abrams et al. (New York: Norton, 2000), p. 1760.
45. Ann Rosalind Jones, 'Surprising Fame: Renaissance Gender Ideologies and Women's Lyric', in *Feminism and Renaissance Studies*, ed. Lorna Hutson (Oxford: Oxford University Press, 1999), pp. 317–36 (p. 334).
46. See Michel Foucault, *The History of Sexuality: Volume One*, trans. Robert Hurley (Harmondsworth: Penguin, 1990), p. 61.
47. Kalamu ya Salaam, 'In Defense of SLAM! Nation – slam Poetry', *Black Issues Book Review* (March 2001); accessed 19 September 2006 at: http://findarticles.com/p/articles/mi_moHST/is_2_3/ai_72275232.
48. Jean 'Binta' Breeze, quoted in Rees-Jones, *Modern*, p. 339.
49. C. L. Innes, 'Accent and Identity: Women Poets of Many Parts', in *Contemporary British Poetry: Essays in Theory and Criticism*, ed. James Acheson and Romana Huk (New York: State University of New York Press, 1996), pp. 315–41 (p. 322).
50. Tom Paulin (ed.), *The Faber Book of Vernacular Verse* (London: Faber and Faber, 1990), p. x.
51. Bob Holman, 'The Room', in *Poetry Slam: The Competitive Art of Performance Poetry*, ed. Gary Mex Glazner (San Francisco: Manic D Press, 2000), pp. 15–21 (p. 21).

52. Jeffrey McDaniel, 'Slam and the Academy', in Glazner, *Poetry Slam*, pp. 35–7 (p. 35).
53. Meta DuEwa Jones, 'Slam Nations: Emerging Poetries, Imagined Communities', *How2* 1: 5 (March 2001). Accessed 19 September 2006 at: http://www.scc.rutgers.edu/however/v1_5_2001/current/index.html.
54. Frye, *Anatomy*, p. 273.
55. Greer, *Slip-Shod Sibyls*, p. 53.
56. Landry, *Muses*, p. 119.
57. Mary Russo, *The Female Grotesque: Risk, Excess and Modernity* (London: Routledge, 1995), pp. 25, 70.
58. Adrienne Rich, *What is Found There: Notebooks on Poetry and Politics* (New York: Norton, 2003), p. 84.

CHAPTER 3

Private Voices

The notion of privacy sits at the heart of any discussion of poetry by women. To talk about privacy in this context is to recognise the significance in and to women's poetry of the intimate and personal, of the quiet voice communicating to an immediate audience. These elements are apparent in poetry across many periods and cultures ranging from the love lyrics of Sappho through to the meditations and devotions of the Renaissance poet Mary Sidney, from the apparently hermetic exercises of Emily Dickinson to the personal confessions of Anne Sexton and contemporary American poet Sharon Olds.

It is worth noting that in turning our attention to some women poets' evocation of the private, introspective or local, we risk conceding the validity of a largely – but not exclusively – masculine critical tradition which has argued that the private sphere is women's proper and only concern. Even Catherine Reilly, in the introduction to her recent anthology of women's war poetry (poetry which, as Chapter 5 shows, offers some profound insights into the history and politics of its time), asserts that 'women always excel when writing about human emotions'.[1] Given that a primary concern of many recent studies in the field has been to refute the assumption that women's poetry is best occupied with the small-scale, with the personal, or with the self, this chapter's focus on the intimacy and quietude of poetry by women may seem an unexpected, even counterintuitive concern.

It is important to cut through critical preconceptions of women's work in this field, and to ask what women poets have made of their private moments or concerns, whether self-consciously chosen spaces or enforced sites of separation. In thinking through these issues, one needs to define, evaluate, and if necessary redefine the term 'private' and thus to consider not only conventionally private themes and subjects (childbirth, loss, love and so on) but also the aesthetics of privacy. What are the private choices, hermetic techniques or strategies by which women poets have sought to close down easy public access to intimate moments? Only by reading privacy as deliberate, rhetorical and artful, rather than as some kind of default position uniquely suited to women, can these writers be credited with the creative skill they require and continue to display in turning the private sphere into a positive domain of their own choosing. So women poets refuse to speak only in and from a position of privacy, just as they claim the right to do so if they so wish.

The lyric mode of poetry which has so dominated Western poetics in the modern period is an important vehicle for the mediation of issues and concerns relating to the private and intimate moments of experience. Women poets' use of the lyric has been the key concern of recent critics writing in the field (for example, Bertram's *Gendering Poetry* and Dowson and Entwistle's *A History of Twentieth-Century British Women's Poetry*). And although I, too, will spend some time looking at women poets' use of the lyric mode, this is not my only concern. This chapter also explores women's treatment of private concerns in a range of other forms.

My intention is to enquire about women poets' treatment of the small-scale, the immediate, and the close at hand. This might mean identifying the effect of conventional expectations and restrictions on women's choice of material and form and on their ability to find a market. Do women poets all or always write about the private, and for those who do, is this a choice or a symptom of unwritten rules about their proper 'sphere'? It might, as we will see later, mean rethinking our understanding of the connotations, scope and historical specificity of the term 'private'. In other periods than our own, modern notions of privacy and agency would appear very different. In the early modern period, for instance, 'all life was public [. . .] or at least had public, social or communal dimensions'.[2]

It may be, as for example in the work of Lorine Niedecker or Louise Glück (whose poems 'Illuminations' and 'Children Coming Home from School' are particularly resonant), that the everyday, the quotidian, the private and ordinary prove to be richly ideological and thus public and historical spaces.[3]

SEPARATE SPHERES

The 'separate spheres' metaphor has operated through successive generations and achieved particular currency in the Victorian age. It posits a distinction between the private sphere ('the female, domestic, sentimental, collective private space' or 'the world of home') and the 'male, individualistic, public sphere of commerce and politics'.[4] The concept of separate spheres has its roots in a much older set of binary perceptions (nature/art, emotional/rational and so on) which read women as silent, passive objects and men as active, authoritative subjects. In the mid-nineteenth century, as Kaplan has shown, there emerged a 'liberal "separate but equal" argument' which ostensibly eschewed the hierarchy implicit in the private/public dichotomy while maintaining many of its restrictions.[5]

Many women poets, as will be seen below, have contested the fixity of 'separate spheres' ideology and the hierarchy of values which underpins it. For some, the private, the domestic, the 'world of home' is a place rich with interest. In establishing this, writers from Cavendish and the eighteenth-century poet Mary Robinson (discussed below) to contemporary poets U. A. Fanthorpe, Kathleen Jamie and Jackie Kay have reclaimed the value of the local, the particular and the everyday. Entwistle has argued of the later poets that 'the confined and confining domestic interior' is transformed into an 'enabling and even transgressive space'.[6] In Jamie and Kay in particular, the vernacular, colloquial cadences of their native Scottish tradition, or the oral and arguably feminised language of the home, seep onto the page, effacing the distinctions between speech and writing, private and public. It is clear from the work of the women poets discussed in this book that they are not confined to one sphere. One might add that by redefining what we mean by 'private sphere' and by looking again at what goes on in it, we can read the private and domestic as profoundly political. Housework, childrearing and so on are all, in their own way, ideological. In the 'suburban' poems of, say, Boland or 1950s American poet Phyllis McGinley, the private sphere represents both a retreat from a larger public context of anxiety, surveillance and threat, and a space in which all sorts of new conflicts and pressures come to a head. In McGinley's 'June in the Suburbs' or 'Spring Comes to the Suburbs', for example, we find an undertow of tension, violence and latent aggression (the sound of whimpers, roars and explosions in the former) and of competitive consumption and display (the distinction between begging, mending, earning, giving and conspicuously spending in the latter). In her 'Sonnets from the Suburbs', we find a catalogue of grotesques to surpass those of Sherwood Anderson's *Winesburg, Ohio*.[7]

Similarly, in Sexton's 'The Death Baby', the suburban family home with its modern domestic conveniences becomes a place of abjection, punishment and despair, the place where the female subject feels herself to be always at fault and always under threat of violence. In Plath's 'Lesbos' (which in its title looks back to Sappho's native island) we find the hitherto safe, idealised, female-only private sphere exposed in all its gothic horror – 'Viciousness in the kitchen!' as the poem begins – before running through a nightmare incantation of chaos, confusion and despair. The poem vilifies children, husband, in-laws, appliances, animals, food and finally the abject self.

Rees-Jones says of contemporary British writer Selima Hill that 'the domestic is not a secure place, but rather one of dramatic confrontations and invasions'. In Hill's twelve-part poem 'Chicken Feathers' (1984), for example, the rituals of everyday life are juxtaposed with memories of a personal and cultural past. The poem opens with an idiomatic, colloquial expression, 'What a picture!', which serves both to ground the narrative in immediate experience and to frame it (hence 'picture') as something unfamiliar, aesthetic, special. Thereafter, there are references to 'Brunhilde', to the 'Chelsea Ball' where the mother danced in a 'leopard costume', to the father's 'Harlequin suit' and his tiny 'Cinderella'-like shoes. The strangeness of these images (with the animal-like mother and the feminised father) provides an uncanny foundation for the certainties of the everyday. Even in quotidian routines, things might not be quite as they seem. And indeed, as the poem proceeds, we find that death intrudes. In part eight, the father retires to his room 'with an orange / in his hand' and there dies. But even this sudden death is assimilated in the ordinary and everyday: '*Come and sit down*', the mother says, '*And have your tea.*' The language of the poem is languid and steady; it is the language of ordinary speech conversing intimately with its auditors. It is a private voice, yet one which confides so much more than private experience; instead it roots this life and this death in a historical context, and it gestures towards the huge questions – about life, death, family, love, memory, loss, imagination and desire – in ways which belie the apparent introspection of the scene.[8]

In earlier periods, too, women poets have contested the apparent division between private and public spheres, effacing the bound-aries in suggestive ways. Marion Wynne-Davies cites a number of early modern poems, for example, by Jane and Elizabeth Cavendish and by Anne Bradstreet, in which although 'the home of the female poet is a site of security and stability', that security has been 'desta-bilised through betrayal, death, poverty, war or destruction'.[9] Margaret Cavendish's 'Nature's Cook' (1668) uses the experience and idiom of the private domestic sphere to comment on larger metaphysical concerns such as disease, suffering and dying. The private domestic kitchen proffers a set of complex conceits. 'Death is the cook of nature,' the poem begins. And Cavendish proceeds to construct a succession of increasingly unpleasant, literally dis-tasteful, elaborations on this theme. The frisson of the poem comes, in part, from our sense as readers of the female author's unexpected and rebellious delight in using this hitherto hidden, private, female space in so grotesque – but also so intellectually provocative – a way:

> Some, Death doth roast with fevers burning hot:
> And some he boils, with dropsies, in a pot.
> Some are consumed, for jelly, by degrees:
> And some, with ulcers, gravy out to squeeze.[10]

As Rees argues in connection with Cavendish's use elsewhere of motifs of spinning and needlework, it is precisely 'through an adroit manipulation of domestic images' that she 'negotiates her position as a writing woman'.[11]

THE LYRIC

The lyric mode of poetry is typically a relatively short poem, often spoken in the first person or adopting a specific subject position and usually taken to convey the intimate thoughts of the speaker about his or her object. For Northrop Frye, the lyric is 'the genre in which the poet [. . .] turns his back on his audience'.[12] The word 'lyric' comes from the Greek term for lyre and denotes the musical instrument which in the classical tradition accompanied the performance of this kind of song. The lyric mode represents a long and widespread tradition, and one that has dominated Western poetry from the Renaissance to the present day with a particular efflorescence of the form since the Romantic period. In Antony Easthope's words, Romanticism 'consistently assumes that language is all but transparent to experience [. . .] the inward can be made outward without any changes because it passes into it as though through a clear medium'.[13]

For Kaplan, the lyric poet is 'obsessed with the twists and turns of private feeling', while for Frye, the lyric is 'an associative rhetorical process, most of it below the threshold of consciousness'.[14] It encompasses a moment of epiphany as experienced and conveyed by the person best equipped both to tell and to interpret its significance – the speaker/poet who has ostensibly lived through it. I hesitate over the terms 'speaker/poet', and I use the qualifier 'ostensibly' because one of the characteristics of the lyric is its pretence to a subjectivity, experience or emotion which either may never have happened (that is, it may be pure fabrication) or may never have happened to the actual poet (in other words, there may be a general but not an autobiographical truth). A great deal of energy has been expended by women poets in disavowing their relationship with the speakers and perspectives presented in their poems. Emily Dickinson explains in a letter of 1862: 'When I state myself, as the Representative of the Verse – it does not mean me – but a supposed version.'[15] The private voice, or the 'I', may itself be a form of masquerade or invention. The previous chapter examined women poets and forms of performance, and it is important to extend this argument and to recognise that the first-person subject may herself be produced performatively. The 'I' of women's poetry may not be expressing any originary identity or providing access to private experience. It might, itself, be a construction or invention – a 'fiction which can be shared', in Helen Carr's words.[16]

In Helen Farish's 2005 collection *Intimates*, in 'Look at These', 'Treasures' and many of the other poems which seem so intimate (to take the collection's title in the way it invites one to), one is never certain to whom the 'I' refers.[17] These might be imagined moments or performed subjectivities. This having been said, and bearing in mind my earlier comment that women poets 'refuse to speak *only* in and from a position of privacy, just as they claim the right to do so if they so wish', we might turn to the work of another contemporary British poet, Kate Clanchy, for an example of a book which embraces the private, the intimate and the domestic. Her collection *Newborn* (2004) offers a challenging example for the reader who wants to assert the non-coherence of speaker and poet, but who also wishes to validate this collection's achievement in putting this coherence at its heart. Here we have poems whose impact comes in part from their apparently simple, but in fact devastatingly clear-sighted, vision of the complexity of everyday life as a mother of infant children. There are poems of celebration here, but more intriguing still are the poems which expose and explore the ambivalence of motherhood, and in particular which examine the highly charged divisions between self and other, private and public – a particularly fraught area in these circumstances. 'The Other Woman', for example, tells a different story to the one the title seems to promise. The 'other woman' here is both the present self (who is quite separate from the self before) and the 'other woman' who is not a mother, and therefore retains an independence which the new mother envies. The poem mourns not the failure of a relationship (the 'other woman' is not the archetypal mistress fighting for the male lover's attention) but the loss of the old self, the 'I' which existed before motherhood took over. If anything, it is the boy child here who has seduced the 'other' (mother) woman, leaving the original subject – the self which existed pre-children – alone to cope with the despair.[18]

It is not only women poets who have paused to make a point of the distinction between poet and speaker. T. S. Eliot's essay 'Tradition and the Individual Talent' is at pains to point out the necessity of separating the poet from the poem: 'Poetry is not a turning loose of emotion, but an escape from emotion; it is not the expression of personality, but an escape from personality.'[19] John Berryman prefaces his *Dream Songs* with the caution that it is 'essentially about an imaginary character (not the poet, not me)'.[20] Nevertheless, the necessity of establishing a separation between poet and lyric voice has been particularly urgent for women. One of the characteristics of the criticism of women's poetry over the centuries has been the assumption that in lyric poetry by women, the 'I' does represent the lived experience or felt emotions of the actual author. As an extreme example, in an extreme context, Al Alvarez says of Plath's *Ariel*: 'In these last poems [. . .] the poet and the poems become one.'[21] Assumptions such as this have permitted the disparagement of poetry by women which comes to seem little more than the unmediated outpouring of overwhelming feeling. In the final chapter, I turn to some of the many ways in which women poets over the generations have sought to confound, escape or rework these expectations, often by devising radical new forms.

The lyric mode of poetry, then, has offered women writers a valuable aesthetic framework within which to examine issues of private and intimate concern, and they have worked and reworked that framework in original and effective ways. But it is a mode which is not without difficulties; first, because some of the male-dominated conventions associated with its use have seemed hostile and alien to women's representations of their own subjectivities. Second, and perhaps paradoxically, women poets have resisted being automatically ascribed to the realm of the private and personal, and have wished sometimes to work in larger and more varied fields. Nevertheless, in making the lyric mode their own, women poets have reshaped its parameters, showing just how fluid the boundaries between private and public might be. For Vicki Bertram, the lyric mode is not solely or uncomplicatedly a private form. Instead it occupies a 'crepuscular position [. . .] on the boundary between personal and public discourse'.[22] Poet Sarah Maguire explains:

> Of all literary genres, lyric poetry is the most subjective, personal and private. And if we think of subjectivity as something secret and individual, separated from history and society and

politics, then there's every chance for lyric poetry to be con-
servative, costive, narcissistic and smug. But if we understand
that, as Jacqueline Rose puts it, 'There is no history outside its
subjective realisation . . . just as there is no subjectivity
uncoloured by the history to which it belongs', this special
focus on the self can be lyric poetry's most radical strength.
'The personal,' as that definitive feminist statement has it, 'is
political.'[23]

POETIC CONVENTION

The lyric is the major, but not the only, form which women poets
have engaged with in their writing. There are also other conven-
tions which women poets from at least the Renaissance onwards
have appropriated, developed and otherwise rendered their own. Of
particular note is the way in which they have made personal, imme-
diate and relevant a range of otherwise largely impersonal poetic
conventions. Looking at Renaissance poetics, for example, the
courtly love rituals, declarations of love, and exchange of love
tokens characteristic of the male-authored poetry of the age become
in the work of some of their female contemporaries rather more
than rhetorical flourishes. Often it is the reversal of agency which
renders these poems striking and thus successful.

In Elizabeth Cavendish's c. 1644 poem, the short and melodious
'Spoken Upon Receiving a Cake of Perfume Made up in the Shape
of a Heart', the immediacy of the voice is striking.[24] The soft sibi-
lance of the 's' sounds and the slow and gentle assonance, particu-
larly in the aa, bb, cc end rhymes, lend musicality to the piece.
There is a directness of address here, from speaker to addressee,
subject to 'my dear', 'I' to 'thee' and, even more intimately, to 'you'.
The range of first and second-person pronouns enforces the bond
between the two participants, connoting an ease and familiarity free
of formal restraint. Similarly, the almost completely monosyllabic
diction suggests an intimate, unguarded moment of communica-
tion. This is all the more genuine for refusing the trappings of
Elizabethan love convention: 'My dear, I thank thee, in it you hast
so well / Showed me the place wherein thy love doth dwell.' The

simple, singular words subtly anticipate and thereby confirm the point made in the poem's closing line, that 'you and I are one, not two'.

In a similar vein and from a similar period, Anne Bradstreet's poem 'A Letter to Her Husband, Absent Upon Public Employment' offers a striking perspective.[25] Bradstreet was born in England into a Puritan family at a time when to live as a Puritan was extremely difficult; she married in 1628 and in 1630 sailed for the New World with her extended family. Her father and her husband both served as Governors of Massachusetts, and the family moved several times within the colony. Bradstreet had eight children, and against the expectations and conventions of her age, wrote and published in a variety of forms.[26] Her poem 'A Letter to Her Husband' plays with the same convention as that with which the Cavendish poem closes (that the two lovers should be regarded as one). More specifically, though, it registers the inapplicability of that conceit in these two lovers' case.

The poem opens ebulliently with a list of the subject's own physical and emotional properties – her selfhood, uniquely and enthusiastically praised by the self. This marks a radical intervention in a tradition in which poetry by men, from the conventions of courtly love ritual onwards, had assumed responsibility for cataloguing – and thereby objectifying – female body parts. In several of Shakespeare's sonnets, for example, and in poems such as Sir Walter Ralegh's 'Love and Time', we find the female body carefully laid bare for male scrutiny and celebration. Moira P. Baker comments on Sir Philip Sidney's use of this form (known as the blazon). In the first song of his c. 1591 *Astrophel and Stella*, for instance, 'scrutinized by the gaze of the male lover who objectifies her body and makes of its fragments a poem, the woman remains the silent and passive other, merely a collection of parts without human subjectivity'.[27] Dowson and Entwistle suggest that it is traditions such as this (or the 'disempowering effect of the male gaze traditionally inscribed in lyric poetry') which render the use of the mode particularly problematic for women writers.[28] In Bradstreet's 'A Letter to her Husband', though, we find a female speaker emphatically defining her own body. She starts with the head or, metaphorically, the mind/intellect:

My head, my heart, mine eyes, my life, nay, more,
My joy, my magazine of earthly store,
If two be one, as surely thou and I,
How stayest thou there, whilst I at Ispwich lie?

The rub here though, or the point the opening lines are making, is that in the absence of the husband which the poem is lamenting, the female speaker must cast off the role of object and has no choice but to assume the place of the self-defining subject. The conditional words 'if' and 'surely' and the question in line four indicate how strange a state of affairs this is, not only that wife and husband are separated but that the female subject must eulogise herself.

The poem proceeds to construct sequences of ever-expanding metaphors to convey the impact of this separation. From the immediate loss registered and felt at the level of the 'head' and 'heart' in line five, the focus moves out from 'the Earth' to the 'Sun' to the 'Zodiac' (lines six to eight). But then it moves back again to intimate and personal experience: 'His warmth such frigid colds did cause to melt. / My chilled limbs now numbed lie forlorn.' The effect is to assert both the immediacy and specificity of this speaker's loss, and the comparative inadequacy of conventional metaphors (Earth, Sun, stars) to convey its real impact.

From its opening lament for its own speaker's solitude, the poem moves to a closing assertion of husband and wife's inalienable union. Lines twenty-one and twenty-two revert to the emphatic 'my' of the opening lines, although the possessive 'my' in this case is there primarily to welcome and succour the other, thus 'my glowing breast' promises a welcome haven to 'my dearest guest'. The final lines lose that self-assertive 'my' and posit in its place a union of 'I' and 'thou', not two but one: 'Flesh of thy flesh, bone of thy bone, / I here, thou there, yet both but one.'

Some 200 years later, the American writer Emma Lazarus's c. 1880 poem 'Echoes' stakes a claim to a woman-centred poetics, a private poetics of 'solitude and song'.[29] However, the assertion of female poetic identity is rather more ambivalent than may, at first, appear. The speaker's gender is declared defiantly in the opening words of the first line, 'Late-born and woman-souled', but this assertion of female identity is already subject to qualification, restriction and curtailment. As the opening line continues, being 'woman souled I dare not hope'. The references to being 'Late born' and in the subsequent line to 'elders' lend an ambivalence to the whole poem, commensurate with the ambiguity about the value of gender in the opening line. Is it good (a blessing) to be 'Late born'? Does the 'freshness of the elders' (line two) persist in perpetuity or does the fact that it 'lays' ('the freshness of the elders lays') mean that it is in decline or subsiding? By these same tokens, is it a virtue or a disadvantage to be 'woman-souled'? The poem leaves these implicit questions unanswered.

From the title onwards, 'Echoes' suggests the necessary co-existence of women and men, of new and old, of 'Late born' and 'woman-souled' and 'manly' and 'modern'. Just as the voice of the echo in classical mythology speaks only in answer to the call of Narcissus (Echo in Ovid's *Metamorphoses* can only speak in response to Narcissus's cry), so too in this poem the voice of the speaker is called into being, or interpellated, by that of the implicitly male addressee. The poem posits a retreat on the part of the female subject/speaker. She does not dare to 'hope' that inspiration will strike her (or that 'modern passion shall alight / Upon my Muse's lips'), and she fears that she will be unable to 'cope' if it does. As a woman, she lacks experience and education ('veiled and screened by womanhood must grope'), and she is alarmed by the ostentatious, aggressive idiom of her masculine peers: the 'world's strong-armed warriors' with their stories of 'the dangers, wounds, and triumphs of the fight', couched in the 'Twanging' notes of the 'full-stringed lyre'.

The speaker offers a caricature of masculine poetics which she turns her back on, annexing instead the private, quiet space of 'some lake-floored cave' (Ovid's Echo, when rejected by Narcissus, retreats to the woods and the caves). The important point here is that the female speaker's turn away from the loudly, belligerently masculine is self-willed; it is a female choice rather than a male imposition. This female speaker rejects the dominant masculine order rather than being rejected by it. Nevertheless, the ambivalence noted above remains. The speaker spurns the orthodoxies of male poetry, yet remains subject to and speechless without its command:

But if thou ever in some lake-floored cave
O'erbrowed by rocks, a wild voice wooed and heard,
Answering at once from heaven and earth and wave,
Lending elf-music to thy harshest word,
Misprize thou not these echoes that belong
To one in love with solitude and song.

PRIVACY IN HISTORY

During the modern period and in particular from the Enlightenment through Romanticism into the modern day, Western poetry, as we have seen, has been dominated by lyric modes and predicated on the free expression of a homogenous, identifiable and authoritative selfhood. Any earlier than this (and, arguably, any later into the postmodern era, a point to which Chapter 7 will return), ideas about selfhood, privacy, agency, expression and freedom would have sounded rather different. Laurence Stone explains:

> Individualism is a very slippery concept to handle. Here [in the early eighteenth century] what is meant is two rather distinct things: firstly, a growing introspection and interest in the individual personality; and secondly, a demand for personal autonomy and a corresponding respect for the individual's right to privacy, to self-expression, and to the free exercise of his will within limits set by the need for social cohesion: a recognition that it is morally wrong to make exaggerated demands for obedience, or to manipulate or coerce the individual beyond a certain point in order to achieve social or political ends. Because these are now such familiar tenets of Western society, they should not be taken for granted. They are culturally determined values, which most societies in world history have despised or deplored, and which most still do.[30]

Even in the Romantic period, as Meena Alexander argues, 'the centrality of the poet's self was crucial to an art that tried to free itself of pre-determined orders, whether literary or political. The world could not be remade without visionary freedom.' However,

> for women writers this Romantic ideal of selfhood and its visionary freedom was not easy to come by. Nor did it always seem to be singularly appropriate to women. The Romantic self presupposed a self-consciousness that had the leisure and space to enshrine itself at the heart of things. Brought up with a very different sense of the self, with constant reminders of how their lives were meshed in with other lives in bonds of care and concern, women could not easily aspire to this ideal.[31]

Privacy, then, has entirely different significations and effects in different contexts and for different genders, and a study of poetry by women needs to be attuned to these diverse ideologies and aesthetics. It needs, too, to recognise women poets' engagement with conditions which, while uncomfortable, may also have seemed inalienable.

Bradstreet's 'On My Dear Grandchild Simon Bradstreet, Who Died on 16 November, 1669, Being But a Month, and One Day Old' must be understood within the overlapping contexts of literary convention (the elegy), spiritual expectations (providing comfort in the belief that such a loss is part of God's plan) and practical experience (high infant mortality rates would have rendered this death at least partly foreseeable).[32] Nevertheless, the poem reveals a speaker struggling to come to terms with all of the tenets outlined above. She cannot simply accept her lot. The brevity of the twelve-line text is paradoxically an indication of the immensity of the experience it conveys. The poem gives the impression that the emotion can only be addressed if very strictly contained. Yet the fractured sentences which are broken into taut, heavily punctuated clauses, particularly in the opening lines, imply an overwhelming set of emotions which cannot so easily be controlled and threaten always to break through the limitations the form imposes. According to Celeste Schenck, 'Women poets from the first refuse or rework the central symbolisms and procedures of elegy mainly [. . .] because the genre itself excludes the feminine from its perimeter.' For two of Bradstreet's near-contemporaries, Katherine

Philips in 'Orinda Upon Little Hector Philips' and Anne Finch in 'The Losse', 'excruciating loss [. . .] exceeds elegiac convention' and proves inadequate to the task which confronts them.[33] In Bradstreet's elegy, disorder and chaos threaten life, faith and poem alike:

> No sooner came, but gone, and fall'n asleep,
> Acquaintance short, yet parting caused us weep;
> Three flowers, two scarcely blown, the last i' th' bud,
> Cropt by th' Almighty's hand; yet is He good.

In line four, the speaker attempts to find consolation in the convention of God's beneficial plan. Thereafter, though, the poem seems unable to credit this comforting solution, the only one which contemporary belief systems can offer. Instead, it merely voices a set of conventions which it cannot credit, thus exposing their inadequacy: 'With dreadful awe before Him let's be mute.' The repeated use of the form 'let's', although it has biblical precedents, for instance in the antiphonal structure of the Psalms, indicates in the end an attempt at self-persuasion ('let's not dispute', 'let's say') which makes the speaker's assimilation of these religious orthodoxies seem provisional. The speaker is very consciously attempting a leap of faith. Although not necessarily convinced that the terrible loss of the child is justified in any realm, she nevertheless has little choice but to assay belief. She must attempt to draw some sort of comfort from the conventions, both poetic and doctrinal:

> Such was His will, but why, let's not dispute,
> With humble hearts and mouths put in the dust,
> Let's say He's merciful as well as just.

Although the poem attempts a form of final blessing – 'Go pretty babe, go rest with sisters twain; / Among the blest in endless joys remain' – the reminder that this is the last of three children to be taken in this way, coupled with the allusion in the antepenultimate line to the 'bitter crosses' borne by those who remain in this world to grieve, denies any comforting resolution. Schenck sees a similar 'critique of transcendence' in Aphra Behn's 'On the Death of the Late Earl of Rochester', suggesting that 'a continuous mourning, a refusal to be compensated for his death' is more fitting.[34]

When thinking about the relationship between poetry written by women and contemporary notions of privacy, we need to be alert to the changing histories of women's reading practices. From the early modern period, women's behaviour was 'carefully policed by the dominant male hierarchy of their age: the ideal woman was chaste, silent and obedient'. It is little surprise then that, as Wynne-Davies goes on to explain, women tended to circulate their manuscripts only within their own families or close circles of acquaintances, and that they tended – although there are exceptions – towards the 'private discourses of love poetry and elegies'.[35] Women poets of the literate classes read and were read within private contexts which, although from a present-day and external perspective might seem constrained, one might also think of as familiar and secure. When women poets assumed a public voice, this was done in a highly self-conscious and rhetorical style, as we have already seen in relation to, say, Margaret Cavendish and in the example which Wynne-Davies provides from Anne Dowriche's dramatic verse play *The French History* (1589): 'For here I do protest, if I had been a man, / I had myself before this time this murder long began.'[36]

Dowriche's poem confutes orthodox expectations, including those raised at the beginning of this chapter, about the necessary connection between women's poetry and a privacy of perspective. *The French History* offers a sustained, comprehensive and allusive account of religious conflict in mid-sixteenth-century France. It is a political, even a polemical poem, deeply imbued in its place, time and ideological contexts. As we will see in Chapter 5, it is not alone in this. Her poem, like others of its period, also confirms the point made in the first chapter about the deep self-consciousness which characterises poetry by women across different periods and forms. Whatever their ostensible theme or concern, almost all of the poems discussed in this book reflect in some way on the curiosity, daring or challenge arising from their very status as female-authored texts. More specifically, and perhaps more frustratingly, they must use the private space afforded to them as women poets in

whichever way they can to address and often confute a public dis-
course which would label women as inadequate, subordinate and
sinful.

Aemilia Lanyer's 1611 *Salve Deus Rex Judaeorum*, for example,
opens thus:

> Renowned Empress, and great Britain's Queen,
> Most gracious mother of succeeding Kings;
> Vouchsafe to view that which is seldom seen,
> A woman's writing of divinest things:[37]

The poem posits a female subject (the speaker) and a female
object/addressee (the Queen). Thus it asserts a contiguity between
femininity and forms of authority – between divine author-
ity (*Salve Deus Rex Judaeorum*), political authority ('Renowned
Empress, and great Britain's Queen') and textual authority
('A woman's writing of divinest things'). It delivers all this, though,
in a voice which, while largely rhetorical and declamatory, is also
intimate and direct in its address from woman to woman. Moreover,
this affirmation of a shared authority (authority of subject and
object) is couched in the figure of maternity. The poem's claim to a
voice and to a hearing is predicated finally on an appeal to the values
of the small-scale, the intimate and the domestic. Motherhood is
posited as the quiet core from which all consciousness emerges and
to which all experience returns.

The poem develops a model of an ideal motherhood which is
representative of spiritual, moral and aesthetic value and embodied
both by addressee/Queen (the 'most gracious mother' of line two)
and by subject/text. The model is sufficient once and for all to con-
found the age-old stories of Eve's culpability:

> Behold, great Queen, fair Eve's apology,
> Which I have writ in honour of your sex,
> And do refer unto your majesty,
> To judge if it agree not with the text:
> > And if it do, why are poor women blamed,
> > Or by more faulty women so much defamed?[38]

The syntax in the first two lines quoted here is ambivalent, indicating both that the poem 'Which I have writ' comprises sufficient apology, and that the Queen herself is its ultimate embodiment ('great Queen, fair Eve's apology'). The figure of the mother in this poem is, arguably, recuperated or restored in all her potential glory as the ideal point of origin and guide and, as in the stanza quoted above, wise judge. The poem as offspring or creation of the subject/mother takes its own place as evidence of the value of the maternal.

The 'great lady' of stanza fourteen, quoted below, signifies both Eve and the poem itself. Both are carefully presented in order to demonstrate their latent perfection, hence 'richest ornaments of honour'. The metaphor refers both to the glorification of Eve and to the aesthetic effects of the poetic text:

> And this great lady I have here attired,
> In all her richest ornaments of honour,
> That you, fair Queen, of all the world admired,
> May take the more delight to look upon her:

Lanyer implies that Eve and the poem validate and praise each other. In a further development of this motif and of the bond between women, the following stanza unites Queen Anne of Denmark (the poem's primary addressee), her daughter Elizabeth of Bohemia (the poet/speaker) and behind them Eve in a shared celebration of female dignity:

> And she that is the pattern of all beauty,
> The very model of your majesty,
> Whose rarest parts enforceth love and duty,
> The perfect pattern of all piety:
>   O let my book by her fair eyes be blest,
>   In whose pure thoughts all innocency rests.

This is a mutually affirmative relationship, confirming the mother/daughter bond established at the beginning of the poem. The penultimate stanza of the first part of the poem confirms the point and affirms the relevance of such a relationship to poetry itself (hence the reference to the 'Muse' who is here rescued from barrenness and made fertile):

And since all arts at first from Nature came,
That goodly creature, mother of perfection,
Whom Jove's almighty hand at first did frame,
Taking both his and hers in his protection:
> Why should not she now grace my barren Muse
> And in a woman all defects excuse?[39]

'I COULD NOT FIND A PRIVACY': EMILY DICKINSON

When Dickinson's speaker laments 'I could not find a privacy' (Poem 891), she is also regretting that she is unable to find a rhetorical position in and from which to be private. Privacy, or the adoption of an intimate and personal voice, is, then, a poetic choice – not an inadvertent and female-specific position. More recent poems by American and English authors exemplify the deliberate assumption of the position of loner and outsider where the retreat into the wilderness represents a form of personal, intellectual and aesthetic freedom. The speaker of Sexton's 1960 poem 'Kind Sir: These Woods' declares herself to be 'lost' at night in the woods. Yet she revels in her own disorientation; becoming lost is a purposive strategy, not an accident. It permits the speaker a form of liberty and access to self-knowledge ('I search in these woods and find nothing worse / than myself caught between the grapes and the thorns'). Stevie Smith's 'I Rode with my Darling' (1950) pictures a female subject torn between the safety of companionship with a solicitous, if domineering, man ('My darling grew pale he was responsible / He said we should go back it was reasonable') and the attractions of the unknown 'dark wood at night'. Yet in Smith's poem, the dark wood does not immediately offer the insights expected of it; the poem closes with a succession of rhetorical questions and the emphatic line, 'All all is silent in the dark wood at night'. Nevertheless, in a final twist, it may be precisely this silence, or privacy, that the harassed woman seeks.[40]

Dickinson draws on the metaphor of the woods in defence of her own poetics in an 1862 letter to her mentor T. W. Higginson. She justifies her retreat into 'the Core of Woods' and very deliberately eschews conventional wisdom about the dangers for young women of being alone in the forest:

> When much in the Woods as a little Girl, I was told that the Snake would bite me, that I might pick a poisonous flower, or Goblins kidnap me, but I went along and met no one but Angels, who were far shyer of me, than I could be of them.[41]

In the case of Dickinson, Sexton and Smith, the privacy afforded by the forest represents, metaphorically, the freedom to be found in poetry – a freedom that will be won only by those who dare to transgress prohibitions which curtail women's lives and writing. Karen Jackson Ford suggests that 'what Dickinson discovers in the woods is authorization for her own waywardness, solitude, instincts and impulses'.[42]

In Dickinson, we find an interesting case with which to explore the meaning of privacy for women poets. She was born in 1830 into a close-knit New England family. Her grandfather, father and brother were all actively involved in education, politics and local civic affairs. As a young girl, she would have been party to this wide and active social circle, but would also have been at least to some degree marginalised and cut off. In 1852, when all the men of the family were involved in active political campaigning and she was left behind at home, she wrote to her then friend (and later sister-in-law) Susan Gilbert to protest her exclusion from the public sphere: 'Why can't *I* be a Delegate to the great Whig convention? – don't I know all about Daniel Webster, and the Tariff, and the Law?' In 1847, Dickinson studied for a year at Mount Holyoke female seminary, although she seems not to have felt entirely comfortable there. Her studies coincided with a great wave of religious enthusiasm (Revivalism or 'the Second Awakening'), yet Dickinson herself felt unable to make a public declaration of her private faith: 'Christ is calling everyone here [. . .] and I am standing alone in rebellion.'[43] She returned to the family home at Amherst and, apart from occasional local visits and trips to Boston and Washington, was to remain there for the rest of her life.

Throughout her life, Dickinson was a prolific writer, producing at least 1,700 poems and over 1,100 letters. A tiny handful of these poems were published in her own lifetime. Of the rest, over 1,000 were copied by Dickinson into 'fair copy' (or final form), and over 800 of these she carefully stitched into forty 'fascicles' (tiny booklets comprising five or six sheets of paper gathered and sewn together). These were only discovered after Dickinson's death by her family, who proceeded to unbind the bulk of them, rearrange their order and publish them, first in 1890 and 1891 as small volumes and subsequently in larger collections. In every case, standard punctuation was restored.[44] This is an important point to make. The strangeness of Dickinson's original punctuation is crucial to an understanding of the work, its unique perspective, its attempt to tackle huge subjects and to convey the experience of a restricted, tormented, fractured subject or the fluidity of a lively and idiosyncratic mind at work, depending on one's point of view. Certainly, early readers of Dickinson were not sure what to make of her work. Even hostile critics, though, recognised its strange daring (one critic called it 'a new species of art').[45] Readers realised that they needed to rethink the conventions of poetry if they wished to comprehend Dickinson's oeuvre.

It was not until the publication of Ralph Franklin's 1981 edition that the original punctuation was restored. Readers could now see the strange repertoire of dashes, some almost vertical, which punctuate the poems and act like a form of code. Readers could also see the original order of the poems as prepared in Dickinson's own fascicles; Franklin was able to show that there were thematic and tonal connections across and between poems. As an example, in one fascicle (fascicle 34), Dickinson had presented poems which we might read as being about the process of writing poetry, including Poem 754 'My Life had Stood – a Loaded Gun –' and Poem 758 'These – saw Visions'.

From the ashes of this biography has emerged over the years an influential and lasting image of Dickinson as some kind of recluse (or the 'hermit from Amherst' as she has become known). The situation is, however, far more complex than this suggests. Cynthia Griffin Wolff argues, 'Dickinson seems to have begun writing seriously in about 1848, and there was nothing in the least secretive about it: she enjoyed a local reputation for great wit, and many of her poems were read by family and friends.'[46] For Suzanne Juhasz, the role of the hermit or recluse, of the woman who has turned her back on public life, should be read as a strategic 'choice' and not an instinctive 'retreat from "real life" ' '.[47] Moreover, the position of the recluse may, as Alicia Ostriker has proposed, offer Dickinson a valuable mask or disguise the better to protect her own time, her subjectivity and her practice as a writer: 'In adopting the persona of the shy recluse, delicately afraid of strangers, too sensitive for the marketplace, Dickinson did precisely what the ideal poetess was supposed to do.'[48] Camille Paglia makes a similar point, saying that Dickinson thinks in 'theatrical or masquelike terms'.[49] Thus Dickinson deflects attention, offering a surface 'self' which obscures rather more complicated depths. It is a moot point whether she does this in conformity with contemporary expectations, in order to expose and undermine the ideology which underpins such expectations, as a strategy for protecting a private self from public display, or as a playful gesture simply because she can.

In any of these cases, the effect is that Dickinson frees herself to write. Even if we do want to read her as some kind of recluse, as protected by choice or compulsion from the public sphere, we should note that she lived a vigorous life of the mind. Her poems are radical and provocative in their rebellious flights of fancy, and her keen observational powers (particularly for small and uninvited visitors: the spiders and birds which populate many of her poems) show that she was sufficiently alert to the outside world to find some real significance in every detail, every move. She was also deeply exercised by huge abstract questions of life and death, faith and despair, love and loss. And she was a wide reader; although perhaps physically rooted in a small Amherst community, she knew the work of Elizabeth Barrett Browning, the Brontës and George Eliot, amongst others. She was also a prolific correspondent, communicating frequently with a wide circle of letter acquaintances; these included Thomas Wentworth Higginson, a man of letters to whom Dickinson sent her poems in 1862 with a plea for him to let her know whether they 'breathed'.[50]

Higginson and Dickinson struck up a literary relationship which was to last until Dickinson's death some twenty-six years later. She tested her ideas out on him, wrestled with his ideas about women writers and challenged his views. Dickinson's brother Austin was also an important sounding board. Dickinson seems to have thrived on their criticism, developing ever more ingenious ways of undermining, subverting, resisting or rebutting their expectations, first, of how women should write and, second, what poetry should look and sound like. To quote Karen Jackson Ford:

> Both Austin and Higginson had customary notions of writing – Austin of women's writing and Higginson of poetry – that conflicted in an extremely productive way with Dickinson's own view of herself as a writer.[51]

Gilbert and Gubar see Dickinson's life as a re-enactment of some of the contradictions implicit in women's writing in the nineteenth century: 'The fantasies of guilt and anger that were expressed in the entranced reveries of the fiction-maker by writers like Rossetti and Barrett Browning [. . .] were literally enacted by Dickinson in her own life, her own being.' Gilbert and Gubar have a point, but it is the poetic performances (the voices and perspectives, the roles and the scenes played out in the poems) which are of more interest. It is in the poetic text itself that Dickinson is able to examine and test both the minutiae of life and its biggest and toughest abstractions. Gilbert and Gubar suggest that 'through an extraordinarily complex series of manoeuvres, aided by costumes that came inevitably to hand, this inventive poet enacted and eventually resolved both her anxieties about her art and her anger at female subordination'.[52] This, I think, is only part of Dickinson's subject matter; her scope is altogether broader.

The critic Dennis Donoghue has said, 'Of her religious faith virtually anything may be said, with some show of evidence. She may be represented as an agnostic, a heretic, a sceptic, a Christian.'[53] Certainly, one might read the poems and letters in entirely contradictory ways as both confessing and denying a faith. Poetry offers Dickinson a private space in which she can contemplate these issues without necessarily being restricted to any one position. As a young girl, she professed a profound faith, writing in a letter to a friend: 'I never enjoyed such perfect peace and happiness as the short time in which I felt I had found my saviour [. . .] I feel I shall never be happy without I love Christ.'[54] Even here, though, we can see that her sense of faith is shadowed by fear, by the risk of losing what she has so fleetingly found. We might trace this electric tension between fear and hope, despair and faith, to the Calvinist tradition of New England. Looking back to the Puritans, Calvinism stressed the total depravity (evilness) of humans, the principle of unconditional election (God alone chooses whom to save), limited atonement (the presence of Christ has helped a little to redeem humans to the extent that they are now able, at least, to worship God), irresistible grace (God bestows this and it cannot be removed) and perseverance (the elected few will stay committed). One can see how this framework might have generated some of the extremes of religious faith and doubt we see in her work.[55]

The short Poem 1551 ('Those – dying then'), for example, invites the reader at one and the same time to envy those who, in the past, died in confidence of their destination at God's right hand, and curiously to pity those who still live. There is a comfort, the poem implies, in having died consumed by a faith which, by implication, has been lost to the present generation: 'Those – dying then, / Knew where they went – They went to God's right hand.' The poem is more explicit in respect of its delineation of the destination than is usual in Dickinson's writing (she is more likely to work by suggestion or intimation), but it is characteristically elliptical in its delineation of who precisely 'Those' are, and when precisely 'then' is. Thus, it leaves the reader uncertain and unsettled.

These first three lines are fairly clear and, to an extent, fairly conventional; they draw on the well-worn image of 'God's right hand'. But any complacency of vision is radically interrupted by the deadpan statement of lines four and five: 'That Hand is amputated now / And God cannot be found –'. How disturbing an image this is! How hopeless (the hopelessness is emphasised by the pause, or almost an end-stop, at the end of each of these two lines). The use of those frank monosyllables coupled with the disyllabic 'cannot' in line five further enforce the point. The notion of 'amputation' is rather more than simply a metaphor for a loss of connection. It may signify a form of punishment (the image derives from the story of Acteon in Greek mythology; Acteon was a hunter who was torn apart by his own hounds as punishment for seeing the goddess Artemis bathing). What, we must ask, has God been punished for? If

God has behaved so badly, what does this suggest about the lives of mortals? Where does this leave the faithful, or indeed the faithless?

It is the believers, or non-believers, to whom the poem now turns. The allusion to God's right hand is implicitly also an allusion to his throne and his divine authority. Stanza two suggests that it is the failure of faith, the 'abdication of Belief' which is at the root of God's downfall. Thus the lost majesty of God surmised in the opening stanza is undermined; power (and the power, by implication, to shape one's destiny in death) lies in the hands of the potential believers. God is the servant of the people, not their master. The only hopes of restoring God to his position and of ensuring a safe passage to his right hand lie in continual belief. To believe in anything is potentially more rewarding than not to believe at all: 'Better an ignis fatuus / Than no illume at all –'. Written in the same period, Emily Brontë's 'I am the only being whose doom' is equally startling in its evocation of the speaker's ultimate isolation and loss of faith. The poem opens with a sequence of negatives ('doom', 'mourn', 'no tongue', 'no eye') and the speaker seems numbed, despairing and vulnerable. She feels herself to be abandoned even by God; his promise (represented by the rainbow) has failed: 'fancy's rainbow fast withdrew'. Worse still, it is the subject's own failure of belief which is responsible for this horror: 'worse to trust to my own mind / And find the same corruption there'.[56]

Dickinson's Poem 280 ('I felt a Funeral, in my Brain') also challenges orthodox expectations and systems of belief. This is visible at the level of form; written in a version of the ballad stanza of which Dickinson was particularly fond (the ballad stanza typically comprises four lines with alternately four and three stressed feet), it promises the direct narrative account of a specific episode or experience. However, the ballad form is broken up, for example, by half instead of full rhymes ('seated' / 'thought' in stanza two) and by the use of the very visible silences encoded by Dickinson's dash (–) such that the line struggles to contain the metre ascribed to it. In line three of stanza two, for example, the poem can barely contain its own rhythm: 'kept beating – beating – til I thought / My Mind was going numb –'.

'I felt a Funeral' is a poem about connection and disconnection. It makes emphatic use of alliteration both within and between lines and stanzas ('felt a Funeral', 'Sense' // 'seated' / 'service' and 'dropped down, and down –') to suggest a certain fluidity of intellectual movement. It also uses the technique of anaphora (repetition of words or phrases) which builds successively throughout the poem from one use of the initial word 'and' in each of stanzas one and two, to two in stanzas three and four, and four in the final stanza. Thus the momentum, but also the dreadful insistence of the poem, is established and reinforced. Dickinson exploits both the aural qualities of the poem and the visual. We hear the alliteration, and the accretion and the half rhymes mentioned above. We see some of these on the page, and we also see the suggestion of rhymes which the visual form of the words invites but then withholds (for example, 'creak' and 'lead'). The effect of this is to unsettle our sense of the flow of the poem; we see rhyme in places where we cannot hear it.

From the first line of 'I felt a Funeral', there are multiple images of containment. The focus moves from the 'Brain' to the 'Box' to the 'Heavens' (if 'Heavens were a Bell'). Is Dickinson suggesting some form of bell jar: a place of containment and experimentation or display? As elsewhere in her work, the poem starts by focusing on the small (the 'I' and the 'Brain') and slowly widens its sphere, moving outwards and upwards. Poem 712 ('Because I could not stop for death') similarly begins with the self and moves on to the School, the 'Fields' and the 'Setting Sun'. In 'I felt a Funeral', the use of the present participle form 'treading', 'beating' and finally 'knowing' emphasises the draining relentlessness of the experience the poem represents. However, when used alongside the past-tense form of the title and of key sections in the poem ('And then I heard' and 'And I dropped'), it serves further to convey the speaker's, and at this point the reader's, sense of confusion. This is invoked, too, by the synaesthesia (or mixing of senses) throughout the text, with touch and sound playing a particularly important role. And although I have mentioned the importance to the reader of the visual qualities of the words on the page, it is clear that for the speaker sight is of minimal importance; indeed, the poem reads as though a nightmare scene where the speaker is precisely unable to see what is going on around her. As though blinded or held in a dark room, buried alive in the 'Box' of stanza three, she can only listen to what is going on around her, trying to make sense of the aural clues. It is this, perhaps, which makes the poem so terrifying, so claustrophobic, so uncanny in Freud's sense of the term.[57]

The fractured perspective and fractured subjectivity represented in the poem are replicated in the fractured syntax. For example, stanza four can only hint at the vision it sees:

> As all the Heavens were a Bell,
> And Being, but an Ear,
> And I, and Silence, some strange Race
> Wrecked, solitary, here –

Is the poem suggesting that all humanity (that 'being' itself) is just an 'ear' (that is, we can only passively absorb that which goes on around us), or is she saying that she alone, the abject speaker, is only an ear (that is, her senses are stripped away such that only the power of hearing remains)? How do we explain that the speaker is alone and silent, but also that she is part of 'some strange Race'? How do we account for the fact that, as the poem itself demonstrates, she is not silenced? If the 'Heavens' were a 'Bell', does this suggest, as indicated above, a form of entrapment like a bell jar, or is the bell a sign of warning or call to Christian worship? There are numerous alternative readings here, and these work to place the reader in the same state of confusion and uncertainty as the subject.

Existence throughout this poem is felt to be profoundly physical. The emotional and spiritual journey the text describes is felt on the bodily and material levels. The 'Mind' is the victim of a sequence of bruising encounters, and in the final stanza the very physical sensation of mental or spiritual breakdown (whether personal or, as suggested a moment ago, a more shared condition of 'being') is emphatically realised:

> And then a Plank in Reason, broke,
> And I dropped down, and down –
> And hit a World, at every plunge,
> And Finished knowing – then –

'The Fall' that the poem describes is experienced literally. The final line is enigmatic, and paradoxical. From one point of view, it suggests that the speaker has stopped knowing anything. From another, one might say that she ends up knowing something. One might also say though that the closing line confirms what a self-excoriating poem this is. The speaker describes the most profound physical and mental torment which is, finally, a kind of personal punishment – or just rewards for her own attempt to understand, rather than simply to accept, divine will. 'Knowing' (or using 'my Brain') to reason with one's circumstances is here the grounds and also the object of punishment. There is almost a resolution at the end of this poem that, knowing now how painful it is to apply the 'Brain' to comprehend God (metonymically 'the Heavens'), the speaker commits never to attempt to know again.

In Dickinson's ostensibly private and hermetic poetry, then, are a breadth of scope and a wealth of concerns which belie the apparently private nature of her work. Thus the boundaries in poetry by women between private and public, intimate and social experience become blurred.

CONCLUSION

We come here to the paradox by which even the most closed, intimate and private of poetic lines is finally and inevitably to some extent also public and shared. In this sense, the private voices of women's poetry might be read as resisting both relegation to the realm of the private and more broadly the system of thought (phallogocentrism) which would see these binaries as functional, necessary and explanatory. In exposing and complicating the set of binaries (in this case private vs. public, personal vs. social, quiet and intimate vs. rhetorical and authoritative), women's poetry also critiques the problematic and essentialist binary of male vs. female.

SUMMARY OF KEY POINTS

- A traditional view of poetry by women might characterise it as being concerned primarily with the exploration of private, intimate concerns.

- Assumptions such as this need to be addressed and questions asked about how exactly women poets have integrated private and public concerns, perhaps effacing any simplistic distinction between the two.
- To this end, women poets have used conventional forms and modes (for example, the lyric and the elegy) in unexpected ways.

NOTES

1. Catherine Reilly (ed.), *Chaos of the Night: Women's Poetry and Verse of the Second World War* (London: Virago, 1984), p. xxv. See also her *Scars Upon My Heart: Women's Poetry and Verse of the First World War* (London: Virago, 1981).
2. David Cressy, quoted in Stevenson and Davidson, *Early Modern*, p. xxxxviii.
3. Glück, *First Five*, pp. 120, 255.
4. Cathy N. Davidson, 'Preface: No More Separate Spheres', *American Literature* 70: 3 (1998), 443–63 (444).
5. Kaplan, 'Introduction', in Barrett Browning, *Aurora Leigh*, p. 9.
6. Alice Entwistle, '"Scotland's New House": Domesticity, Domicile and Contemporary Women's Poetry', in *The Edinburgh Companion to Contemporary Scottish* Literature, ed. Berthold Schoene (Edinburgh: Edinburgh University Press, 2007), p. 96.
7. Phyllis McGinley, *Times Three: Selected Verse from Three Decades* (New York: Viking, 1960).
8. Rees-Jones, *Consorting*, p. 171; Selima Hill, 'Chicken Feathers', *Saying Hello at the Station* (London: Chatto, 1984), p. 45.
9. Wynne-Davies, *Women Poets*, p. xxi. For more on Elizabeth and Margaret Cavendish and on Anne Bradstreet, see also pp. 367–73.
10. Cavendish, 'Nature's Cook', in Bolam, *Eliza's Babes*, p. 72.
11. Rees, *Margaret Cavendish*, p. 171.
12. Frye, *Anatomy*, p. 272.
13. Easthope, *Poetry as Discourse*, p. 123.

14. Kaplan, *Salt*, p. 274; Frye, *Anatomy*, p. 272.
15. Quoted in Camille Paglia, *Sexual Personae: Art and Decadence from Nefertiti to Emily Dickinson* (London and New Haven, CT: Yale University Press, 1990), p. 638.
16. Carr, 'Poetic License', p. 89.
17. Helen Farish, *Intimates* (London: Cape, 2005).
18. Kate Clanchy, *Newborn* (London: Picador, 2004), p. 44.
19. T. S. Eliot, *The Sacred Wood: Essays on Poetry and Criticism* (London: Faber and Faber, 1997), pp. 48–9.
20. John Berryman, *Dream Songs* (London: Faber and Faber, 1993), p. vi.
21. Al Alvarez, 'Sylvia Plath: A Memoir', in *Ariel Ascending: Writings About Sylvia Plath*, ed. Paul Alexander (New York: Harper and Row, 1985), pp. 185–213 (p. 199).
22. Bertram, *Gendering Poetry*, p. 42.
23. Sarah Maguire, 'Poetry Makes Nothing Happen', in Herbert and Hollis, *Strong Words*, pp. 248–51 (p. 250).
24. Wynne-Davies, *Women Poets*, p. 259.
25. Ibid. p. 266.
26. See Wynne-Davies, *Women Poets*, pp. 370–3. See also Adrienne Rich, 'Foreword', in *The Works of Anne Bradstreet*, ed. Jeannine Hensley (Cambridge, MA: Belknap Press, 1967), pp. ix–xxi.
27. Moira P. Baker, ' "The Uncanny Stranger on Display": The Female Body in Sixteenth- and Seventeenth-Century Love Poetry', *South Atlantic Review* 56: 2 (1991), 7–25. Accessed 19 August 2006 at: http://www.radford.edu/~mpbaker/bodyart.html.
28. Dowson and Entwistle, *A History*, p. 3.
29. Kaplan, *Salt*, p. 177.
30. Lawrence Stone, *The Family, Sex and Marriage in England 1500–1800* (Harmondsworth: Penguin, 1979), p. 151.
31. Meena Alexander, *Women in Romanticism: Mary Wollstonecraft, Dorothy Wordsworth and Mary Shelley* (Basingstoke: Macmillan, 1989), pp. 5–6.
32. Wynne-Davies, *Women Poets*, pp. 260–1.
33. Celeste Schenck, 'Feminism and Deconstruction: Re-Constructing the Elegy', *Tulsa Studies in Women's Literature* 5: 1 (1986), 13–27 (13, 14).

34. Ibid. 20.
35. Wynne-Davies, *Women Poets*, p. xxvi.
36. Anne Dowriche, *The French History*, in Wynne-Davies, *Women Poets*, pp. 18–57 (lines 1435–6).
37. Aemilia Lanyer, *Salve Deus Rex Judaeorum*, in Wynne-Davies, *Women Poets*, pp. 99–147.
38. Ibid. lines 73–8.
39. Ibid. p. 297. For more on Lanyer, see *Poems of Aemilia Lanyer*, ed. Susanne Woods (New York: Oxford University Press, 1993).
40. Stevie Smith, 'I Rode with my Darling', in Couzyn, *Contemporary Women Poets*, p. 46.
41. Quoted in Jackson Ford, *Gender*, p. 32.
42. Ibid. p. 34.
43. *The Letters of Emily Dickinson*, ed. Thomas H. Johnson, vol. 1 (Cambridge, MA: Belknap Press, 1965), p. 213. Paul Crumbley, 'Emily Dickinson's Life'; accessed 17 March 2006 at: www.english.uiuc.edu/maps/poets/a_f/dickinson/bio.htm.
44. See Thomas H. Johnson, 'Introduction', in *The Complete Poems of Emily Dickinson* (London: Faber and Faber, 1970), pp. v–xi. See also Susan Howe, *My Emily Dickinson* (Berkeley, CA: North Atlantic Books, 1985) and *The Manuscript Books of Emily Dickinson*, ed. R. W. Franklin, two vols (Cambridge, MA: Belknap Press, 1981).
45. Crumbley, 'Emily Dickinson's Life'.
46. Wolff, 'Emily Dickinson', pp. 121–47 (p. 121).
47. Quoted in Nancy Walker, '"Wider than the Sky": Public Presence and Private Self in Dickinson, James and Woolf', in *The Private Self: Theory and Practice of Women's Autobiographical Writings*, ed. Shari Benstock (London: Routledge, 1988), pp. 272–303 (p. 272).
48. Alicia Ostriker, *Stealing the Language: The Emergence of Women's Poetry in America* (London: Women's Press, 1987), p. 38.
49. Paglia, *Sexual Personae*, p. 648.
50. Dickinson, *Complete*, p. v.
51. Jackson Ford, *Gender*, p. 26.
52. Sandra M. Gilbert and Susan Gubar, *The Madwoman in the Attic: The Woman Writer and the Nineteenth-Century Literary*

Imagination (New Haven, CT: Yale University Press, 1984), p. 583.

53. Quoted in David Yezzi, 'Straying Close to Home – Author/Poet Emily Dickinson's Religious Beliefs and Spirituality', *Commonweal*, 9 October 1998, n.p.

54. Ibid.

55. See Donna M. Campbell, 'Calvinism in New England Puritan Culture'; accessed 19 March 2006 at: http://www.wsu.edu/~campbelld/amlit/calvin.htm.

56. Emily Brontë, 'I am the only being whose doom', in Reeves, *Five Late*, p. 112.

57. See Freud, 'The Uncanny', in Strachey, *Standard Edition*, vol. 17, pp. 219–52.

CHAPTER 4

Embodied Language

A persistent question for readers of women's poetry has been the relationship between cultural production and biological experience (or, perhaps more importantly, interpretations of that experience). To what extent, if at all, does women's biological existence inform the production, and indeed the reception, of their work? How do we account for themes of dislocation, dismemberment and physical abjection in women's writing? To talk about women, poetry and the body is to raise a number of apparently discrete (although perhaps inevitably connected) concerns. In addressing these vexed issues, I will be examining three key areas: first, the effect of a shift from women's bodies being perceived as the objects of the male poetic gaze to women being either the subjects of their own vision or the same-sex objects of the visions of others. Second, theories of a distinct female writing, tied in with biological experience or the rhythms of the body – from Woolf's 'feminine sentence' to the 'écriture féminine' of French feminist thought. Third, the link between physical and literal creativity, or the production of children and the creation of poetry: how have women read this apparent relationship?

In relation to all of these concerns, it is important, as has already been argued with respect to concepts of privacy and of the private 'self', to note that the significations of the female body change in different historical and cultural contexts. An English Renaissance viewpoint, for example, schooled in classical, mythological and biblical traditions, would be quite different from a Victorian angle

and different again from a Chicana perspective. To enquire about
the relations between women, poetry and the body is *not* to posit any
essentialist, universal or timeless set of preoccupations. Diana Fuss
in her valuable study *Essentially Speaking* distinguishes two
positions: the essentialist, in which 'the body occupies a pure,
pre-social, pre-discursive space [. . .] is "real", accessible and trans-
parent', and the constructionist in which 'the body is never simply
there; rather it is composed of a network of effects continually
subject to socio-political determination'.[1] Both of these categories
are evident in the argument below. More important, though, than
these two new binaries is the identification and examination of the
complex and shifting registers which subtend the field. This
chapter asks what women poets have made of these concerns in
their own particular places and times.

OBJECTS/SUBJECTS

'Thought has always worked by opposition [. . .] by dual, *hier-
archized* oppositions.'[2] So comments the French feminist and
philosopher Hélène Cixous. And the 'opposition' between the mind
(logic, reason, rationality) and the body (irruptive, uncontrollable,
irrational) is an opposition which has been taken as foundational to
the male/female, active/passive, subject/object divide critiqued
already in this book. This part of the chapter takes biological exist-
ence as its main focus and analyses the many ways in which poetry
by women has engaged with these apparent binaries. Such poetry
interrogates the adequacy and accuracy of these binaries, the
assumed privileging of one party over another, and the wider epis-
temology on which they are based.

If the tradition of Western poetry has objectified women, aes-
theticising and fetishising parts of the female body as evidence of
male desire and as potential reward for his poetic skill (the male poet
who demonstrates sufficient ability might seduce and win over the
female object), what is at stake for women poets as they reclaim their
own bodies and assume the place of subject? What difference does it
make for women as poets and as readers given that, as Moira P. Baker
has argued of poetry from the Renaissance (here she is concurring

with Nancy J. Vickers), 'The canonical tradition of description of the female body was "shaped predominantly by the male imagination for the male imagination" '?[3] It is the transgressiveness of female representations of physical experience, of sexuality and of desire which is significant. The shock of some of this poetry (some of Olds's work, for instance) lies not in the fact that women's bodies are being exposed, which is, after all, a long-standing poetic convention, but that it is women who are doing the exposing. As an example, one might compare Olds's writing about self, mother, sister, daughter and other women with the work of some of her near-contemporaries: Allen Ginsberg or Craig Raine, for instance.

An early Olds poem, 'Indictment of Senior Officers' (1980), suggests that subjectivity and identification are primarily physical; that it is biological experience which shapes both self and other and the relationship between the two.[4] Female identity, while physically rooted, is formed and controlled in relationships of power, hence the 'Senior Officers' of the poem's title. The bond between the two sisters who are the key figures in the poem is biological or genetic; what unites them, as lines three and four explain, is their dark hair and eyes, their 'bodies / like twins'. Like in Jacques Lacan's mirror stage and rather like in the dual relationships of speaker and mother and speaker and daughter in Sexton's 'The Double Image', the image of one 'living body' provides proof of the existence of the other. One might go on to argue that what separates and thus weakens these twin female bodies, although at first secure in the semiotic order (hence 'we did not talk'), is their necessary entry into the masculine symbolic order of language, dominated by the 'doctor husband' and the 'soldier'.

The cultural, medical, historical and political context implied in this poem is important. Femininity, or the female body, is here pathologised by a culture which condemns and punishes it. The second stanza describes in detail the physical injuries inflicted on the female body by the male 'doctor husband's beatings' and by the 'scars' of operations. There are two forms of violence, the poem suggests, the domestic and the medical. The effects on the female body are equivalent in both.

In a subsequent poem, 'The Sisters of Sexual Treasure', the sisters are again united, this time against their mother.[5] They delight in transgressing her taboo against the expression of sexuality, against the exploration of the (male) body and against the emergence and display of female desire. The sisters' sexual licence is displayed by their very explicit reversal of the conventional poetic tropes (the blazon which was touched on in the previous chapter) whereby the bodies of women are atomized, fragmented and laid bare for public scrutiny. Here it is the male body which is thus treated, spread out like so many pieces of animal flesh, the 'hocks, flanks, thighs'. The poem cannot, however, be read as a simple celebration of an uninhibited female sexuality, not least because the sisters' erotic fulfilment is gained at the expense of the mother. Her needs and desires, obscured perhaps by repression, fear and denial, are viciously vilified. The mother's weak and fragile body (realised in lines four and five with metaphors of tiny birds and insects) represents everything which must be jettisoned in favour of the strength and richness of the male form. What kind of free expression of the body is this, the poem in part is asking, if the physical liberation of some is gained at the cost of the annihilation of others? The desires in 'The Sisters of Sexual Treasure' are complex. Which, if any, of these positions (mother's or daughters') expresses a true female sexuality? Who is more shackled and more inhibited, the mother whose prohibitions are grounded, perhaps, in her wish to protect her daughters from male sexual exploitation, or the daughters who believe themselves to have escaped her anxious restrictions only to find themselves performing, in lines ten and eleven, a phallic sexual fantasy?

British poet Carol Ann Duffy's 2005 collection *Rapture* plays with the reader's expectations of subject and object positions. In so doing, it re-energises some of the conventions of romantic, lyric and courtly love poetry. One of the final poems in the collection, 'The Love Poem', does this explicitly and self-consciously. In telling of this new love, it samples some of the canonical works of poetic tradition, from Shakespeare's Sonnet 130 ('My mistress' eyes are nothing like the sun') to John Donne's 'To his Mistress' with its celebratory line 'O, My America, My Newfoundland' to Barrett Browning's 'How do I love thee? Let me count the ways'. Throughout the book, it appears that the voice is that of a female subject, but the gender of the addressee, or object, is not always certain and is never fixed (for example, 'Answer' and 'Venus' seem to connote a male and a female addressee respectively).

In 'Whatever', the lover's body is first disassembled or disembodied, even fetishised (note the carefully delineated 'hand', 'breast', 'finger' and 'lips'). But in each case the synecdochic representation of the other is also the synecdochic representation of the self, hence the emphatically repeated 'my' which is always as emphatically answered by 'your'. There is a succession of complex doublings at play here: the left hand of the other meets the right hand of the self; the 'finger' (which may be the speaker's or the lover's) meets 'my lips' which then meet 'your lips'; the reader's attention is directed first to 'my eyes' and then to 'your eyes'. Subject and object are mutually defining, and mutually reliant.[6]

WRITING THE BODY

When thinking about gender, writing and the body, it is useful to distinguish between a tradition of poetry by women which takes as its explicit concern or theme the private bodily experiences of women's daily lives (childbirth, menstruation, sexual pleasure, illness, for example) and a reading of poetry by women which attends to the ways in which the female body speaks implicitly. The distinction is between physical, biological experience as a chosen theme and physical, biological experience as the basis of a fundamental poetic language. Turning to the latter definition, there are problems for some readers in accepting both the abstraction and the usefulness of the French feminist thought which proposes such a reading. If one concedes that women voice themselves – their desires, their subjectivities – in and through the body, does one not simply return to the biological essentialism that successive waves of feminism have sought to rebuff? Having said this, although French feminist thought may at first appear confusing, misguided or plain unhelpful, if we suspend our scepticism for just a moment, we might find that it offers a surprisingly productive way of thinking about individual poems and thereby about the field in general.

A key element of Luce Irigaray's argument in the essay 'This Sex Which Is Not One' is that female sexuality is not amenable to a phallogocentric system which thinks in terms of singularity. Female desire 'does not speak the same language as man's desire, and it probably has been covered over by the logic that has dominated the West since the Greeks'.[7] Female sexuality is, she suggests, plural, multiple and fluid: 'The geography of her pleasure is much more diversified, more multiple in its differences [. . .] than is imagined – in an imaginary centred a bit too much on one and the same.'[8] Sexton's 1974 poem 'The Fierceness of Female' offers an example of what Irigaray might mean.

'The Fierceness of Female' is in constant movement, fluidity and flux.[9] The title alone sets up an alliterative sequence and initiates a rocking movement; the stresses on '*Fierce*ness' and '*Fe*male' set the rest of the poem in motion. The first line 'I am spinning' establishes a further movement, this time circular. The use of the present participle form anticipates that used throughout the poem and connotes constant energy or a kind of centrifugal force rooted in the female body. Subsequent metaphors of circularity (clock, breast, melon, bubbles, the 'lunatic ring' of the lips) keep this idea in play. In tandem with these motifs of circular movement, which signify a rejection of the masculine, phallogocentric, singular order, we find metaphors of plurality or twoness. At the level of structure, the poem comprises two long stanzas. More specifically, line two refers to 'lips' (female labia? the voice of the woman poet?) which generate the centrifugal energy. Later in this stanza, more explicitly still, we find that 'all is two, / touching like a choir of butterflies'. In place of lack (where 'all was absent') we now find a female presence or, more properly, multiple female presences – hence 'choir' of butterflies. This whole sequence takes place in a context which is both plural (that is, the ebb and flow of the tides signified by the ocean which is 'pushing toward land / and receding') and ceaselessly circular. Hence we have a sustained representation of Irigaray's model of female subjectivity: 'Within herself she is already two – but not divisible into ones.'[10]

The poem evokes a moment of pure jouissance (a term used by Cixous, Julia Kristeva and others to describe sheer unrepressed pleasure).[11] As stanza two opens, we see that the symbolic order of language is subsumed within the semiotic: 'I unknit. / Words fly out of place.' For Irigaray, 'Woman finds pleasure more in touch than in sight [. . .] she has sex organs just about everywhere.'[12] In section two of the poem it is these multiple senses (the 'hands that stroke each other', the 'nipples', 'lips' and 'fingers') which dominate. The poem celebrates female sexuality and female subjectivity, but as much as this is a poem about female embodiment and desire, it is also a poem about female writing – hence images of lips and tongues. The 'words' that 'fly out of place' may, indeed, be 'out of place' in terms of conventional signifying systems (or the symbolic order of language), but they establish their own place here, telling 'the truth', in the penultimate line, of the female body.

DESIRE: CHRISTINA ROSSETTI

One of the aims of 'l'écriture féminine' is the full articulation of female sexuality. As Hélène Cixous asks, 'What is feminine *sexual pleasure*, where does it take place, how is it inscribed at the level of her body, her unconscious? And then how is it put into writing?'[13] In addressing these questions, and in further assessing the value of this approach to poetry by women, it is fruitful to consider Christina Rossetti's 1859 poem *Goblin Market*. Christina Rossetti was born in 1830 into an Anglo-Italian family and was a near-contemporary of the Brontës, Dickinson and Barrett Browning. She was educated intermittently at home. Her brother, Dante Gabriel Rossetti, along with William Morris and others, was one of the 'Pre-Raphaelite Brotherhood', an informal coterie which rejected what they perceived as the lifeless conventionality of most contemporary art and looked back to a 'golden age' before the time of the Renaissance painter Raphael. Christina Rossetti worked briefly as a governess, and in the 1850s and 1860s she assisted at a home for 'fallen women' (the fallen woman, or prostitute, was a figure of much concern and agitation to Victorian culture, often seen at one and the same time as a symptom of moral degeneracy and a threat to the sanctity of married life).[14] She was fleetingly engaged to be married to a Roman Catholic but called off the engagement, apparently because of religious differences. A case might be made that Rossetti was dominated, patronised or oppressed by some of the men in her life; like others of her generation, she chafed against the absence of opportunities for women of her age, class and abilities.

It is against this backdrop of desire, potential and ambition tempered by repression, convention and containment that *Goblin Market* should be read. This long poem seems, at first, like a bizarre and unconventional folk or fairy story. As Rossetti's brother William reports: 'I have more than once heard Christina say that she did not mean anything profound by this fairy tale.' However, as he goes on to say, there is significantly more to the poem than meets the eye: 'The incidents are such as to be at any rate suggestive, and different minds may be likely to read different messages into them.'[15] Is *Goblin Market* simply a whimsical tale? Is it a story about literal or metaphorical 'sisterhood'? (As we have seen in the case of Lowell's 'The Sisters' and Olds's 'The Sisters of Sexual Treasure', the figure of the sister stands both for a literal familial relationship and a wider gender bond, and has been embraced in this latter form as a key motif of the second wave feminist movement.) Is this a story about self-sacrifice in the sexual or emotional sense, or in the physical or spiritual sense? What does it tell us about young women's relationship to power and authority in this or any other period? Is it possible to read the poem as the articulation of a split or divided subjectivity?

Goblin Market, as has been suggested, is a more complex and nuanced poem than the apparently straightforward narrative and the ballad-like format seem to suggest. A close look at just the first part of the poem shows how effective the poetics of the text (rhyme, rhythm, metaphor, imagery and alliteration) are in suggesting some of its multiple meanings. The opening words 'Morning and evening / Maids heard the goblins cry' indicate from the outset both how timeless this scene is (it is ceaseless, having no regard for the clock) and, paradoxically, to suggest that time is passing, that evening follows the morning, heralding the end of the day. By line seventeen, the cyclical nature of time is reaffirmed: 'Morns that pass by, / Fair eves that fly'. Again, the effect is to reassert the paradoxical timelessness and transience of existence. There is a further subtext though, for if the 'fair eves fly', the suggestion is that 'Eves' (note the difference the addition of a capital letter makes) or, metonymically, innocence, virginity and maidenhood, are transient things: there one minute and gone the next.

The intrusion of the 'goblins' at the end of line two startles the reader as much, presumably, as it did the 'Maids'. It takes us from the world of the everyday (the diurnal course which the opening phrase has established) instantly into the realm of the fantastic and imaginary. The confident ease with which the poem does this causes an elision of the difference between the real and the imagined, the empirical and the fantastic. The goblins' 'cry' too works in multiple, and at this point undetermined, ways. This is the cry of the costermonger, selling his wares, or a cry of pain – pain perhaps wrought by denial or suffering – and it is the cry of desire, even sexual desire. It is a cry, crucially, which although here associated with the goblin is later, in all of the connotations suggested above, identified with or displaced onto the 'maids'. Those who now hear the cry are later the ones who utter it. Thus again, barriers are distended or collapsed; the poem takes the reader into a strange liminal space where the certainties one lives by, for example about gender and identity, can no longer be relied on.

The goblins' cry, 'Come buy our orchard fruits, / Come buy, come buy', with its insistent repetitions conveys the intrusive pressures of the market and, by association, of desire. The 'orchard fruits' of line three, confirmed as 'apples' in line five, symbolise the fruit of 'the tree of knowledge of good and evil' (Genesis 2: 9). Here again, as elsewhere in the poem, archetypally sinful women such as Eve and Pandora drawn from ancient mythology, the Bible and other sources are indicted. In lines eighty-one and eighty-two, which introduce Laura's downfall, she is likened to a swan. The simile paradoxically brings to mind the story of Leda and the swan from classical mythology. In that legend, Leda was seduced or raped by Zeus, who had assumed the form of a swan. The image stands here as a representation of a forbidden sexual encounter; its reversal such that Laura becomes the swan, rather than the swan's victim, implies some culpability on her part, some sexual avariciousness (hence the closing line of the section quoted below):

> Laura stretched her gleaming neck
> Like a rush-imbedded swan,
> Like a lily from the beck,
> Like a moonlit poplar branch,

Like a vessel at the launch
When its last restraint is gone.

The comparison is ominous. A further palimpsest in the poem is the story of Orpheus and Eurydice, with Laura in the role of Eurydice, cast down into a dangerous underworld, and Lizzie acting as Orpheus, compelled to go down and reach her. Unlike Orpheus, as the poem shows, Lizzie is able to resist the temptation to look back which, if succumbed to, would cast Laura permanently into Hades.

Returning to line three, the postponement in identification of precisely what fruits these are is supremely effective in placing us as readers in the same position as the 'Maids' and, by implication, as Eve in the book of Genesis. The reader, too, desires to know their true identity. We want our thirst for knowledge to be satisfied; we want our experience to be enriched. Given a glimmer of insight, we seek more. The poem thus solicits a reading process which re-enacts the very procedure it is describing. We are made to thirst for knowledge about Laura and Lizzie's thirst for knowledge. In Peter Brooks's terms, we encounter a 'dynamics of desire animating narrative and the construal of its meanings'.[16]

It is increasingly clear as the poem proceeds that sexuality is at stake. From morning, connoting daylight, freshness and a secure and social world, to evening, connoting darkness, danger and the private, we sense a growing sexual thread in the narrative. The description of the fruits to which the maids are privy becomes confused in the long opening cry uttered by the goblins to the extent that the characteristics of the fruit are displaced onto the maids. Figuratively, it is the two young women, and not just the literal fruits, who are 'unpecked' ('plump unpecked cherries'), who are 'bloom-down-cheeked' and 'swart-headed'. The images, while redolent of the bounty of luscious fruits, work also to suggest the fecundity and sexual ripeness of the young women. Yet beneath the tantalising, luscious surface we find fruits which are potentially dangerous – bitter, sour or prickly fruits such as the 'crab-apples', the 'sharp bullaces', 'Damsons' and 'fire-like-barberries'. In all of these ways, *Goblin Market* establishes a rhetoric of difference, from plenitude to lack and from innocence to experience, which is also, crucially, about the co-existence and finally the inseparability of the two terms.

Goblin Market warns about the peril embedded in temptation, about the risk of succumbing to the Goblins' repeated cry. Thinking in economic and material terms, the goblins entice the sisters (and readers) with the abundance of the market. They show the sisters, and us, far more than we could possibly eat. We are numbed by the profusion of goods and thus rendered immune to the danger lurking beneath the opulent surface. The numbing effect is produced, in part, by the use of repeated line endings 'cherries', 'raspberries', 'cranberries', 'dewberries', 'blackberries' and so on. So, too, the synaesthesia running throughout the poem (the confusion of senses such that the sisters' experience is conveyed through touch, taste, sound and sight) works to confound our senses, leaving us helpless amidst a cornucopia of pleasures. We are spoiled for choice, made greedy and avaricious and thus powerless and vulnerable to temptation. Thus the text offers a commentary on contemporary capitalism and on the seemingly unstoppable market forces which in post-Industrial Revolution Victorian Britain shaped every dimension of people's lived experiences, including, in this poem, their sexuality. These market forces, as the poem shows, entice (or, in Marxist terms, interpellate) people, stimulating desire and promulgating excess. It is significant that it is ostensibly wild and natural fruits which the goblins are selling, not manufactured goods such as sweets or pastries. The implication is that every area of life, even the free-growing fruits of the earth, is vulnerable to capitalist exploitation.

The first section of the poem (to the end of line thirty-one) represents a positive inducement, or temptation, to taste and buy. The second section, beginning 'Evening by evening', represents negative constraint. Punctuated by images of shame ('Laura bowed her head' / 'Lizzie veiled her blushes'), the poem warns us about the dangers of looking, tasting and buying. In repeated negations ('we must not look at goblin men, / We must not buy their fruits') the young women unwittingly indicate how preoccupied they are by what the goblins have to offer, how tempted they are, how much they desire that which they are denying. In Freudian terms, 'The content of a repressed image or idea can make its way into consciousness, on condition that it is negated.'[17] In other words, in identifying all of the things which the girls must and will not do, they reveal the strength of their temptation and desire.

The plenitude and contentment promised by the opening section of the poem is fractured in this second section, not least because it is here for the first time that the 'maids' are named and thereby individuated. From a Lacanian perspective, it is here that they leave the semiotic order (represented by the lush, sensual, natural excesses of the fruits) and enter the symbolic order of language. Just as the women are now identified and defined, so too are the goblins. For the first time we see beyond the fruits they bear to the 'merchant man' beneath. Rat-like, cat-like and snail-like, they seem nevertheless to enchant the young women. The men's power over Laura and Lizzie consists, in part, of their possessing material wealth which the women are denied (in Marxist terms, the goblins' economic capital determines their social power). While the goblin men display a 'golden weight / Of dish and fruit', the women can only long for what they cannot afford: Laura 'stared but did not stir, / Longed but had no money'. Thus the poem comments on the dispossession and enforced passivity of women. Without financial means, Laura's only option is to realise the economic value of her own body. Without coins to give, she can give physical tokens of her female self – a 'golden curl' as the goblins put it, or a 'golden lock' in the narrator's terms. The change of noun is significant, connoting the bondage under which Laura is now placed.

It is relevant at this point to return to the historical context in which this poem was written, a context which, as Isobel Armstrong explains, features social concern about 'illegitimacy, fallen women, the fierce legal bond of marriage, the sexual fate of the woman who waits' and 'the experience of exclusion'.[18] Rossetti's own experience as a visitor to homes for 'fallen women' forms a specific subtext. As Elizabeth Helsinger suggests, *Goblin Market* sets up a set of apparent contraries: private sphere of the home vs. public sphere of the market, domestic work vs. alienated labour, self-sufficiency vs. the market economy. Bridging, or conflating, these oppositions is the figure of the prostitute. She transgresses these boundaries, operating in both spheres. Like Laura, she is an object to be bought and sold and she is an agent of consumption. She, too, does the buying and the selling.[19]

Lizzie is different. She retains a modicum of power. Because she has money (unlike Laura, who in line 116 confesses 'I have no coin') she is able legitimately to pay for goods. Her 'silver penny' (line 324) renders her immune to the goblins' temptations. In a sense, it is Lizzie's economic wealth that gives or buys her moral value. She can afford to withstand temptation in a way that her penniless sister cannot. Thus the poem intervenes in Victorian debates about working-class women's morality. Virtue, *Goblin Market* suggests, does not come cheap. Morality, innocence, and the ability to resist temptation are shown to be symptoms of economic position and not, as mid-century Victorian values would have it, a sign of spiritual worth. To quote Elizabeth Helsinger again, this is 'a transgressive poem that denies (or at least defers) a series of linked distinctions constructed on the fiction of moral woman's difference from economic man'.[20] The poem's moral message is, then, a mixed one. Market forces are thoroughly vilified but nevertheless at least partially redeemed as the possible route out of the kind of trap the sisters find themselves in. However, we should also note that the price Lizzie pays for Laura's release from the goblins' grasp is far more than an economic price. Her sister's freedom is bought at the cost of her own humiliation, her willingness to sacrifice herself, and ultimately her own physical and implicitly sexual torment:

> They trod and hustled her,
> Elbowed and jostled her,
> Clawed with their nails,
> Barking, mewing, hissing, mocking,
> Tore her gown and soiled her stocking,
> Twitched her hair out by the roots,
> Stamped upon her tender feet,
> Held her hands and squeezed their fruits
> Against her mouth to make her eat. (lines 399–407)

The final section of the poem is ambivalent, too, in the message that it conveys about Lizzie and Laura and, by extension, about the position of women in their culture. Laura, who is now assimilated into the conventional world of domesticity, marriage and motherhood, seems merely to have exchanged one set of dangers for another. Life as a wife and mother is 'beset with fears' (line 546) of a different kind. And when she calls her children to her to tell them all about the goblin men and her sister's bravery in saving her from them, one cannot help but see a twinge of nostalgia, a residue of longing, in her recollection of the 'quaint fruit-merchant men, / Their fruits like honey to the throat'. In this way, perhaps, desire lives on. For some readers, the end of *Goblin Market* disappoints. We began the poem being positioned by the very language of the text as avaricious punters. We too wanted to see and know and possess those forbidden fruits which were so tantalisingly offered to us. The closing lines of the poem leave us, perhaps, unsatiated. Our desires have been stimulated, even overstimulated, and the safe, quiet life of the home no longer seems satisfying. Metaphorically, we have eaten of the fruit. Our eyes and senses are now awoken, and our punishment for our earlier greed is to be left feeling forever unfulfilled.

From Rossetti in nineteenth-century England we turn to American poet Amy Lowell's 1921 'Witch-Woman'.[21] This equally incantatory poem of passion and desire seems to confirm the point which Kristeva makes in her essay 'About Chinese Women': 'Woman is a specialist in the unconscious, a witch, a bacchanalian, taking her jouissance in an anti-Apollonian, Dionysian orgy.'[22] 'Witch-Woman' is explicit in its celebration of all forms of sexuality – of physical and emotional relationships between women and between women and men – but nevertheless confusing in some of these representations. Although the poem plays with conventional tropes (the moon signifying female fertility, for example), it does this almost entirely in order to reverse or expose orthodox homologies. Later in the century, Duffy's 'Wintering' and 'Quickdraw' also explore female desire; in the former, the moon – although ostensibly a metaphor for female fertility and sexuality – is depicted as a weapon: 'Night clenches in its fist the moon, a stone.'[23] 'Quickdraw', too, although tongue-in-cheek, portrays the lover's much desired phone calls as a painful, masochistic pleasure. The speaker portrays herself as a quick-draw cowboy (cowgirl?), holstering her telephones like pistols, and paradoxically enduring both the pain of waiting for a telephone call from her lover and the equal pain which the long-awaited call finally delivers. Like 'silver bullets', each word hits home: 'take this . . . and this . . . and this . . . and this . . .'.

Lowell's poem, rather like 'The Captured Goddess' and 'Sisters' discussed earlier, begins by reclaiming and embracing the transgressive figure of the witch. The identity of the speaker or speakers of the poem is unclear. The poem at first seems to report the popular accusations of the crowd (' "Witch! / Witch!" ') but then slips into the rather more intimate and amatory tones of a lover:

'Thighs and breasts I have loved;
Lips virgin to my thought,
Sweeter to me than red figs;'

The poem is explicit in its evocation of lesbian sexuality (the 'red figs' connoting perhaps the open vagina?), but it is also explicit about the taboo against this kind of relationship and the social price it demands. "Is my heart wicked?" the speaker asks, demanding of herself a response to the criticisms implied of her by others. It is explicit, too, about the pain attendant on the breakdown of such a relationship. This pain is experienced physically, viscerally with 'kisses shot through with poison / [. . .] cutting me like red knives'. 'Witch-Woman' looks to the conventions and rituals of the mythic past and to poetic tradition in its attempt to ease this pain. The long opening section of the poem, delivered in reported speech, reads as a form of incantation or prayer with its repetitions, its biblical idiom (' "my sons, and my sons' sons, and their sons after" '), its performative ' "Let me be as iron before this thing" ', and its appeals to the ' "Lord" ': ' "O just and vengeful God" '.

The second section takes an entirely different form. Long prose stanzas narrate a mysterious night-time world where night and day, dark and light, witch and human, man and woman, are entirely interchangeable: 'body touches body' as this section opens, black is entwined with gold, the woman takes on the phallic form. She is dominant, visible and powerful: 'The woman stands like an obelisk, and her blue-black hair has a serpent whisk as the wind lifts it up and scatters it apart. Witch-heart, are you gold or black?' The man is passive, prone, immobile. All action and all desire are performed by the women: 'matron moon' and 'obelisk' come together as one. Again the imagery celebrates female sexuality. The woman is simultaneously associated with red ('Scarlet is the latter dropping from the moon') and with green. Thus she encompasses both; she is pure fire and pure peace, pure danger and pure fertility. The poem portrays sexual desire in increasingly urgent and fervent tones. Each prose stanza grows in length and becomes more incantatory, featuring ever more internal rhymes as though a spell is being cast on subject, object and reader alike. As the poem reaches its climax (I use the word advisedly), it is as though it can no longer do justice to the sublime experience it is attempting to convey. The speaker struggles to find a language to describe the hitherto unseen. The tradition of love poetry attends to the eyes and lips, perhaps to an idealised breast. This poem goes further, seeking the images and metaphors with which to evoke the intimate physical attributes of the object of desire – the female lover: 'The moon?' it asks (in other words, shall I liken the female object of my desire to the moon of poetic convention?). 'No moon', the poem answers itself, but then struggles to find any adequate mode of representation: 'No moon, but a crimson rose afloat in the sky. A rose? No rose, but a black-tongued lily. A lily? No lily, but a purple orchid with dark, writhing bars.'

The final stanza of the poem represents a bitter and disappointed return to the everyday, the real and the phallic, and to the unidentified reported voice or voices of the opening section. It offers obeisance to the 'white sword' to the 'vengeful and cruel Father / God of Hate'. Freud's 'reality principle' has taken hold. Most dispiritingly of all, the speaker recognises that she must hand over the body of the woman/lover to a patriarchal society and sexual order, a gesture which she can make, but not without bitter regret:

> 'Take my drunken sword,
> Some other man may need it.
> She was sweeter than red figs.
> O cursed God!'

CREATIVITY AND FEMININITY

This section turns to the ways in which women poets have exploited the metaphorical connections between physical and literary creativity. Audre Lorde is explicit about the relationships between these processes: 'It is through poetry that we give name to those ideas which are – until the poem – nameless and formless, about to be birthed, but already felt.'[24] Her recent poem 'To the Poet Who Happens to be Black and the Black Poet Who Happens to be a Woman' reinforces these links. It begins with a birth and thus with the bond between mother and daughter, but that bond is put to the test, both by the circumstances of the birth (on a cold Harlem night) and by the mother's own confusion about the gender of the child she has borne. Gender is confirmed, and affirmed, partly by sisterhood (which may be literal or figurative: 'the first time I touched my sister   alive / I was sure' [typography in the original]) and partly – and more importantly – by the writing process. It is this which makes the poet. Synecdoches and metonyms of writing ('fingers', 'song', 'language') figure throughout the poem, and the final stanza insists that creativity is a specifically female act – one which unites self, language, birth and blood.[25]

How might we read the work of male poets who have appropriated images of pregnancy such as these to evoke their own nascent creativity, thus annexing a space which we might otherwise see as belonging uniquely to women? Moira P. Baker notes male Renaissance poets' (specifically Sir Philip Sidney's) use of 'a range of rhetorical stratagems for (dis)embodying female power and thus attempting to master it, textually, at least, if not sexually'. In Sonnet 1 of *Astrophel and Stella*, as Baker goes on to explain, Sidney appropriates the image of pregnancy and labour to describe his own creative processes:

> Thus, great with child to speak, and helpless in my throes,
> Biting my truand pen, beating myself for spite,
> 'Fool,' said my Muse to me, 'look in thy heart and write.'[26]

For Baker, 'The conflation of the womb image and male speaker suggests his attempt to control the generative powers of the feminine.'[27] Elizabeth Gregory reads some recent American poetry by men in a similar way, arguing that John Berryman's use of metaphors of childbirth, for example in his 1953 poem 'Homage to Mistress Bradstreet', signifies his 'engagement with the authority questions at stake for male poets'. Berryman, Gregory says, is negotiating a position – in some respects an abject one – in relation both to the austere, impersonal and largely masculine modernist aesthetic which still dominated American poetry and to the emergent personal and direct (and thereby nominally 'feminine') confessional mode which succeeded it. Berryman, perhaps like Sidney, 'claims access to poetic power via the analogy of literal (pro)creativity with that of literary creativity that the birth scene provides'. In neither case, though, is it enough to use this female model; both poets are at pains to assert their mastery over it. In Berryman's 'Homage to Mistress Bradstreet', his speaker alludes to Bradstreet's 'bald / abstract didactic rime'.[28] In so doing, as Gregory points out, he 'affirms his continued masculinity through contrast of his "better" poetry with hers, signalling his continued anxiety about identification with Bradstreet's gender and distinguishing himself from it at the same time that he puts it to use'.[29]

Turning to Bradstreet herself, her c. 1666 poem 'The Author to her Book' is fascinating for the way in which it simultaneously exploits and problematises any straightforward association between female author and poetic text. Although a poem which ostensibly uses metaphors of parturition and child-rearing to signify literary production, the relationship between the 'mother' of the text (in other words, the speaker) and her literary and literal offspring is far more complex than might at first be thought.

The poem is believed to have been written for the second edition of Bradstreet's *The Tenth Muse, Lately Sprung Up in America*; the first edition having been published some years earlier without Bradstreet's knowledge and to her subsequent displeasure. In more ways than one, 'The Author to her Book' reads as an assertion of personal and female authority. First, the poem asserts the poet's right to bring her own poems to bear as she chooses, in her own time, and under her own stamp or seal. Second, and more interestingly, it affirms the female speaker's right to use, interpret and refigure metaphors of childbirth, motherhood and creativity in her own way. This way, as it transpires, may suggest some quite different meanings to those suggested by the surface employment of such images. 'The Author to her Book' fascinates because of its refusal to deliver what it seems to promise or, more properly, because although it seems to rely on archetypal connections between biological and literary creativity, it in fact questions those associations. The effect of this is that it is the female poet, with the emphasis on 'poet' not on the gender, who shapes and controls the text. It is Bradstreet's artful rebuttal of the mother/poet connection which finally demonstrates her aesthetic skill and disproves the poem's own initial assertion of its 'feebleness'. The admission of 'feebleness' concedes while it disavows the brother-in-law's presumptuousness in proceeding with the publication of Bradstreet's poems without her knowledge or permission. More broadly, it acknowledges and confounds a set of cultural assumptions which would see women's primary and essential function as maternal and which views the writing woman as an aberration.

The poem, then, works in two quite contradictory ways. That it succeeds finally because of this dialectic is apparent from the outset. The title alone asserts the speaker's gender and her authority, in the sense of both her authorship of this piece and her rights of possession over her own poetry. Thereafter, the opening line seems simultaneously to conform to gendered expectations of women's productivity and to refute them. It conforms in that it concedes that, if produced by a woman, it will be 'ill-formed'. Moreover, it implies that both the woman speaker and by a process of displacement the poem, or 'offspring', are to be regarded as 'feeble'. Yet it refutes these readings in that by addressing her progeny as 'ill-formed' and subsequently as 'rambling' (line eight), 'unfit for light' (line nine) and 'irksome' (line ten), the speaker acts utterly in contradiction to, and thus undermines, the orthodox expectations of the mother's role which the poem ostensibly establishes at the outset. Here, instead of being the child/poem's staunchest defender, she is its harshest critic. The artful rhyming couplets demonstrate that instead of instinctively demonstrating her love, the speaker is instinctively repelled: 'I cast thee by as one unfit for light, / Thy visage was so irksome in my sight.'

Thus Bradstreet rewrites the convention whereby the poem is the helpless offspring of the female bearer. The association is neither passively nor simplistically used. The relationship between female author and poem both is and is not like the relationship between mother and child. It only *is* like it to the extent that, like biological motherhood, it is complex, critical and requires endless diligence and care. Again and again, the speaker is at pains to point out the hard work it has taken to render the child/poem presentable. It is not the moment of birth which is significant as a metaphor in such a context; it is the labour which ensues (the endless round of washing, dressing and healing which is the mother's lot). The drudgery and ceaselessness of this role is particularly, perhaps uniquely, effective in the work of women writers as a figure for their own creative practices. The poem, like the infant, requires endless nurturance and effort:

> I washed thy face, but more defects I saw,
> And rubbing off a spot, still made a flaw.
> I stretched thy joints to make thee even feet,
> Yet still thou run'st more hobbling than is meet.

The allusions to 'feet', running and 'hobbling' refer both to the mother's role in guiding her child as it learns to walk and, more pertinently, to the 'feet', metre and flow of the poetic line (the word 'hobble' used to denote a faltering line of verse was in use from 1522).

A further significant metaphor in the poem is that of costume or dress. The infant/poem appears first dressed in 'rags'. In order to make it presentable to an audience of readers, the speaker recognises the need to send it out in 'better dress'. But, in a domestic metaphor which implicitly speaks volumes about the woman's restricted access to education and to the public world of a cultural elite, the 'author' concedes that 'nought save home-spun cloth, i'th'house I find' (line eighteen).

The conclusion to the poem is as contradictory or duplicitous as the opening. In a return to the rejection or disowning of the progeny of the opening lines, the speaker again seems to disavow her creation, sending it off into the cruel world (line nineteen) albeit with a blessing of sorts: 'in critics' hands, beware thou dost not come'. This time, her motives are less instinctive and more culturally and materially determined. It is a kind of modesty which persuades the speaker apparently to rescind her responsibility for her poem/child. More importantly, though, it is the absence of other options. Speaking of herself in the third person, the 'author' explains: 'And for thy mother, she alas is poor, / which caused her thus to send thee out of door.' Yet the speaker reserves two important powers. She reserves the power to name the child bastard. This is the power to deny paternal authority and thereby in an arguably perverse way to assume her own: 'If for thy father asked, say thou hadst none' (line twenty-two). One might almost read this as a specific riposte to Bradstreet's brother-in-law, the one-time usurper of the role of father to the text. She also retains power and authority over her own work. The offspring which she has apparently rejected, reluctantly taken back, attempted to improve, and is now apologising for, is finally an artfully constructed, ingenious and wholly effective exemplification of her female art. The shift to the present tense in line eighteen of the poem makes this particular labour immediate; the apostrophe from 'the Author to her Book' is also much more than this. It takes and revises the conventional association of female poetry and childbirth, and it complicates both poetic and biological creative processes. It speaks not just to 'the Book' but to its readership and to a larger (critical) culture. Its apparent modesty is patently unrequired, but all the more effective because it both performs the self-effacement demanded of 'the Author to her Book' and disproves its necessity.

Metaphors of procreation and maternity figure at the outset in the later poet Barrett Browning's *Aurora Leigh* (1857). However, it is their very failure or absence which is the focus of attention. In the opening lines, the speaker compares creative endeavour, born of an acute sensitivity, to the experience of innocent babies. The poem laments the loss of the speaker's own mother who died, we are told, when the speaker was but four years old: 'As it was, indeed, / I felt a mother-want about the world.' More specifically, later, the poem uses images of lactation – 'udders warm and full / of mystic contemplations, come to feed / poor milkless lips of orphans' (lines 114–16) and of suckling babes (line 161) – in order to foreground the maternal and creative function. The poem traces the development of a mature female sexuality, but one born in conflict, constantly tested, and repeatedly under attack (lines 1033–59). Kaplan glosses it thus: 'Approved and taboo subjects are slyly intertwined so that menstruation, childbirth, suckling, child-rearing, rape and prostitution, are all braided together in the metaphorical language.'[30]

Throughout, female sexuality is inextricably tied up with images of writing (line 1265), of books and reading (line 1005), and of the power which accrues to those who control the language.

Modern poet Ruth Fainlight's poems 'Another Full Moon' and 'Anticipated' yoke the female body with a latent or emergent creativity. 'Anticipated' sees the subject (the emphatically rendered 'I') attempting to weigh up the moon, and its creative potential. There is an assumed contiguity between female self and moon, and the speaker attempts to read the moon for signs of her own latent powers: 'perhaps I, too, have reached an acme', as stanza two puts it.[31] 'Another Full Moon' uses a single, free-verse form with emphatic caesura juxtaposed with successive waves of enjambment to convey, first, the speaker's disappointment (presumably, at not being pregnant; the onset of another new moon signalling the onset of menstruation) and thereafter her necessary reconciliation with the inevitability of her situation. The speaker explains that she would 'much prefer not to be absolutely / in thrall to the rhythm of ocean'. She is subject to the demands of the calendar (specifically her own monthly cycles), and the tone of the poem – laconic, diary-like, contemplative – mirrors this situation.[32]

The modernist poet Mina Loy's 'Parturition' (1914) visits similar ground, but in so doing so radically exposes the female poetry/childbirth analogy as to completely undermine it.[33] Like Sexton's 'The Fierceness of Female', Loy's poem opens with the female speaker at the heart of the creative process: 'I am the centre', she declares. Yet this is emphatically not a positive and purposive place. To quote the first three lines in full:

> I am the centre
> Of a circle of pain
> Exceeding its boundaries in every direction.

The poem proceeds in fragmented lines with numerous pauses and aporia. There are multiple gaps on the page, successive waves of long and short lines, fragments of overheard and barely comprehensible language, unanswered questions, shifting perspectives and parenthetical dashes. Thus the poem conveys a compelling vision of the confusion and trauma of labour and childbirth and of the creative act of writing poetry. This is at one and the same time brutal ('I am climbing a distorted mountain of agony'), animalistic ('impression of small animal carcass / covered with blue-bottles') and wholly corrupted by being assimilated into a culture which wishes to sanitise, sentimentalise and thereby defuse its power:

> Each woman-of-the-people
> Tip-toeing the red pile of the carpet
> Doing hushed service
> Each woman-of-the-people
> Wearing a halo
> A ludicrous little halo
> Of which she is sublimely   unaware.
> [Typography in the original]

The shift is akin to what Susan Bordo describes as 'the docile, regulated body practiced at and habituated to the rules of cultural life'.[34] This poem, like others, for example the collage-like 'Love Songs to Joannes', 'highlights[s] the objectification and denial of women and the body that the myth of romance requires'. According to Alex Goody, in Loy's work, 'Loss of autonomy is inextricably linked to loss of language.'[35] In the placid conventionality of the last lines of 'Parturition' when, post-parturition, the woman is returned to the everyday symbolic order and loses touch with the ineluctably more powerful language of the (female) order, such a loss is made explicit.

CONCLUSION

There are a number of important objections to reading poetry by women in terms of its conscious or unconscious evocation of biological experience. Key among these is the objection that to speak of women's poetry in this way is to bow to a kind of essentialism. To suggest that women speak or write their own bodies, this argument goes, is to suggest that women's identity both as individuals and as a group is essentially, naturally, inevitably and timelessly tied to their physical existence. It assumes a homogeneity in difference (women's difference from men) which effaces or denies other differences, for example, of race, ethnicity, class, sexual orientation, disability and so on. Another important objection is that to think solely or primarily in terms of the body is to obliterate crucial material, economic and political factors. However, this objection is, in part, a misunderstanding of the breadth and nuances of French feminist thought. As Luce Irigaray insists, 'In order for woman to arrive at the point where she can enjoy her pleasure as a woman, a long detour by the analysis of the various systems of oppression which affect her is certainly necessary.'[36]

A poem such as Olds's 'May 1968' indicates just how indivisible the apparently divergent discourses of the body and of politics actually are. Here, the female body in crisis is a metonym for larger political crisis. Implicitly Olds feminises an entirely contradictory tradition which has at one and the same time associated politics with masculinity (in this poem, she emphatically makes it a female space), and she reads the geography of the nation as feminine. 'May 1968' first feminises political experience and then appropriates the authority to speak from and for the position of nation-as-female. The poem opens with resistance to authority (the speaker very deliberately does what she is told not to do), which has the effect of heralding further waves of authority. These are represented by New York City skyscrapers, denotative of the power of commerce but here emasculated or castrated by seeming to be cut off at sky level, and mounted police almost magically kept at bay by the power of singing and counting. The whole edifice is centred by the woman speaker, literally grounded, lying on the earth and sheltering the foetus which may or may not be growing in her. She is like the Omphalos of Greek legend, and it is the nascent power of her body, her femaleness, her potential fertility which commands, controls and finally calms everything around her. Her songs and numbers weave a spell around those near her until everything 'dropping, dipping' (itself akin to the castrating images of the opening lines and the pointed reference to the 'gelding' in line nineteen) gives way to her command. All are hypnotised by her presence, encircling the central dyad of mother and unborn child.

From the point of view of French feminism, the poem is interesting in its use of images of twoness (mother and daughter, head and tail, human and horse, earth and sky) and of circles or cyclical periods: the round 'o' of the mouth, the menstrual cycle ('one month'), the 'curve' of the horse's belly, and the closing 'circle around my body and my daughter'. These subtly, but nevertheless emphatically, register the female identity of the speaker and the biological rootedness of her experience. The poem precisely exemplifies the aims of 'l'écriture féminine' as illustrated by Hélène Cixous's assertion, 'Woman must write herself: must write about women and bring women to writing [. . .] woman must put herself into the text.'[37] More than this, though, it demonstrates the historical and political rootedness of female subjectivity. To draw on Elaine Marks and Isabelle de Courtivron, we might say that the poem works by 'decentr[ing] the reigning phallus [represented in Olds's poem by the Dean, the skyscrapers, the cops, everyone who towers over the mother and unborn daughter] from its dominant position in the symbolic order.'[38] This is a woman writing her body, but writing that body in cognisance of the specificities of space and time.

SUMMARY OF KEY POINTS

- The relationship between female bodily experience and poetic creativity has a long, complex and contested history.
- What difference does it make when women poets assume the role of active, speaking subjects rather than passive, silent objects?
- Recent French feminist theory (the work of Kristeva, Cixous and Irigaray, amongst others) is helpful in exploring the possibilities of a distinctive female language (or l'écriture féminine').
- Another way of thinking about this issue is to explore women poets' own readings and representations of the relationship between women's poetic and biological creativity.
- Women's poetry has arguably been used both to express and to disguise forms of desire.

NOTES

1. Diana Fuss, *Essentially Speaking: Feminism, Nature and Difference* (London: Routledge, 1990), p. 5.

2. Hélène Cixous, 'Sorties', in *New French Feminisms: An Anthology*, ed. Elaine Marks and Isabelle de Courtivron (London: Prentice-Hall, 1981), pp. 90–8 (pp. 90–1).

3. Baker, '"The Uncanny Stranger on Display"', 14.

4. Olds, *Strike Sparks*, p. 3.

5. Ibid. p. 4.

6. Carol Ann Duffy, *Rapture* (Basingstoke: Picador, 2005), p. 45.

7. Luce Irigaray, 'This Sex Which Is Not One', in Marks and de Courtivron, *New French Feminisms*, pp. 99–106 (p. 101).

8. Irigaray, 'This Sex', p. 103.

9. Sexton, *Complete*, p. 546.

10. Irigaray, 'This Sex', p. 100.

11. See Cixous, 'Sorties', and Julia Kristeva, 'Women's Time', in Belsey and Moore, *The Feminist Reader*, pp. 197–217.

12. Irigaray, 'This Sex', pp. 101, 103.

13. Cixous, 'Sorties', p. 95.

14. For an account of campaigns to assist fallen women, see Duncan Crow, *The Victorian Woman* (London: Allen & Unwin, 1971) and Jane Jordan, *Josephine Butler* (London: John Murray, 2001). For more on the economic context see Angela Leighton, *Victorian Women Poets: Writing Against the Heart* (Hemel Hempstead: Harvester, 1992).

15. Quoted in Kathleen Jones, *Learning Not to be First: The Life of Christina Rossetti* (Cassell: London, 1990), p. 91.

16. Peter Brooks, *Bodywork: Objects of Desire in Modern Narrative* (Cambridge, MA and London: Harvard University Press, 1993), p. xi.

17. Sigmund Freud, 'On Negation', in *The Freud Reader*, ed. Peter Gay (London: Vintage, 1995), pp. 666–9 (p. 667).

18. Armstrong, *Victorian Poetry*, p. 346.

19. Elizabeth Helsinger, 'Consumer Power and the Utopia of Desire: Christina Rossetti's "Goblin Market"', in *Victorian Women Poets: Contemporary Critical Essays*, ed. Joseph Bristow (Basingstoke: Macmillan, 1995), pp. 189–222 (pp. 189–90). See also Isobel Armstrong, '"A Music of Thine Own": Women's Poetry' in Bristow, ed., pp. 32-63.

20. Ibid. p. 190.

21. 'Witch-Woman', in Bernikow, *The World*, pp. 228–32. The poem was first published in Amy Lowell, *Legends* (Boston: Houghton Mifflin, 1921).

22. Julia Kristeva, 'About Chinese Women', in *The Kristeva Reader*, ed. Toril Moi (Oxford: Blackwell, 1986), pp. 138–59 (p. 154).

23. Duffy, *Rapture*, pp. 36, 30.

24. Audre Lorde, 'Poetry is not a Luxury', in Herbert and Hollis, *Strong Words*, p. 137.

25. Audre Lorde, 'To the Poet Who Happens to be Black and the Black Poet Who Happens to be a Woman', *Callaloo*, 24: 3 (2001), 813–14.

26. Sir Philip Sidney, *Astrophel and Stella*, in *Silver Poets of the Sixteenth Century*, ed. Gerald Bullett (London: Dent, 1982), p. 173.

27. Baker, ' "The Uncanny Stranger on Display" ', 7, 8.

28. John Berryman, *Collected Poems: 1937–1971* (London: Faber and Faber, 1989), pp. 133–48.

29. Gregory, 'Confessing the Body', p. 43.

30. Kaplan, 'Introduction', *Aurora Leigh*, p. 15.

31. Fainlight, 'Anticipated', in Couzyn, *Contemporary Women Poets*, p. 136.

32. Fainlight, 'Another Full Moon', in Scott, *Bread and Roses*, p. 155.

33. Mina Loy, *The Lost Lunar Baedeker: Poems of Mina Loy*, ed. Roger L. Conover (New York: Noonday Press, 1997), p. 7.

34. Susan Bordo, 'The Body and the Reproduction of Femininity: A Feminist Appropriation of Foucault' in *Gender/Body/Knowledge: Feminist Reconstructions of Being and Knowing* (New Brunswick, NJ: Rutgers University Press, 1992), pp. 13–33 (p. 13).

35. Alex Goody, 'Gender, Authority and the Speaking Subject, or: Who is Mina Loy?', *How2*, 1: 5 (2001) 8, 12. Accessed 19 September 2001 at: http://www.scc.rutgers.edu/however/vi_5_2001/current/in-conference/mina-loy/goody.html.

36. Irigaray, 'This Sex', p. 105.

37. Cixous, 'The Laugh of the Medusa', in Marks and de Courtivron, *New French Feminisms*, pp. 245–64 (p. 245).

38. Marks and de Courtivron, 'Introduction', p. 36.

CHAPTER 5

Public Speech

As we have already seen, one persistent perception of poetry by women has been that it belongs in and focuses on the private sphere, on intimate, personal and domestic experience (of Plath, for example, one critic applauds the masculine qualities of her writing, saying 'something muscular shows up in her work, as unusual in women poets as visceral self-pity seems common').[1] The public sphere of politics and history, so this perception goes, belongs to men. Ann Rosalind Jones cites fifteenth-century restrictions on women's education in the culturally valued skills of rhetoric 'because it belongs to the public realm, the sphere of law, politics, and diplomacy, which was firmly defined as off-limits to women'.[2]

There are a number of immediate responses to make to this charge. The first is that designations as to who belongs in or out of the public sphere of politics depend very much on how one defines 'private', 'public' and 'politics'. It depends where, if at all, one draws the boundaries. I say 'if at all' because, as this book has already argued, one of the hallmarks of poetry by women and of the new range of theories which have arisen to explicate it is a refusal, or at the very least a rethinking, of the kinds of binaries which would see public and private, political and personal as opposite poles. So although it seems feasible to argue, as Bertram does, that 'many women poets encounter difficulties in relation to asserting an authoritative public voice', such a proposition raises a number of problems. First, it immediately provokes the reader into suggesting exceptions to this general rule, from the contemporary black British writer Grace Nichols (who Bertram herself cites as a poet whose 'espousal of such a persona seems effortless') back to Browning and forward again to current American, Native American and Chicana writers Adrienne Rich, Joy Harjo and Lorna Dee Cervantes. Second, and perhaps more importantly, it requires one to rethink one's ideas of what an 'authoritative public voice' might sound like. Rachel Blau DuPlessis's comments about T. S. Eliot's poetry and his practice of 'absorb[ing] social issues into his poetry inside the poetic texture itself' stand, I would argue, for the procedure of many of the poets discussed in this chapter.[3]

AUTHORITY

Early modern English poet Isabella Whitney strives to make an authoritative claim to an agency recently denied to women by the imposition of a 1544 Act of Parliament. This Act 'reaffirmed the long-standing legal prohibition upon the writing of wills by certain groups or classes of people: those groups included persons under the age of twenty-one, idiots, madmen – and wives'.[4] Whitney's 'Will and Testament' (1573) invokes and mocks this prohibition. The poem begins with a faux lament for the speaker's relative poverty ('I whole in body and in mind, / But very weak in purse') and with a provocative apostrophe to London, the city which seems to give so little but to which the speaker, it transpires, figuratively owes so much. The 'Will and Testament' opens out into an affectionate celebration of London life, displaying a deep intimacy born of experience travelling the streets, galleries, markets and merchants' stores. Underpinning the fantastic benevolence of the speaker's plans (the legacy of the whole of London that she plans to leave in her will) is the rather more sobering sense of the prohibitions against her leaving anything. Look, the poem is saying, at the bounty I could bestow and at the generosity with which I might act if only it were not for the restrictions which prevent me, as a woman, giving or owning anything. As the poem concludes, the tone becomes more solemn, austere and melancholy. It moves away from the rich fantasies it has enjoyed creating and reflects instead on the 'nothing[ness]', the 'shame' and the 'oblivion' which characterise the speaker's real experience. London now stands for the dominant forces which refuse her participation in economic life and thus full, free subjectivity.

Phillis Wheatley's 'To the Right Honourable William, Earl of Dartmouth, His Majesty's Principal Secretary of State for North America' (c. 1773) weaves the personal and the political, the humble and the brave to create a poem of significant authority. Wheatley was born in Africa in the mid-eighteenth century. She was enslaved, shipped to America and sold to John Wheatley of Boston. Wheatley's wife Susannah and daughter Mary decided to educate Wheatley, and she soon showed great promise as a poet. In her early work she assimilates the racial ideologies of the period, but with a growing awareness of her own situation and that of other black slaves, she began subtly to voice anti-slavery sentiments.[5] As a number of commentators have shown, however, Wheatley's freedom to speak was severely circumscribed by the conditions in which her work was received and promoted:

> Not only did Wheatley's dependence on white patrons who countenanced slavery make it impossible for her to write unambiguously about her experience of oppression, but the transatlantic promotion of her poetry deliberately directed readers away from the interpretative frame supplied by her servitude.[6]

'To the Right Honourable' opens with a positive inducement to share in the speaker's well-being: 'Hail, happy day, when, smiling like the morn, / Fair *Freedom* rose New-England to adorn.' Few, it seems, can refuse to approve the 'freedom', geniality and contentment which the poem seems to promise. Yet the text does not shirk from reminding its readers of a different set of conditions – of 'wrongs', 'grievance', the 'iron chain' of '*Tyranny*'. This connotes both the condition of America as the once-colonised subject of English rule and, more specifically, the speaker's own personal situation, revealed in stanza three, as an enslaved African. The poem asserts its authoritative and public voice, finally, by its appeal to God to validate its message.[7]

As this suggests, it is important to give a historical and cultural perspective to these terms. The parameters of 'public' (and conversely of 'private' as we saw in Chapter 3) shift and change from culture to culture, historical period to historical period. What this means is that in order to understand, say, Elizabeth I's (Elizabeth Tudor's) poems, one needs to be alert to the complex, and to a present day culture quite alien, significations of the sixteenth-century discourses in which they work. Elizabeth I's poems 'On Monsieur's Departure', 'Written with a diamond on her window at Woodstock' and 'The Doubt of Future Foes' reveal a speaking subject raging against powerlessness, constraint and imprisonment. Even an ostensible love lyric such as 'On Monsieur's Departure' is characterized by oppression. The opening stanza is crowded with negatives; it enacts a kind of self-surveillance. The positive qualities which the speaker burns to share ('I love', 'I do', 'I see', as the beginning of each of the first few lines asserts) are instantly annulled: 'I love and yet', 'I do, and dare not', 'I am and am not'. The speaker has learned to police her own emotions: 'I grieve and dare not show my discontent, / I love and yet am forced to seem to hate.'

In stanza two the speaker struggles under the burden of constant observation. On one level she rues the anxiety or 'care' attendant on the loss or absence of her lover. On another level, she speaks of the pressure of living within a society which requires constant self-monitoring and self-scrutiny. By stanza three, though, the poem has moved into a different realm. The language is no longer self-negating, clipped and terse. Instead, in lines slowed down by assonance, by the assonantal internal and end rhymes ('mind' // 'kind', 'snow' // 'float', 'low') and by a whispering sibilance ('some', 'soft', 'snow', 'sink', 'sweet'), the speaker seems to abandon the fight and to lay bare the emotions she has hitherto felt under pressure to conceal.

In other poems, too, the structure and form of the text serve to exemplify the political restrictions under which it was produced. In the case of 'Written with a diamond on her window at Woodstock', the minimal space taken up by the three-line poem mimics the enclosed space of the prisoner's confinement (as Robyn Bolam explains, Elizabeth I was held under house arrest by her half-sister Mary Tudor):

> Much suspected by me,
> Nothing proved can be,
> Quoth Elizabeth prisoner.[8]

'The Doubt of Future Foes' is emphatic in its denunciation of the speaker's perceived enemies.[9] The poem is rich in metaphor, specifically in metaphors of entrapment and constraint ('snares', 'web' and so on) which it uses in order to assert a claim to territory, authority or inherited right ('root', 'anchor') as opposed to the falsity and mutability of 'grafted guile' and 'changed course'. The poem is performative in its declaration of what will and will not be permitted. (I use the word 'performative' here in J. L. Austin's sense of the term: 'the issuing of the utterance is the performing of an action'.)[10] Such a performative simultaneously describes and enacts its authority: 'No foreign banished wight shall anchor in this port; / Our realm brooks not seditious sects, let them elsewhere resort.' The forceful clipped language and, in particular, the use of the terse monosyllables which dominate the final lines ('My rusty sword through rest shall first his edge employ / To poll their tops that seek such change or gape for future joy') demonstrate the speaker's command of language, her political and her poetic power.

In a slightly later period, and a different culture, the same inter-penetrability of private and public can be demonstrated. Kaplan notes of Bradstreet's apparently intimate verse that her Puritan background permitted

> no psychological separation of the divine and material world. In her religious and domestic writing Anne Bradstreet often achieves the integration of these things and perhaps moves toward the much more difficult integration of her role as woman and poet.[11]

In the present day, too, as Deborah Nelson argues of the work of the 'confessional' poets, in order to comprehend their apparent immersion in and revelation of the private and intimate, one must understand and historicise the Cold War culture of containment in which they were produced:

> The autobiographical and confessional trend in American culture erupted simultaneously with this ideological inflation of the value of privacy. Moreover, confessional poetry was not merely the personal in public. It was always the most secret, violent, damaging and disruptive elements of private life on display. Plath and her fellow confessional poets provided a counter discourse to the official ideology of privacy in the Cold War.[12]

Plath's poem 'Nick and the Candlestick', for instance, which is ostensibly an intimate poem of private and familial contemplation, embodies what Robin Peel has called 'an assault on the world' – on religion and on the prospect of nuclear annihilation (the poem was written in the shadow of the Cold War and the Cuban Missile Crisis).[13] This is, surely, a public voice, and its authority comes from its relatedness to the immediate and the real. Private and public, then, may mean vastly different things in different contexts. As we will see in the poetry discussed in the rest of this chapter, by rethinking what we understand 'politics' to mean, and by being alert to shifts in its signification, it is possible to recuperate as 'political' a number of poems by women which might otherwise not have been read in this light.

THE ROMANTIC MOVEMENT

The work of women writers from the Romantic period is useful in exemplifying the issues outlined above. To recap, it is important to understand the historical and cultural specificity of our terms and to be aware of a body of hitherto hidden poetry by women which may, itself, overthrow stereotypes of gender and genre. So, too, one must think sceptically and creatively about the public/private binary and be aware of the ways in which the poetics of the text (its use of metaphor, rhythm, rhyme, form) might confuse or conflate the two, offering political commentary under the guise of an intimate narrative. If one stops reading poetry by women purely in terms of its revelation of private and intimate emotion, and looks instead for its political dimensions, one might find entirely different significations at play.

The English Romantic period (usually taken to run from the mid-1780s to around the 1830s) offers interesting grounds for testing the ways in which we think about gender, genre, politics and authority. How do we explain the rise of Romanticism and the change which it underwent from initial idealism to retrenchment and despair? The movement marked an enormous break with the past. It emerged from a time of great crisis and articulated through its own disparate forms, concerns and intentions ways of responding to, understanding, contesting or escaping massive social change. In particular, it used the ostensibly intimate and personal voice to explore the relationship between the individual and the masses. In Western societies, long-established systems of thought, government and belief were being contested, and this ideological upheaval inevitably inspired and was reflected in aesthetic change. The movement asked innovative questions about the self's responsibility (personal, literary and political) to a larger social order and vice versa. It uses an apparently personal, lyric voice but it demonstrates that this could be of broad relevance, engaging with larger questions of concern to the wider culture.

Romantic poetry, in particular poetry written by women in this period, registers such changes very acutely. How are we to read the Romantic spirit – archetypally the spirit of social change, equality and freedom – with the conditions of women in mind? As far as the specific context for women poets in the Romantic era is concerned, Enlightenment ideals of progress, improvement and emancipation are an important influence. Mary Wollstonecraft's pioneering study, *A Vindication of the Rights of Woman* (1792), both recorded and stimulated the experiences and aspirations of a generation of overlooked women. In Louise Bernikow's words:

> After the drought of the eighteenth century, women's writing
> in the nineteenth was a deluge [. . .] the actual change in
> women's lives had much to do with the sudden explosion of

writers and the appearance among the scores of a few great ones. The world into which Mary Wollstonecraft dropped her bombshell book, *The [sic]Vindication of the Rights of Woman* – this world in which women were the most exploited class of laborers, the least educated children, the most disenfranchised adults – such a world convulsed again and again through the course of this century.[14]

And although, ultimately, Romanticism might be said to have turned its back on many of the foundational principles of Enlightenment thinking (the importance of rationality, empiricism, reason), it does retain and embrace fundamentally Enlightenment ideals of freedom, individual potential and egalitarianism. These are ideals which, arguably, speak particularly to women poets of the period. Nevertheless, as the first poem I will discuss here shows, the relationship between some women poets and dominant discourses of the eighteenth and nineteenth centuries – whether Enlightenment or Romantic or both – is complex. Here, as in earlier (Renaissance) and subsequent (Victorian) periods, one must not overlook the influence of religious ideologies.

To take Anna Laetitia Barbauld's 1795 poem 'To the Poor' as an example, unusually here we have a poem specifically addressed to a marginalised and displaced group, 'the poor'. Written in clipped rhyming couplets which work to convey the righteous anger of the speaker, the poem opens with a devastating exposé and critique of a society structured around class distinctions and divided according to material wealth. This is a society which tolerates the subjugation of the weakest and most vulnerable (the 'child' with which the first line opens) by the privileged few, or the 'fellow-men' of line two. The poem is biblical in its idiom as it seeks to convey the bitter injustice of the society it describes:

> Who feel'st oppression's iron in thy soul,
> Who dragg'st the load of faint and feeble years,
> Whose bread is anguish, and whose water tears;

Yet in advocating a spiritual solution (Barbauld's speaker urges the poor passively to 'bear' their 'afflictions' in the hopes of divine deliverance), the poem fits uneasily into either Romantic or Enlightenment paradigms. In seeking neither a self-divined nor a socially-engineered solution, 'To the Poor' rather unsatisfactorily marries a complex social problem with a set of religious beliefs inadequate to the task of resolving it. The poem offers a devastating critique and a brave social challenge (in line eighteen, for example, it distinguishes between the malign 'lords below' and the benign 'Lord above'), but cannot, or is unwilling yet to, advocate a social solution to the oppression it describes.[15]

The poems in William Wordsworth and Samuel Taylor Coleridge's *Lyrical Ballads* (1798) mark a major and very visible break from the poetic orthodoxy which preceded it. Although there had been poetic innovation and experimentation in the eighteenth century, for example, in the use of the ballad – a form derived from a base oral tradition – and in the proto-Romantic and radical poetry of Thomas Gray and William Blake, that century has been typified since by the ornate, rational poetry of Alexander Pope and the other Augustans. We might also generalize that the poets of the eighteenth and earlier centuries were, by and large, speaking to and about their own kind and took for granted a like-minded and homogeneous readership. *Lyrical Ballads*, in contrast, goes out of its way to address a new audience (the common people): 'What is a poet? To whom does he address himself? And what language is to be expected from him? He is a man speaking to men.' Wordsworth and Coleridge used a new poetic language, which they described as 'a selection of the language really spoken by men', and they selected a new field of subject matter, that of 'incidents and situations from common life'.[16] These principles, declared in the manifestoes which formed the preface to the 1805 *Lyrical Ballads*, should be understood as much more than simply aesthetic preferences; they are radical, egalitarian gestures.

Wordsworth and Coleridge's manifesto was anticipated some years earlier by Joanna Baillie, who was best known as a dramatist but who was also an accomplished poet. In the lengthy preface or 'Discourse' to her 1798 *Series of Plays*, she advocates the use of ordinary, common, natural language. The writer, she said, should avoid 'the enchanted regions of simile, metaphor, allegory and description'. Instead, they should reveal 'the plain order of things in this everyday world'.[17] Born in Scotland but resident in Hampstead, London, Baillie's poems have been said to have exerted an influence on Wordsworth. Her evocation of rustic experience and of childhood perception pre-empt the concerns displayed in his *Prelude* and in the poems of *Lyrical Ballads*. Other characteristically Romantic concerns, such as an interest in nature and the sublime, in experiences from ordinary life, in human perception (or 'emotion recollected in tranquillity' as Wordsworth so famously put it), shape and in turn are shaped by women poets' writing of the period. Each of these concerns reads slightly differently when seen from the point of view of women poets.

Sara Coleridge's (Samuel Taylor Coleridge's daughter) poem 'Blest is the Tarn' (1837) celebrates the sublime natural landscapes also to be found in, for example, Wordsworth's *Prelude*.[18] Indeed, 'Blest is the Tarn' seems specifically to write back to, or enter into a dialogue with, Wordsworth's poem (part one of the 1799 version). In 'Blest' and in *Prelude*, we see a calm lake or tarn overshadowed by cliffs or mountains and overlooked by a moon above. A personified nature works on human emotions, first to stimulate, and then to sooth and restore. The difference in this poem, of course, is that where the young Wordsworth in the *Prelude* actually enters into the scene, taking a boat and rowing out into the lake, Sara Coleridge's speaker specifically does not do this. As line three specifies, 'Nor voices loud, nor dashing oars invade.' Her speaker is in a peculiarly liminal position. Unable physically to participate, she gains all her insights from those other key Romantic strategies of observation and imagination. Charlotte Smith's rather earlier 'Sonnet XXXIX: To Night' (1784) operates in a similar way, although this time with a far more melancholy tone (emphasised by the low, slow assonance and soft alliteration: 'mournful sober-suited' and 'moon'). This is a poem which also hovers in a liminal space – hence its images of interrupted or hesitant movement ('lingering', 'uncertain', 'restless'). It is a poem of denial – hopes and ideas are repeatedly negated, hence the suffix '-less' ('restless', 'viewless', 'cheerless', 'hopeless').[19] Its only hope is in a final appeal to some higher spiritual good. Smith's *Elegiac Sonnets*, from which this poem was taken, were published some fifteen years before Wordsworth's *Prelude*. They went through several editions and were enthusiastically read by poets of her generation.

Similarly, Felicia Hemans's 1827 poem 'The Wings of the Dove' recalls John Keats, for example, in its yearning for release from everyday life: 'Darkling I listen; and, for many a time / I have been half in love with easeful Death', to quote the well-known lines from stanza six of Keats's 'Ode to a Nightingale'. The cadences of Keats's poem (the low, languid, mourning assonance) are echoed or answered in Hemans. However, where Keats can imagine release, Hemans, writing as a woman, must recognise the ties that bind her to earth. In the last three stanzas of the poem, she suggests that there is an 'other', an unspoken, unspecified 'you' (a lover, a child or a family member?) which pulls her back home:

> Wild wish, and longing vain,
> And brief upspringing to be glad and free!
>   Go to thy woodland rein!
> My soul is bound and held – I may not flee.
>
>   For even by all the fears
> And thoughts that haunt my dreams – untold, unknown
>   And burning woman's tears,
> Poured from mine eyes in silence alone;
>
>   *Had* I thy wings, thou dove!
> High midst the gorgeous Isles of Cloud to soar,
>   Soon the strong chords of love
> Would draw me earthwards – homewards – yet once more.[20]

Keats, although unable finally to follow the nightingale's flight to freedom, is returned only to his 'sole self'. Thus masculinity represents autonomy. Femininity is constructed in social relationships with family, lovers, and home.

Defining features of Romantic verse, as we have seen, include the use of experiences from common life and the foregrounding of private perception and contemplation ('emotion recollected in tranquillity'). Ann Candler's 'Reflections on my own Situation' or L. E. L. (Letitia Landon's) 'Lines of Life' speak of women's dislocation and isolation. Both use versions of the ballad form (four-line stanzas typically rhyming abcb or abab). The form is of particular resonance in the hands of women poets, in part because, as John Lennard notes, it has long been used for 'accommodating private tragedy to public interest' and in part because of its origins in oral and folk traditions.[21] At a time when female literacy rates would have been significantly lower than those of men, the ballad form exemplifies the way in which stories have been handed down from generation to generation through the female line.

L. E. L.'s 1824 poem 'Home' paints a similar picture of an idealized rustic life to that found in some of Wordsworth and Coleridge's *Lyrical Ballads*. Recollected in tranquillity, this childhood spot ('home') assumes a huge symbolic importance. It comes to stand for everything familiar, permanent and true such that regardless of where the speaker is in the world, 'home' remains in her imagination, fixed and meaningful:

> Years past by,
> But still that vale in silent beauty dwelt
> Within my memory.[22]

However, the poem is not as simplistic as this might at first suggest. The expectations built up in the first part of the poem anticipate the disappointment at the end. Here progress and change, including the commercialization and increasing mechanization of country life, the spread of towns and the urbanization of the landscape, conspire to spoil the past, and the speaker's recollection of it, forever. This poem, then, protests about social and economic change. But the closing scene also reads as a metaphor for the dangers of too close a reliance on the past. So, while it is horrified by the impact of the present, it recognises the folly of nostalgic longing: 'Where were the willows, where the cottages? / I sought my home: I sought and found a city.' Thus Landon's 'Home' clearly belongs in the later Romantic period when the golden promise of Romanticism had begun to tarnish, when the early hopes and expectations had given way to ugly reality.

It is vital at this point to ask whether the grand principles which underpinned Romantic thinking meant different things for women and for men poets. More properly, we need perhaps to complicate the kind of framework I have just set up, and to think more broadly about gender and genre and about the ways in which Romantic poets of either gender manipulated expectations about appropriate voices and forms. Male and female Romantic poets alike are writing in a historical context which defines masculinity and femininity in particular ways. Notions of masculinity in late eighteenth and early nineteenth-century England are tied up with ideas about self-assertion, power, commerce, urbanization, public life, rationality and progress. Notions of femininity are tied up with ideas about passivity, intuition, home and family, privacy, nature, sentiment and tradition. Catherine Stimpson, citing the work of Margaret Homans, shows how these patterns have persisted into the modern period. In Lacanian theory, explains Stimpson, the boy child must make a transition from the semiotic order (associated with the female) into the symbolic order of language (associated with the male): 'Once there he must regard and guard women only as objects, as matter. He must transmogrify the lost maternal presence into "Mother Nature". Romantic poetry, as Homans so clearly shows, emblematizes this pattern of thought and action.'[23]

How, then, are we to read the complicated and in some cases transgressive gender perspectives adopted by male poets in this period? As we have already seen, a defining feature of Romanticism is its radicalism. Arguably, nowhere is the movement more radical than when male poets cross the culturally ascribed gender divide and, implicitly at least, adopt a feminine subject position or when women writers, as what Margaret Homans calls 'imitation sons', make the journey in the opposite direction.[24] Much of what we now recognise as Romantic (the interest in the small-scale and intimate, the emphasis on emotion and intuition, the assumption of the role of passive imbiber of the scene) is also culturally in this period defined as feminine. For female poets of the Romantic era, what is most radical is their entry into the male-dominated field, their taking up the pen and finding a voice. An early poet of the period, Anna Laetitia Barbauld, noted this and commented that she had 'stepped out of the bounds of female reserve in becoming an author'.[25] In doing this, female poets enter the masculine domain or the public world of speech, authority and power.

Thus, when considering Romanticism, and indeed other poetic periods, it is useful to think about the ways in which it offers both male and female poets the opportunity to rethink expectations of masculinity and femininity, of class and place, of genre and of history. It would be a mistake to read a male-defined and male-dominated Romanticism as the norm, and not to recognise, first, that the movement offered both sexes a chance, albeit perhaps an unconscious one, to experiment with different gender roles and, second, that female writers and female perspectives were implicated in the project from the outset. Nevertheless, the tenets of Romanticism which have been taken as definitive of the movement (the interest in selfhood, emotion and the sublime) had different meanings, and promised quote different outcomes, to women and men poets. To go back to Sara Coleridge's 'Blest is the Tarn', the Romantic epiphany experienced by a lone male in a rowboat in the middle of a lake at midnight has only a fraction of the impact when watched by a woman through a distant window.

OPPRESSION

The work of the eighteenth-century poet Mary Leapor exposes what Donna Landry describes as 'the operations of class difference, conflict, and deliberate or unconscious repression' specifically from the hitherto unheard perspective of the labouring or working-class woman.[26] Women in the eighteenth century, in writing at all, were overcoming tremendous forces; 'Against the silencing and objectification of female labor to be found in high literary discourse, we can place a counter tradition of poetic production by working class women. It is a discourse marked by many constraints.'[27]

Leapor was born in 1722 and worked as a kitchen maid in Northamptonshire. Although there is evidence that she borrowed books from her employer and other acquaintances and that she possessed a small number of books of her own, her route to becoming a poet was not a straightforward one.[28] Indeed, her parents, although proud of her abilities, recognised that she would be more profitably employed as a servant.[29] Her success, when it came, was born in part because of the eighteenth-century 'vogue of "uncultivated genius", which aided the success of poets like Clare and Burns', but also embraced the work of women and working-class poets such as herself.[30] In her work, she manipulates conventions (for example, those attached to the pastoral or the country house poem) and thereby lays bare the structures of class and gender oppression which mark the working-class woman's experience. According to Donna Landry, Leapor 'more sharply and thoroughly than any other plebian poet of the period [. . .] mounts a critique of the manifold injustices perpetrated by men against women'.[31]

Leapor's 'An Essay on Woman' swiftly delineates the multiple prohibitions within which working-class women operate. These restrictions are pointedly not only imposed by men.[32] Although one might infer from the poem's opening lines that all women (wives, maids, ugly, fair) are subordinated to and by men, it transpires that some women are less subordinate than others and that economic power – which determines class position – is the key determinant of working women's outcomes: ''Tis wealth alone inspires every grace.' As the poem sardonically notes, all feminine virtues can be overlooked when property comes into play: 'What numbers for those charming features pine, / If blooming acres round her temples twine?' The same, as Wynne-Davies shows, is true of Renaissance women poets:

> although it is undoubtedly true that women writers of the early modern period did not have the same opportunities as men, they did not always form a separate and distinct group on the basis of their sex. Instead, they correspond quite closely to the same economic and rank divisions as male authors [. . .] class was an essential factor in determining the female poetic subject during the English Renaissance.[33]

One of the ways in which 'An Essay on Woman' achieves its resistant effects is by its very knowing deployment of sentimental poetic conventions against themselves. Thus the poem exaggerates the construction of the feminine object, using hyperbole to expose its own insubstantiality. Leapor sets up a string of metaphors which starts with lilies and turns into tears falling on the ground. These stimulate romance and then marriage (hence Hymen in line fifteen) followed by death. Marriage, the poem cynically suggests, heralds the end of love. Thus the poem shows us the skull beneath the skin or the feet of clay ('and turns the goddess to her native clay' in line eighteen) which undermine the idealisation of the married state.

The poem laments the lot of the intelligent, aspirational working woman. She is despised by other women (the 'babbling kind' who 'view her with malignant eyes') and condemned by envious men who are 'vexed to find an nymph so wise'. Leapor uses heroic couplets to construct a mocking portrait of a society ill at ease with a working woman who so completely challenges their class and gender-riven expectations. In this way Leapor uses the traditions associated with English country verse in order both to expose its artifice and to critique the ideology of the culture for which and to whom it speaks. Landry explains, 'Writing verse that ventriloquises and thus challenges the verse forms and values of the mainstream culture is a way of speaking out, and of altering social discourse.'[34] The final twist of Leapor's knife comes in lines forty-four to forty-nine at the climax of the satirical scene she has drawn. Here the sentimental language of maids, nymphs, Hymen and so on is abandoned. The ugly, poverty-stricken reality of the life of the poor is revealed in all its shocking meanness. Leapor throws down a challenge to bourgeois patrons and sympathizers; those who wish metaphorically to embrace an idealized image of the labouring life are invited to come and see it in its reality:

> Then let her quit extravagance and play,
> The brisk companion and expensive tea,
> To feast with Cordia in her filthy sty
> On stewed potatoes or on mouldy pie;
> Whose eager eyes stare ghastly at the poor,
> And fright the beggars from the hated door;
> In greasy clouts she wraps her smoky chin,
> And holds that pride's a never-pardoned sin.

Later in the century Hannah More enters forcefully into contemporary debates about the slave trade with her 'Slavery, A Poem' (1788). This work is worthy of note not least because of the explicit way in which it sympathises with the enslaved woman; 'She, wretch forlorn! is dragged by hostile hands, / To distant tyrants sold, in distant lands!' More manipulates contemporary ideologies. At the

centre of her poem and thus most at risk of violation by the brutal-
ity of the Atlantic slave trade is the sanctity of the hearth and home,
hence her use of images of the 'babe', the 'child', the 'parent' and
'HOME'. She uses patriarchal systems of thought against them-
selves. How can a culture which so valorises femininity, family and
domesticity simultaneously so cruelly corrupt them?[35]

WAR

As Catherine Reilly points out in the introduction to her 1984
anthology, *Chaos of the Night: Women's Poetry and Verse of the
Second World War*, women's poetry has been 'under-represented' in
most selections of war poetry.[36] Reilly shows that this is not neces-
sarily because women have not been active in war, as service women,
war-workers, drivers, nurses and so on. Neither is it because they
have not been affected by war; those who remained at home during
both First and Second World Wars suffered their own losses in
terms of disrupted family and home life, food shortages, emotional
trauma and so on. Their under-representation may in part, as
Chapter 3 suggested, be explained by dominant binary perceptions
of poetry and gender which see the public world as the masculine
sphere and the private world as the feminine. Such a perspective
may simply have been unable to read women's poetry in terms of
its sometimes oblique representations of contemporary political
experience.

This obliqueness of view, and this reticence about direct naming
or representation, are particularly evident in Edith Sitwell's poem
'Still Falls the Rain'.[37] Edith Sitwell was born in 1887 to a titled
family, and with her brothers Osbert and Sacherevell cut an influ-
ential figure in London literary life throughout the modernist
period and beyond. Interested in the arts, music and literature
(and latterly in spiritual concerns as evidenced in some of the
imagery in 'Still Falls the Rain'), she edited the experimental peri-
odical *Wheels* and developed innovative ideas about poetic tech-
nique, particularly the use of synaesthesia (the mixing of the senses)
to evoke sensations and ideas. This technique is evident in 'Still
Falls the Rain'. The poem reads like a lament or ululation – an effect

which is conveyed by the alliteration of the 'l' sounds in the opening lines and in the persistent refrain 'Still falls the rain':

> Still falls the Rain –
> Dark as the world of man, black as our loss –
> Blind as the nineteen hundred and forty nails.

However, the poem's subtitle, 'The Raids, 1940: Night and Dawn', indicates the possibility of surviving the trauma which the poem records and of learning something from it, come the new day.

Capitalisation is used throughout the poem, paradoxically both to convey the specificity and uniqueness of these days, and to convey their sheer anonymity, their ubiquity. So the '*Rain*', which specifically refers to the barrage of bombs which fell on London in the Blitz of 1940, also alludes more generally to an all-encompassing natural phenomenon. Hence, the poem suggests, the devastation of war is experienced both as a unique, personal and private trauma and as a more ubiquitous, shared, public condition. The capitalization throughout the poem emphasises its sardonic tone. When it appears in unexpected places, it functions as a critique of the glorification of war, of the easy assimilation of euphemistic and thus imprecise descriptors such as 'Field of Blood' in line ten. The word '*Tomb*' is capitalized, gesturing at one and the same time to the Tomb of the Unknown Warrior, dedicated in Westminster Abbey after the end of the First World War (or the 'war to end all wars' as it was known), and to the special significance of each and every soldier's 'Tomb'. All, finally, deserve the respect afforded by the capital 'T'.

The 'Rain' with which the poem opens is more simply than literal rainfall or a metaphor for bomb attack. There are other allusions too. Shakespeare's *The Merchant of Venice* tells us that 'The quality of mercy is not strained / It droppeth as the gentle rain from heaven' and that 'It blesseth him that gives and him that takes' (IV, i, 179). 'Still Falls the Rain' takes from Shakespeare a sense of the contiguity of enemy and victim, war maker and peacemaker, the giver and the receiver of mercy. All are alike under the 'Rain'; all suffer, all might offer and all might gain from the gift of mercy. There is a clear biblical framework in the poem demonstrated by its repeated allusions to Christ's suffering on the Cross, to his martyr-dom and his capacity to 'have mercy on us'. 'Still Falls the Rain' recognises and confesses (the biblical idiom is again apt in this con-nection) everybody's responsibility for the devastation seen around them.

Sylvia Townsend Warner's poem 'Road 1940' is also worthy of note. 'Why do I carry', it opens, 'this child that is no child of mine?' It goes on to list all those who have refused to take responsibility – soldiers, misers and the child's mother. And it asks what point there is in saving a child now who might simply grow up to replicate the violence of which the child itself is now a victim: 'If it grow to hero it will die or let loose / Death'.[38] But in an unsettling, if deeply telling, twist the poem refuses the easy satisfaction of taking the moral high ground. It is too easy, it suggests, to say that we are all equally to blame. It might seem a small shift, but it is far more difficult, if nihilistic, to say that we are all equally evil. As the poem closes, the speaker reveals that her reasons for helping the child are not as altruistic as we might have assumed. Instead they are merce-nary and selfish; the speaker hopes that her own act of goodness will reap rewards, that if she were ever to suffer a similar misfortune as the child, someone else would 'Grant me even to lie down on a bed; / Give me at least bread'.

This raises huge moral and political questions. What kind of world simultaneously pities and attacks the weak (a similar problem is posed, as we have seen, by Hannah More's poem 'Slavery')? The speaker knows that an ill child will attract more pity than a dispos-sessed adult, and implicitly asks what kind of society could tolerate such a hierarchy of suffering. Do the ends justify the means in a case such as this? Is it worse to help for selfish reasons than not to help at all? Townsend Warner's poem transports us to a world in which human kindness cannot be relied upon (hence '*if* we ever should come to kindness' in the final stanza – my italics), where the kind of mercy that Sitwell describes in 'Still Falls the Rain' has disap-peared. This is a corrupt world, a modern civilisation whose values far from being defended have been tainted and denied. H. D.'s mag-nificent *Trilogy* (comprising the 1944–6 poem sequences *The Walls do not Fall*, *Tribute to the Angels* and *The Flowering of the Rod*) exem-plifies this point.[39] Here the catastrophe of the Second World War is explored in the context of individual, localised, immediate experience which is also so much more than that – which has long historical and cultural roots. Birth and death, beginnings and endings, the material and the spiritual, the immediate and the historical, the experiential and the abstract – all are encompassed and explored in this poem which stands alongside, say, T. S. Eliot's *The Waste Land* as an account of modern despair and potential salvation.[40] In Townsend Warner's poem, spiritual salvation, although implicitly available (hence references to the 'child' and the 'bread', images which resonate in Christian iconography), cannot be relied upon and thus remains out of reach for most.

In poems such as these we see women poets imaginatively exploring the complexity of war and its effects on human and social values and relationships. 'Road 1940' and 'Still Falls the Rain' contemplate the choices which ordinary non-combatants might be forced to make. In the latter, the rain falls on each of us alike. Each of us is culpable and each of us, ally and enemy alike, is equally entitled to receive some kind of mercy.

SPEECH

Rita Dove's 1983 poem 'Parsley' examines the place of language both in political repression and in political protest. It bears its frustration in images which promise nascent joy and fertility but which deliver only repression, frustration, deception and fear. The parrot with which the poem opens is only 'imitating spring', and any signs of spring (conventionally connoting hope, new birth, a fresh start) are entirely overshadowed by the heavy metaphors of death throughout the text – the 'skull-shaped candies', the 'artillery' and the 'arrowheads'. 'Cane' (sugar cane) features throughout the poem, representing both the punishing and inescapable lives of the slave workers who cultivate it and the literal threat of violent punishment. The homonym of 'cane' (sugar cane) and 'cane' (stick or weapon) is ominous and pervasive; four of the six stanzas in the poem's opening section close with the reminder 'the cane appears'.[41]

At the heart of this poem lie the political uses to which language is put. Dove's poem makes what might otherwise seem an abstract issue become immediate, compelling and fatal. It imagines the circumstances which led the dictator Rafael Trujillo to order the death of 20,000 black Haitians because of their inability to pronounce the letter 'r' in the Spanish word for parsley (an author's note appended to the poem provides this background detail). In 'Parsley', the general's dictat is rooted in a complex nexus of grief, loss, isolation, anger and misplaced, ugly, irrational revenge. For many readers the poem is deeply disturbing yet gains much of its impact from its evocation, or speaking, of an otherwise hidden moment in history. The Haitians themselves are heard only obliquely in the poem, for example, when 'screaming' as the rain lashes down on the cane in section one. They sing in section two and thus unwittingly give the dictator the kernel of the idea which leads to his plans for their annihilation (when they sing, they inadvertently sing 'Katalina' instead of 'Katarina'). The voice otherwise is the terse, impassionate one of the narrator who is content, because the events reveal their own awful horror, not to offer explicit judgement. For other readers, it is the imaginative retelling of the dictator's story which is precisely what makes the poem so disturbing. This is, arguably, a story we do not want to hear; can we defend the poem's intervention in giving the dictator a voice? Rita Dove defends the position in a subsequent reflection on the experience of reading this poem at the White House:

> Here I was, at the White House at the highest administrative level of power, and I wanted to talk about the uses to which power has been put. I also wanted to talk about how necessary it is in all avenues of life to be able to imagine the other person.[42]

How impossible and how dangerous it is, 'Parsley' tells us, to separate private from public, personal from political, self from other.

A number of other contemporary poems expose and thereby contest the slipperiness of language and its propensity to be used for ideological purposes. Jo Shapcott's 'Phrase Book' is concerned with the euphemisms by which people persuade themselves, particularly in wartime, of the harmlessness or necessity of their actions.[43] Like Herbert Reed's well-known Second World War

poem 'The Naming of Parts', Shapcott's 'Phrase Book' adopts a
clipped, glib tone which seems at first to efface the resonance of its
message. On a closer reading it is apparent that the public idiom
offered by the phrase book of the title is wholly inadequate to
expressing the horror of violence which lies beneath the surface:
'I am standing here inside my skin, / which will do for a human
remains pouch.' More urgently, the language on offer cannot but
misrepresent the female speaker who is left powerless, speechless
and unable to define her own subjectivity: 'Please explain. / What
does it mean? What must I do?' Carol Ann Duffy's 'Poet for our
Times' is about the political evasions of language. Written in the
form of the dramatic monologue and spoken in the voice of a
tabloid journalist, the poem exposes the complicity of language in
the erasure of ideological complexity. In other words, it shows how
both journalistic and poetic languages are guilty of misrepresenting
the truth. The association between the two discourses is reinforced
by the poem's title and by the speaker's comparison of himself to 'a
sort of poet / for our times'. In the guise of a mocking exposure of
some of the excesses of Thatcherism, Duffy makes a rather more
profound point about the responsibility of the poet.[44]

Irish poet Eavan Boland's poem 'An Old Steel Engraving', the
eighth in her twelve-section 'Outside History: A Sequence' (1990),
asserts the importance of bearing witness. History and poetry here
are inextricably interwoven. Understanding is a symptom of
reading and truth is a product of interpretation. The poem opens
with a single command 'Look.' Thus we, as readers, are invited into
the same space as the speaker. Like Keats's 'Ode on a Grecian Urn',
'An Old Steel Engraving' shows us a frozen image, a moment of
stopped time which we must imaginatively interpret. It is signifi-
cant in the context of the violent and negative images which suffuse
this poem, the larger sequence and, to an extent, the collection as a
whole, that the central object – the engraving – is typically pro-
duced by using either a sharp tool or acid to burn out a negative
impression on a plate of steel. Ink is then used to fill the indenta-
tions and to make the impressions. What the speaker in this case
sees is a picture of an awful limbo; the falling man in the engraving
is trapped forever, neither living nor dying, while the witness who
passes by and sees the man falling is 'scared witless' and is thus

powerless to act. The poem/engraving is riddled with metaphors of suffering and loss – of death and drowning (hence the dragged river of lines three and four), 'shadows' and fear. This is couched always in repeated and thus emphatic negatives. Four times in the eleven lines of stanza one, we are told that the object of the engraving, and the passers-by who witness his fall, 'cannot' act. The painful paralysis of object, witness and by extension reader works as a metaphor for the wider political situation in Ireland. As the closing lines of stanza one affirm, 'the ground' (this ground, this Ireland) is 'the origin and reason for it all'. Boland, of course, is writing in and from an Ireland which has been politically independent of Britain since the 1920s, but the central metaphor of the 'Old Steel Engraving' is instrumental in historicising her account – it looks back to a pre-independence Ireland: the Ireland of Yeats, Maud Gonne, Lady Gregory and the 1916 Easter Rising. Yet the survival of this engraving, and the fixity and persistence of the moment of trauma it depicts, indicate that these troubles live on, as indeed they did throughout the twentieth century (and arguably into the twenty-first) in Northern Ireland.

As stanza two explains, the distancing of these troubles by their aestheticisation or reification (in the form of the engraving) is an escape route to be denied. In contemplating these images, we must also consider their context or 'the spaces on the page' as stanza two has it. Our responsibility is to imagine what happened first and what happened next, to construct a past and a future, or a historical narrative. The stories the engraving 'cannot tell' are precisely the spaces we must fill in: 'they widen / to include us'.

In order to bring the past to life, to relieve or at the very least put an end to the suffering encapsulated in the paralysis of the engraving, we must speak or give voice to our circumstances. We must turn 'cannot' into 'can':

> nothing can move until we find the word,
> nothing can move until we say this is
> what happened and is happening

Like W. H. Auden's 'Musée des Beaux Arts', Boland's poem focuses not on the obvious key players in traumatic or historically significant moments, but on the otherwise passive and silent but nevertheless implicated observers who in electing whether to bear witness or to move swiftly on exercise a profound moral and political choice. 'History', as Boland's poem has it, 'is one of us who turns away / while the other is / turning the page' (in Auden's poem, 'everything turns away / Quite leisurely from the disaster').[45] 'An Old Steel Engraving' is a manifesto for an engaged poetry. The act of 'turning the page', of reading and writing, of bearing and sharing witness, is a political act representing not distance (not 'turn[ing] away') but movement.

Clair Wills argues for the importance in the work of modern poets Fanny Howe and Medbh McGuckian of the 'recurrent image of women as witnesses to and recorders of history'.[46] These images, she goes on to say, may be traced in and on the female body as, for example, in Howe's poem 'Monday the First'. In Olds's work, too, as Vicki Feaver points out, the characteristic method 'consists of "reading" a body, or bodies, in a language that is both sensual and exploratory, that discovers meaning by making connections with other bodies and other discourses and texts'.[47] Most important of all, though, for example in Olds's poem 'I Go Back to May 1937', discussed in the next chapter, is the authority which comes with bearing witness: 'I will tell about it'.

Denise Levertov's poems 'The Mutes' and 'The Olga Poems' see public and political concerns inscribed on the female body. Hers is a deeply political oeuvre. Her 1967 collection *The Sorrow Dance*, written in the shadow of the Vietnam War, presents a litany of powerlessness and despair. In many of these poems, for example in 'Life at War' and 'The Pulse', the speaker feels herself to be trapped in some claustrophobic scene. In 'Life at War', the contained body is itself blocked. Wartime existence and the pervasive ideology which persuades us to tolerate it have numbed and oppressed the subject, as shown by the successive metaphors of suffocation, apnoea, smothering and so on: of 'lumps of raw dough // weighing down a child's stomach', of 'pocked' lungs, 'mucous membrane[s]' and 'husky phlegm'.[48] Language is implicated in this deadening process but also, paradoxically, essential to escaping it: 'We are the humans', the poem avows; those whose 'language imagines *mercy*, / *lovingkindness*'. However, the conflation of 'lovingkindness' makes this seem a mere form of words, a cliché without substance or efficacy.

CONCLUSION

The American poet Adrienne Rich has devoted much of her writing life, in poetry and in essays, to examining the relationship between poetry and politics, between private contemplation and the declaration of a public position. In the essay 'Dearest Arturo', for example, she insists that 'poetry and politics aren't mutually exclusive'.[49] As we saw with Dove's 'Parsley', finding and claiming a speaking position is itself inextricably political. It is crucial to Rich that the poet engages from the outset with these debates; politics begins in privacy. In her early and influential essay 'When We Dead Awaken' (an essay which was at the forefront of second wave feminist literary studies), she explains that as a young poet writing in the 1950s and 1960s and moving from a formalist, male-dominated aesthetic, she had to find the space to think independently: 'I needed to think for myself – about pacifism, and dissent and violence, about poetry and society, and about my own relationship to all these things [. . .] I began at this point to feel that politics was not something "out there" but something "in here".'[50] This statement has served as a model for the work of a number of women poets who, as this chapter and Chapter 3 have shown, have made their own ostensibly private concerns the beginning of a politicised debate. The political potential of poetry by women is encapsulated here. Rich's comments serve as a coda to, for example, the situation described in Shapcott's poem 'Phrase Book'. For in that poem, paradoxically, it is the language of the poem which permits a release from the language of the phrase book. This subversively radical potential is, for Rich, one of the propensities of poetry: 'That is one property of poetic language: to engage with states that themselves would deprive us of language and reduce us to passive sufferers.'[51]

SUMMARY OF KEY POINTS

- Historically, the public sphere of politics has been associated with the masculine.
- Women poets have worked in a number of imaginative and transgressive ways to acquire an authoritative public voice.

- The Romantic movement provides a valuable example of the complex relationships between gender and genre. The work of women poets in Romanticism prompts us to rethink the parameters, characteristics and limitations of orthodox definitions of the period.
- Women poets have used their writing to expose, examine and resist various forms of oppression. Self-consciousness about the political effects of language is one of the hallmarks of their work.

NOTES

1. Paul West, 'Crossing the Water', in *Sylvia Plath: The Critical Heritage*, ed. Linda Wagner-Martin (London and New York: Routledge, 1988), pp. 157–61 (p. 158).
2. Ann Rosalind Jones, 'Surprising Fame: Renaissance Gender Ideologies and Women's Lyric', in *Feminism and Renaissance Studies*, ed. Lorna Hutson (Oxford: Oxford University Press, 1999), pp. 317–36 (p. 318).
3. Bertram, *Gendering*, p. 134. Rachel Blau DuPlessis, *Genders, Races and Religious Cultures in Modern American Poetry, 1908–1934* (Cambridge: Cambridge University Press, 2001), p. 154.
4. Quoted in M. H. Abrams et al., *Norton Anthology of English Literature*, p. 606.
5. Kaplan, *Salt*, pp. 85–7.
6. Kirstin Wilcox, 'The Body into Print: Marketing Phillis Wheatley', *American Literature* 71: 1 (1999), 1–29 (8).
7. Phillis Wheatley, 'To the Right Honourable William', in Bolam, *Eliza's Babes*, p. 177.
8. Quoted in Bolam, *Eliza's Babes*, p. 28.
9. Ibid. p. 29.
10. J. L. Austin, *How to Do Things With Words* (Oxford: Oxford University Press, 1962), p. 6.
11. Kaplan, *Salt*, p. 28.
12. Deborah Nelson, 'Plath, History and Politics', in Gill, *Cambridge Companion*, pp. 21–35 (p. 23).

13. Robin Peel, *Writing Back: Sylvia Plath and Cold War Politics* (London: Associated University Presses, 2002), pp. 221–2.

14. Bernikow, *The World*, pp. 26–7.

15. Anna Laetitia Barbauld, 'To the Poor', in Feldman, *British Women Poets*, p. 66.

16. Wordsworth and Coleridge, *Lyrical Ballads 1805*, ed. Derek Roper (Plymouth: Macdonald and Evans, 1976), pp. 30–1, 29, 20–1.

17. Joanna Baillie, *A Series of Plays* (Oxford and New York: Woodstock Books, [1798] 1990), pp. 1–72.

18. Sara Coleridge, 'Blest is the Tarn', in Feldman, *British Women Poets*, p. 200.

19. Charlotte Smith, 'Sonnet XXXIX', in Feldman, *British Women Poets*, p. 686.

20. Felicia Hemans, 'The Wings of the Dove', in Feldman, *British Women Poets*, p. 299.

21. John Lennard, *The Poetry Handbook: A Guide to Reading Poetry for Pleasure and Practical Criticism*, 2nd edn (Oxford: Oxford University Press, 2005), p. 56.

22. L. E. L. (Letitia Landon), 'Home', in Feldman, *British Women Poets*, p. 372.

23. Catharine R. Stimpson, 'Foreword', in Margaret Homans, *Bearing the Word: Language and Female Experience in Nineteenth-Century Women's Writing* (Chicago and London: University of Chicago Press, 1986), p. ix.

24. Homans, *Bearing*, p. 20.

25. Quoted in Philip Cox, *Gender, Genre and the Romantic Poets: An Introduction* (Manchester: Manchester University Press, 1996), p. 34.

26. Landry, *Muses*, pp. 1–2.

27. Ibid. p. 3.

28. See Pearson, *Women's Reading*, p. 190.

29. Landry, *Muses*, p. 101.

30. Pearson, *Women's Reading*, p. 187.

31. Landry, *Muses*, p. 81.

32. Mary Leapor, 'An Essay on Woman', in Bolam, *Eliza's Babes*, pp. 140–1.

33. Wynne-Davies, *Women Poets*, p. xx.

34. Landry, *Muses*, pp. 3, 6.
35. Hannah More, 'Slavery, A Poem', in Bolam, *Eliza's Babes*, pp. 160–1. Hannah More served for a time as patron to the 'milkmaid' poet, Ann Yearsley. For more on this relationship and its breakdown, see Landry, *Muses*.
36. Reilly, *Chaos*, p. xxi; see also Reilly, *Scars Upon My Heart*.
37. 'Still Falls the Rain', in Edith Sitwell, *Collected Poems* (London: Macmillan, 1957), p. 272.
38. Sylvia Townsend Warner, 'Road 1940', in Reilly, *Chaos*, p. 123.
39. H. D., *Trilogy* (Manchester: Carcanet, 1973).
40. Ibid.
41. Rita Dove, 'Parsley', in Baym et al., *Norton Anthology of American*, p. 2813.
42. Accessed 5 December 2005 at: www.english.uiuc.edu/maps/poets/a_f/dove/reading.htm
43. Jo Shapcott, *Her Book: Poems 1988–1998* (London: Faber and Faber, 2000), pp. 65–6.
44. Carol Ann Duffy, 'Poet for our Times', in Hulse et al., *The New Poetry*, p. 229.
45. Eavan Boland, *Outside History* (Manchester: Carcanet, 1990), p. 39. W. H. Auden, *Selected Poems* (London: Faber and Faber, 1979), p. 79.
46. Clair Wills, 'Marking Time: Fanny Howe's Poetics of Transcendence', in Mark and Rees-Jones, *Contemporary*, pp. 119–39 (pp. 137–8).
47. Vicki Feaver, 'Body and Soul: The Power of Sharon Olds', in Mark and Rees-Jones, *Contemporary*, pp. 140–56 (p. 144).
48. Denise Levertov, *Selected Poems* (Newcastle: Bloodaxe, 1986), p. 78.
49. Rich, *What is Found There*, p. 23.
50. Adrienne Rich, *On Lies, Secrets and Silence: Selected Prose 1966–1978* (London: Virago, 1980), p. 44.
51. Rich, *What is Found There*, p. 10.

CHAPTER 6

Poetry and Place

In the last few decades, literary studies have been interested in the relationships between literary representations of subjectivity, gender, place and space. 'Place' in this context refers to specific natural or material sites or locations, and 'space' connotes a more abstract and social sense of geographical context and relations. Edward Soja, one of the key thinkers in this area, defines the field thus:

> We are becoming consciously aware of ourselves as intrinsically spatial beings, continuously engaged in the collective activity of producing spaces and places, territories and regions, environments and habitats. This process of producing spatiality or "making geographies" begins with the body, with the construction and performance of the self, the human subject, as a distinctively spatial entity involved in a complex relation with our surroundings.

Soja cites Rich in his explanation of the relationships between private bodies and public spaces: 'Our "performance" as spatial beings takes place at many different scales, from the body, or what the poet Adrienne Rich once called "the geography closest in," to a whole series of more distant geographies.'[1]

Elizabeth Grosz pushes the connection between body and space a little further. She is interested not merely in context, or in reading the body in and against specific backgrounds. Rather, she is interested in the two-way relationship between bodies and spaces or 'the constitutive and mutually defining relation between bodies and cities'. It is important to note that Grosz is not only or specifically talking about the metropolis here. Instead, as she explains, 'The built environment provides the context and coordinates for most contemporary [. . .] forms of the body, even for rural bodies insofar as the twentieth century defines the countryside, "the rural," as the underside or raw material of urban development.'[2] In Lorna Dee Cervantes's 'Freeway 280', contiguities of place mould and define the subject.[3] This place – the freeway and the wild lands concealed but also resurgent beneath it – stands for a particular identity. The language of the poem, with its blending of Spanish and English terms, the commingling of the natural and built environments and its image of the subject/speaker scrambling across the barriers 'that would have kept me out' (stanza three), all work to show the female subject struggling to reconcile different parts of her identity, struggling to find and articulate a selfhood which is rooted in a now-obliterated territory.

Cultural geography offers new ways of thinking (or 'powerful new models and vocabularies') about some of the issues identified thus far in this book: questions of subjectivity and embodiment, about private and public spheres, about the local and domestic and the global and political.[4] For some thinkers it offers an ' " escape from binary thinking", particularly with respect to cultural studies and its ongoing "romance" with alterity'.[5] In this chapter I will be using these new ideas about space, place, identity and representation as a framework for two key points: the first is an assessment of borderland spaces and identities; the second is an examination of specificities of place and motifs of mapping and cartography in women's writing. In the work of the contemporary Anglo-Iranian poet Mimi Khalvati, for example, the speaker seeks to locate and inscribe her place in a geographical – which is also inevitably a historical – context (see her poems 'Amanuensis' and 'A Persian Miniature').[6]

BORDERS

Much of the discourse which surrounds the study of poetry by women is predicated on some notion of boundaries or borders.

Implicitly or otherwise, it presupposes a borderland between the poetry of women and the poetry of men, between the voices or language or subject matter or reading and reception of one gender's poetry as distinct from that of the 'other'. From this point of view, one might think of the history of the study of women's poetry as a history of the struggle to define and police these borders – a struggle which seems doomed to fail given the mutability and variety of its object.

These borders, like geo-political boundaries, might change over time (thus women poets' access to certain forms, themes or idioms does not remain constant). The border might be narrow in some places (the ballad form has been extensively and successfully used by women and men poets alike) and wider in others (the epic, for instance). In some places, it might be carefully monitored, such that certain 'no go areas' are delineated, whereas in others, it might be treated with more laxity. Concessions might sometimes be made or territory annexed. The dramatic monologue, for example, has been enthusiastically adopted by many women poets as they assay numerous otherwise unavailable voices and subject positions. It is a struggle which, in any case, seems self-defeating. To be constantly engaged in a process of negotiating and renegotiating the boundaries or parameters implies enforced passivity. It suggests that someone else has the upper hand in imposing border controls. Arguably, it denies the possibility of self-definition. Such a debate, moreover, is predicated on what I have already characterised as a now-disputed sequence of binaries (major/minor, original/copy, centre/margin, men/women) which recent theorists of women's poetry have chosen to dispute.

Of late, a number of women poets have chosen to focus on boundaries, parameters and borderlands as a way of registering their refusal to be considered merely as marginal or as ex-centric (outside the centre) and of articulating the multiplicity and hybridity of gender, sexuality, language and thus subjectivity. This may, at first, seem paradoxical (the positive embracing of the margins seems a perverse way of refusing to be passively relegated to them), but there are two points to be made here. The first is that this is an active assertion of agency; this is a self-willed claim by women poets in their own terms not necessarily to the right to occupy a marginal space (some sort of pyrrhic victory this!), but of their desire to engage in some meaningful ways with it, to disentangle, question and rearticulate its significations. The second is that this is an attempt not to switch from one position (on the boundaries) to another (in the middle), but to rethink the whole epistemology. Women writers engaged in this process are occupied with rethinking the parameters of the parameter; they assess space and place in terms not just of physical geography but of language, subjectivity, sexuality, race and so on. Gloria Anzaldúa's hugely influential *Borderlands/La Frontera: The New Mestiza* theorises the relationships and cultural meanings of the borderlands and functions as a manifesto for a new generation of – primarily but not exclusively – Chicana poets.[7]

From Anzaldúa's perspective, the borderlands are liminal, undecidable, fluid and indeterminate – they are a perhaps literal 'no *man's* land' – and thus ripe for appropriation and interpretation by women writers. The argument of *Borderlands/La Frontera* is indispensable to this chapter's consideration of a range of problems relating to location and dislocation, specificities of place and abstractions of space, particularly as these relate to language, race and ethnicity. It is important, as postcolonial commentator Homi Bhabha has argued, to recognise the provisional nature of the field: 'The "middle passage" of contemporary culture, as with slavery itself, is a process of displacement and disjunction that does not totalize experience.' Writers in this context, such as the poets discussed below, 'deploy the cultural hybridity of their borderline conditions to "translate," and therefore reinscribe, the social imaginary of both metropolis and modernity'.[8]

For Cervantes, a Californian poet of Chicana origins, the boundaries between a number of different languages – the English language of the dominant North American culture and daily life and the Spanish language imposed on her Mexican ancestors and Chicana heritage by European colonisers – are a major concern. 'Visions of Mexico While at a Writing Symposium in Port Townsend, Washington' examines the split between different languages, different histories, and different subjectivities. The division is articulated first in the title of the poem and then in its bipartite structure with its very firmly located opening section ('Mexico') and second section ('Washington').

Nevertheless, the poem opens with a sense of confusion:

> When I'm that far south, the old words
> molt off my skin, the feathers
> of all my nervousness.
> My own words somersault naturally as my name.[9]

Which is the 'old' language in the context of this move south? The language of the colonial past (that is, Spanish)? Or the language spoken immediately before the journey and now jettisoned (that is, the language of North America)? More urgently, what is the status of the native language of Mexico, erased by colonisation (supplanted first by Spanish and thereafter by the English of North America) and now mostly silent? The true 'old words', from this point of view, cannot be heard. Which are 'my own words': the words of daily discourse (American English) or, as the poem proceeds to make clear, the Mexican words which come as 'naturally' ('Michoacán, / Vera Cruz, Tenochtitlán, Oaxaca')? The opening stanza registers the fluidity of language and thus, by implication, of identity and its capacity to shape and determine consciousness. A post-Saussurean view of language, as we have already seen, teaches that language precedes and determines experience. The speaker here is subject to, not the subject of, language (or, more properly, languages), and either language leaves her confused and excited in turn. The 'new' words which she claims as her 'own' bring with them a new landscape and a new identity. But crucially the 'old' language remains. It is the language (English) in which the poem is expressed and read. This point attenuates the opening ambiguity of the poem. Moreover, the new or recovered identity (the Mexican identity which, it is implied, replaces the old) is itself incomplete and uncertain. A shared language is not necessarily shared experience.

The poem plays with all manner of other boundaries in addition to the primary boundary between languages. Strange things might happen between north and south ('when I'm that far south' and 'coming south'), between genders as we will see in a moment, and between humans and animals. In line two, the speaker implicitly likens herself to a snake or lizard ('the old words / molt off my skin') or to a bird ('the feathers / of all my nervousness'). Both metaphors convey a state of transformation or change. Later, the association of self with seabird is reinforced; the speaker's struggle with a new language (and her motivation for trying to acquire it) is displaced onto the gulls:

> We work
> and watch seabirds elbow their wings
> in migratory ways, those mispronouncing gulls
> coming south
> to refuge or gameland.

The use of this image in the poem is deeply nuanced. It gestures towards, and even inverts, North American perceptions of migration from Mexico towards the north. Here the seabirds are travelling in the opposite direction. It also implicitly assimilates the language and perspective of the north – the 'old words' which would complain about the inability of Mexican migrants to the US to speak the language. The speaker sits in a profoundly uneasy position as both subject and object of criticism, on the side of alien and native at one and the same time. The speaker is always situated in the position of observer/outsider, never truly at home in either context. 'I watch and understand', she says, but she is always excluded by historical circumstance from that which she sees: 'My frail body has never packed mud / or gathered in the full weight of the harvest.' In stanza two: 'I don't want to pretend I know more / and can speak all the names I can't.'

The separation in 'Visions of Mexico While at a Writing Symposium in Port Townsend, Washington' is also one of gender and, inevitably, of power. The women in this poem, Mexican and North American alike, are excluded from the male centre of activity; they are the watchers and waiters, the non-participants. The thin and fragile bond which here transcends boundaries of race and ethnicity is that of gender: 'Alone with the women in the adobe', the speaker confesses, 'I watch men.' There is something uncomfortable, for speaker and reader alike, about this voyeurism. The vignette underpins the theme of power which implicitly runs through the poem. Again, though, any straightforward assessment – and certainly any facile polarisation of powerful and powerless – is undermined. This is so not least because the conventional Western capitalist reading of the female object of the male gaze is so inverted or, more properly, confused. There are degrees of hierarchy and power here; and power, like language and subjectivity, is a relative and mutable thing.

Denied access to the dominant language (or to the symbolic order), the subject must 'speak' in a different way. Not all languages are equal, the poem suggests (Sujata Bhatt's poem 'Search for my Tongue' makes a similar point). If we turn to Lacan, we see that power in Western culture is tied up with access to the symbolic order of language and the law of the father/phallic order (in Lacan's words: 'it is in the name of the father that we must recognize the support of the symbolic function which, from the dawn of history, has identified his person with the figure of the law').[10] Given this, Cervantes's speaker's only recourse is to a pre-symbolic or semiotic language – the language of the body: 'my sense of this land can only ripple through my veins':

> I come from a long line of eloquent illiterates
> whose history reveals what words don't say.
> Our anger is our way of speaking,
> the gesture is an utterance more pure than word.

Again, the poem sets up an apparent set of binaries (symbolic/semiotic, old/new, human/animal) but then refuses, or at least complicates, them: 'We are not animals,' she insists. But this section closes with an assertion of her bardic and aesthetic function which is also a sign of her animalistic core: 'We hear them / and the poet within us bays.'

In the 'Washington' section which mirrors 'Mexico', the speaker records her sense of dislocation or unease as she travels 'north'. The birds, in the first section, had offered a metaphor for ease of movement, the freedom to travel and the instinctive ability to make both 'north' and 'south', in turn, their homes (a claim which the speaker, too, had tried to make). Now, though, the birds can only offer a mirror to, or transposition of, her own sense of dislocation and unease. In the north, speaker and birds alike seem out of place, dissatisfied: 'The uncomfortable birds gawk at me. / They hem and haw from their borders in the sky.' The physical ease and fluency that the speaker experienced in stanza one (losing the skin and feathers of her 'nervousness') is here parodied and made to look grotesque:

> México is a stumbling comedy.
> A loose-legged Cantinflas woman
> acting with Pancho Villa drunkenness.

Here ethnicity, nationality, gender, sexuality and class are interwoven. Again, this is a way of refusing binary vision. 'Part of the work of that *Mestiza* consciousness', as Sonia Saldivár-Hull puts it in her preface to the second edition of Anzaldúa's *Borderlands*, is to 'break down dualities that serve to imprison women'.[11]

There is a complex network of social, sexual, racial and material relations at play. At the centre or perhaps at the bottom of this hierarchical network (the position is both important and relative to the perspective of the observer) is a 'painting of a woman: her glowing / silk skin, a halo'. The description and subsequent positioning of this vision in the middle of a circle of 'drooling' men makes it unclear whether this is a literal 'painting' of a woman or whether the word is used figuratively to connote some kind of idealised image. Caught in this snapshot-like scene are the transient speaker/narrator, the 'glowing'-skinned woman of the painting, 'dark-skinned men with Jap slant eyes' and 'two Chicana' (significantly, the speaker does not identify herself alongside these). At first, Japanese men and the painted woman are bound together by the men's gaze. The 'two Chicanas' seem excluded, positioned 'below' and marginalised from the central scene (line forty-eight). Yet the stillness of these women ('They were still as foam while the men / fiddled with their asses') suggests a contiguity between their immobility and that of the women in the painting. More complicatedly, though, 'still as foam' suggests the possibility of nascent activity; it is as though pressure is building up beneath the immobile surface. In this respect, all of the women – golden painting, the two Chicana – represent a latent resistance.

Just as there is an implicit bond between the woman at the centre of this scene and those on the margins, so too there are possible connections between Japanese men and Chicana women. One could argue that both, in their way, by active encouragement or passive acceptance, acquiesce in the subjugation of women. Conversely, one might read both, in their own ways, as the objects of racially-motivated vilification. Lines fifty-three and fifty-four ('the bubbles of their teased hair snapped / open in the forced wind of the beating fan') primarily connote the women (and thereby attenuate, in the image of bubbles snapping, the foam metaphor of an earlier line). They might also be read as gesturing towards the men, with their hair slicked back, ready for their night out or what the poem calls 'a caricature of machismo' (line forty-seven). The violent images ('teased', 'snapped', 'forced', 'beating') suggests that both Chicana and Japanese have historically been subjected to violent attack. It is particularly relevant in this context that this section of the poem takes place in the state of Washington on the West Coast; it was on the Western seaboard that Japanese residents were interned as a consequence of the Second World War attack on Pearl Harbor.

It is upon this complex and dispiriting background that the speaker wishes to lay a restorative narrative, to sing songs that could 'drone away / all the Mariachi bands you thought you ever heard'. She suggests that she 'could' (the conditional form is significantly provisional) share an authentic or true account with which to efface the caricature identity hitherto learnt. At this point, the syntax of the poem begins to break down. Visually, there are fractures and aporia on the page – areas or borderlands which lie *between* syntactical meaning but which are nevertheless meaning*ful* in their own way. It is precisely in these gaps, silence and borderlands that the story of Chicana subjectivity is told:

> songs that could tell you what I know
> or have learned from my people
> but for that I need words
> [. . .] words I steal
> in the dark when no one can hear me.

The final stanza of the poem explains and justifies the speaker's own traversal of the boundaries between north and south, English, Spanish and Mexican. In this manifesto for her poetics, Cervantes defends the journey north to Washington as a necessary step towards acquiring the tools (words) required to tell the story of the south. Like the migration of the sea birds, this is a strategy for survival. She *must* go north in order to speak from and for the south. Only then can she turn the conditional 'could' into 'will'.

BORDERLAND BRITAIN

These concerns emerge, too, in the work of a range of modern women poets working in and around an English poetic and cultural tradition. As Dowson and Entwistle have shown, poets from Boland and McGuckian in Ireland and Northern Ireland to Liz Lochead and Jackie Kay in Scotland, Gillian Clarke and Pascale Petit in Wales, Mimi Khalvati and Moniza Alvi from Anglo-Iranian and Anglo-Asian positions respectively, and Jean 'Binta' Breeze, Valerie Bloom and Grace Nichols from British Caribbean perspectives, are exercised in various ways by questions about origins, identity, place, power, subjectivity, language and about the boundaries which demarcate these. As Moniza Alvi puts it, writing itself is 'an act of discovery on the border where inner and outer worlds meet'.[12]

Notions of 'home' are particularly at stake in these contexts. Dowson and Entwistle argue that some women poets identify themselves with an 'often productively uncertain sense of home'. In a number of poets, 'The impulse to use place as a cultural identifier is complicated but enriched by their experience of territorial, social and linguistic alienation.'[13] In Welsh poet Gillian Clarke's 'Border', for example, as we have seen, a succession of violent metaphors reveal that 'ploughland' is 'ripped from the hill', farms are 'broken' and 'fields blur'.[14] There are no certainties of identity or place. In McGuckian's 'The Albert Chain' (1994), a history of division and pain is revisited and, more importantly, recuperated.[15] The 'chain' of the title acknowledges both the servitude of a colonised people and the inevitable links which unite coloniser and colonised, the subject and the subjected. The poem is rooted in the particular and local (in stanza one we see fruit trees and cinders from a dying fire which reinvigorate the fresh morning air), yet this peaceful bucolic scene has its sinister secrets – the fruit hanging from the bullet-marked trees is likened to terrorists, and there are references to skinned wild-cats and a dead squirrel. In stanza two, the speaker portrays herself returning to the scene of war, drawn back to her embattled country as though by the links of a chain. The return to the country is also a return to the self. It reestablishes a personal identity which is also a geographical and historical one. The speaker must relearn her country: 'how every inch of soil has been paid for / by the life of a man, the funerals of the poor'. This is also an identity which is mapped in relation to others and to the speaker's – perhaps fallible – perception of others:

> I met someone I believed to be on the side
> of the butchers, who said with tears, 'This
> is too much.'

Interestingly, McGuckian draws on a specific mythology – the story of Prometheus in stanza three – the better to locate her narrative in a framework connotative of ceaseless punishment and despair. Dowson and Entwistle suggest that the poem 'represents an undecidable space in which historical, cultural and political tensions and oppositions can be resolved and dissolved, if temporarily'.[16]

Russian poet Marina Tsvetayeva's 'The Poem of the End' evokes multiple forms of boundary. It maps a succession of meeting points – the 'single post, a point of rusting tin' which 'marks the fated place' where speaker and other (who may be lover or enemy or both) are to meet. In these sinister places – from the bleak, rusting post of part one of the poem to the bridge, which is transformed implicitly into a bed in the final section – the speaker is exposed and vulnerable. Faced with a terrible choice between life and death (the 'bridge' is metaphorically a bridge across the mythical River Styx into Hades), she finds herself torn. She is trapped in a liminal space which, although marked by crossing points, refuses to grant security or sanctuary:

> This is delirium,
> please say this bridge cannot
> end
>   as it ends.[17]

In contemporary Scottish poet Kathleen Jamie, national identity is inextricably linked with the language one speaks or, more importantly, the language one is spoken by. In 'Mr and Mrs Scotland are Dead' (1994), fragments of language – a language which is open to multiple interpretations – are all that remain.[18] The referents of the poem's title are both suggestive and elusive; 'Mr and Mrs Scotland' signify a specific or an abstract couple and stand as a synecdoche for the Scottish nation as a whole. All are being mourned; their possessions are scattered to scavengers or to the winds at the 'civic amenity landfill site'. Only traces are left behind: phrases on postcards, labels, discarded books. Yet these traces embody a history, a subjectivity, a nation and thereby a hope for the future. What should she do with these ghostly voices from the past, the speaker asks: 'Should we reach and take them?' Should she take them home in the hopes that they will regenerate a newly resurgent sense of Scottish identity, to 'open / to the light our kitchen drawers'? It is significant that this poem couches its sense of a restored nationhood precisely in the realm of the immediate, the domestic and the feminine. Elsewhere, Jamie has said that 'much of writing is about permission. I mean here the long process of becoming a poet of any authority.' She goes on to say that poetry is 'a place of engagement and consumption'.[19] In 'Mr and Mrs Scotland are Dead' she engages with, and acquires her authority from, the presence of her metonymic Scottish ancestors.

Jackie Kay's position is interesting, straddling as it does in her own words, 'two, quite distinct, but, to me, connected traditions'.[20] Kay was born in Scotland to a Scottish mother and a Nigerian father and subsequently adopted by a Scottish couple. Her work plays with the boundaries between races, ethnicities, genders, voices, classes and sexualities as, for example, in 'Close Shave', which confides, in a first-person male voice, a coal miner's love for his barber.[21] The collection from which 'Close Shave' comes, *The Adoption Papers*, begins by noting the importance of distinctions between different positions, but then spends the rest of its time precisely refusing, conflating or exchanging these positions. In 'The Tweed Hat Dream' the speaker lists distinguishing or identifying features: 'a few genes, blood, a birth. / All this bother, certificates, papers', but then asks rhetorically or otherwise: 'it is all so long ago.

Does it matter?'[22] Other poems, for example 'The Telling Part',
turn repeatedly to questions about the differences between 'real'
and other mothers, between black and white skin (does colour
matter, as 'Black Bottom' asks?).[23] Which is more important, in the
words of 'Generations': 'blood', ancestry or nation? The answer lies
in a recognition of the inextricability of all of these factors and
more. The differences which the collection opens with are finally
either so multiple, so contradictory or so mutable as to be indeci-
pherable. They refuse any definitive interpretation. Instead of
answers to questions about origins and identity, the book offers a
continuation of the enquiry and successively more questions:

> What were the faces like
> who were my grandmothers
> what were the days like
> passed in Scotland
> the land I come from.[24]

The absence of any question marks here indicates that these are
questions in the form of endless conversation, a perpetual riddle
not a specific moment of enquiry and understanding.

By the second of the two parts of *The Adoption Papers* (part one is
'The Adoption Papers', part two is 'Severe Gale Eight'), the appar-
ent certainties or binaries which anchored the earlier section (black
and white, real and adoptive, and so on) have given way to a more
shifting and indeterminate set of positions. There are love poems
spoken in the voice of a mother to her child, in the voice of a woman
to her female lover ('Pounding Rain'), in the voice of male lover to
male object ('Dance of the Cherry Blossom', 'Close Shave') and
many others. One dramatic monologue 'Mummy and Donor and
Deirdre' imagines the sequence of events which follows one child's
discovery, and announcement to his school friend, of his conception
by artificial insemination to a lesbian couple. Spoken in the interwo-
ven voices of the young child, his friend's reported comments and the
child's mother, the poem demonstrates the overlapping and confu-
sion of perspectives in any representation of origins. The complexi-
ties are not amenable to straightforward disclosure, the boundaries
which separate and define parents and children are not clear cut.

The last poem, 'The Underground Baby Case', combines apparent reportage (hence the journalistic style of the title) with confession and fairy story to offer a narrative of identity which is finally the story of its multiple, if untraceable, determinants. This mixing of genres to create a new hybrid form is, itself, a characteristic of borderland consciousness as described by Anzaldúa, Bhabha and others. 'The Underground Baby Case' works also as a narrative – or parable – of the stories we might tell ourselves in order to persuade ourselves of our origins, our place and our identity. The elegiac final lines of the poem posit a motive for such self-narration. In a kind of auto-genesis, the capacity to create a story of one's beginnings offers the capacity to beat death, positing in its place a new story of life. The sixth and final section of the poem opens with the same couplet as the first two lines of section one ('There was a couple of things / I wanted to remember'), thus indicating the indeterminacy of ends and beginnings and the circularity of the stories we tell ourselves.

SPECIFICITIES OF PLACE: ELIZABETH BISHOP

In an essay written in 2000, the poet Grace Nichols (who was born in Guyana but moved to Britain as a young adult) explains, 'The poetry I feel closest to has always been the kind that also keeps an eye on the landscape [. . .] a sense of place has always been important to me as a writer.'[25] For Nichols, place is more than the natural and visible world. It is a complex interweaving of history, community, authority and subjectivity. In the poems of *i is a long memoried woman* (1983), she explores the conditions which shape the self – specifically the colonised self.[26] The poems pit urgent life forces (the 'vengeful chi' of the opening poem, 'One Continent / To Another') with the powers of repression. Female creativity struggles again and again, as for example in 'Ala', against forces which would annihilate it. Ritual and dream sequences, such as 'One Dream', show the speaker avoiding repressive forces by making recourse to unconscious modes of expression. The language of these poems, with their musical and choral rhythms and refrains (sometimes concretised on the page as in 'Drum-Spell') and with their interwoven idioms drawn from biblical, oral and other sources, roots the poems firmly in the landscape referred to above. It is more proper, perhaps, to speak of landscapes in the plural because this is very much a poetry of motion – here of enforced movement under conditions of slavery from one continent and culture to another. It is a form of hybrid identity which the collection finally celebrates, insisting in its closing poem 'Epilogue' that, in this new place, a new subjectivity and a new language have come into being:

> I have crossed an ocean
> I have lost my tongue
> from the root of the old
> one
> a new one has sprung.

Specificities of place lie at the heart of the work of a quite different poet, Elizabeth Bishop. In successive collections, *North and South*, *Questions of Travel* and *Geography III*, themes of location and dislocation, of the experience of place and of travel between places, dominate. In a brief autobiographical sketch which Bishop wrote in 1961, she emphasises geographical change, particularly her own experiences of movement from place to place first as a displaced child (her father died when she was an infant, and her mother was hospitalised several years later; Bishop therefore spent her childhood with and between different relatives) and then as an adult who lived in the US and Brazil. This is a trajectory which, she suggests, has its roots in family history: 'My mother's family seems to have had a taste for wandering, also for writing and the arts.'[27] For Bishop, as for other poets (for example, Boland with her poem 'That the Science of Cartography is Limited'), cartography – the science of mapping – becomes central to an understanding of a gendered identity in place and time, or what Rich has termed 'a politics of location'. In Rich's words, 'I need to understand how a place on the map is also a place in history within which as a woman, a Jew, a lesbian, a feminist I am created and trying to create.'[28]

Cartography is, at bottom, a method of interpretation. It is the way in which we draw equivalences between what we see and the specific location from which we view. Moniza Alvi's poem 'I Would Like to be a Dot in a Painting by Miró' offers an abstract representation of what this process means.[29] And if, as for example the critic Leigh Gilmore suggests, the maps available to women writers and readers derive from a landscape charted by men, women may find themselves excluded or mislocated. The challenge for women is either to draw up new maps or to reconcile themselves to the challenges (and sometimes the unexpected rewards) of getting lost, as, for example, in the poems by Dickinson, Sexton and Smith discussed earlier:

> To keep from getting lost in the usual ways – frequently by over relying on traditional theories of interpretation and history which were developed to describe the literary characteristics of texts by mostly white, male, heterosexual-identified, non-working-class writers [. . .] one must follow a route of estrangement from dominant codes of meaning and look again at the micro history of cultural production and the critical histories of reception.[30]

The task for women's poetry is to develop a new cartography – one which brings place, time and subject position into convergence.

A number of Bishop's poems proceed by geographical or cartographical methods or take these as a theme. The early poems 'The Map' (1946) and 'Over 2,000 Illustrations and a Complete Concordance' (1955) are some of the most obvious examples. In other poems she is interested in anthropology and cultural difference, and is concerned as much with the process and ethics of observation as with the thing observed (what David Kalstone has accurately labelled 'the crises of observer and observed').[31] We see this interest in observation, recording and assessing in, for example, 'Questions of Travel' (1965), which closes the gap between literal and imaginative journeys. In this and many other poems, Bishop adopts the stance of uncertain observer, and invites a sense of distance, loss, solitude and isolation. This separateness is also apparent in poems which are not obviously about travel, but which centre around the same distinct outsider's look in, for example, 'In the Waiting Room' (1976), where travel pictures from the *National*

Geographic magazine are the catalyst for a sudden, momentous real-
isation of the terrifying isolation and inevitability of individuality.
In other poems, for example the earlier 'At the Fishhouses' (1955),
the closing lines indicate that all knowledge flows from the earth,
from the natural world which is shown to have vital knowledge to
impart.

To return to the theme of cartography, in 'The Fish' (1946)
Bishop's use of similes (the fish is 'like ancient wallpaper', 'like full-
blown roses', 'like feathers', 'like medals with their ribbons') shows
her attempting to find points of reference, plotting what she sees
against a fixed point of comparison, in order the better to map the
object and moment of vision. However, 'The Fish' is a poem about
the difficulties of such a process. In spite of the speaker's desire to
understand and describe or to 'plot' the fish, the fish refuses that
process and will not return her stare. Notwithstanding her best
attempts at assimilating it, at making it familiar and comprehensi-
ble (hence the similes of flowers and wallpaper quoted above), the
fish will not be humanised, will not be mapped against the points
she seeks to impose.

'The Moose' (from the 1977 collection *Geography III*), written
for Bishop's aunt in Nova Scotia, displays a strong narrative voice
which is also the voice of the curious outsider, looking at and lis-
tening to an unfamiliar (*unheimlich*, in Freud's sense of the word)
world.[32] The poem opens with a broad and abstract outline of the
scene, but it gradually narrows and sharpens its perspective, fixing
its focus in stanzas five and six on a bus and a traveller moving west.
The stanzaic form and rhyme scheme reflect the regularity and
monotony of the journey. Yet the apparent simplicity of the land-
scape (the 'narrow provinces'), sketched out in the opening stanzas,
proves misleading. The flowing narrative and the descriptive detail
generate suspense until suddenly, in stanzas twenty-two and
twenty-three, we reach a moment of climax. This moment of reve-
lation is sustained over two stanzas as though further to grip the
reader. Out of the closely observed interior and exterior landscapes
(the bus and the forest) steps the object of the poem – the moose.
Yet, like in other Bishop poems (for example, 'The Fish' or 'At the
Fishhouses'), the poem is less about the object itself than about the
human stories behind it and the moment of perception by which it

is first realised and then represented to the reader. For Thomas Travisano, it is the sense of change over time which is important:

> Her narrative technique is subtle in that it has less to do with outward events, although these are generally present, than with the quietly changing attitude of the observer as it responds to the object observed [. . .], the fish, itself unchanging, appears to undergo a transformation as the observer's eye moves over it.[33]

CONCLUSION

Lorine Niedecker's poem 'Paean to Place' exemplifies many of the issues raised above. The poem offers a compelling vision of a particular place, which is also an abstract space and is constitutive of the subject's sense of self. It opens with a vision of fluidity and receptivity, with the alliterative 'f' sounds and the spacing on the page enticing the reader's attention, inviting them to join the flow:

> Fish
>   fowl
>   flood

Before this, though, there is a brief epigraph to the text which reads: '*And the place / was water*'. This, coupled with the images of floods, fish of the sea and fowls of the air (to paraphrase the book of Genesis) suggests a primeval, elemental backdrop to this story. It is in this place that life begins. The subject does not exist alone here, and her identity is presented in relation to the mother figure (who is presented sensually in stanza two with softly sibilant sounds) and to the father who unites all three within this particular place. He is depicted in terms which draw both on the alliteration of the fluent 'f' sounds from stanza one and the soft 's' sounds of stanza two. The father, stanza three tells us:

> thru marsh fog
>   sculled down
>   from high ground
> saw her face

A 'Paean to Place' celebrates this elemental place – this place which is formed of a combination of sights, sounds, touch, memory and interpretation – and which is thus the birthplace of the writing subject. This place is uncluttered, free of vanity and desire (hence the allusions to the biblical flood). Here, the speaker finds language (the palimpsest is God's 'in the beginning was the word' from John 1: 1). Midway through the poem, she is likened to a 'solitary plover' with 'a pencil / for a wing bone' and towards the end declares, 'I possessed / the high word'. In this space, she assumes her identity and becomes empowered.[34]

SUMMARY OF KEY POINTS

- Late twentieth-century theories drawn from the field of cultural geography provide a useful lens through which to view issues of subjectivity, gender, place and space.
- Concepts of borders and boundaries have often been used to define and demarcate differences between genders and between genres.
- Poetry by women – particularly but not exclusively from colonised cultures – has taken the notion of the border as a metaphor for a specifically gendered experience.
- Theoretical work by Chicana author Gloria Anzaldúa, amongst others, provides a valuable way of theorising this borderland consciousness.
- Other women poets have drawn on the science of cartography as a way of identifying and mapping experience and subjectivity.

NOTES

1. Edward Soja, *Postmetropolis: Critical Studies of Cities and Regions* (Oxford: Blackwell, 2000), p. 6.
2. Elizabeth Grosz, 'Bodies – Cities' in *Sexuality and Space*, ed. B. Colomina (New York: Princeton Architectural Press, 1992), pp. 241–53 (p. 242).

3. Lorna Dee Cervantes, 'Freeway 280'; accessed 12 December 2006 at: http://www.poets.org/viewmedia.php/prmMID/ 15602.

4. Sara Blair, 'Cultural Geography and the Place of the Literary', *American Literary History*, 10: 3 (1998), 544–67 (545).

5. Patricia Yaeger, quoted in Blair, 'Cultural Geography', 565, n. 15. 'Alterity' means difference/otherness/being outside.

6. Rees-Jones, *Modern*, pp. 231, 232–3.

7. Anzaldúa, *Borderlands/La Frontera*.

8. Homi Bhabha, 'The Location of Culture', in Rivkin and Ryan, *Literary Theory*, pp. 936–44 (p. 937).

9. Lorna Dee Cervantes, 'Visions of Mexico', in Baym et al., *Norton Anthology of American*, p. 2834.

10. Jacques Lacan, 'The Symbolic Order', in Rivkin and Ryan, *Literary Theory*, pp. 184–9 (p. 186).

11. Anzaldúa, *Borderlands/La Frontera*, p. 5.

12. Quoted in Dowson and Entwistle, *A History*, p. 203.

13. Ibid. p. 197.

14. Gillian Clarke, 'Border', in Rees-Jones, *Modern*, p. 191.

15. Medbh McGuckian, *Selected Poems* (Oldcastle: The Gallery Press, 1997), p. 88.

16. Dowson and Entwistle, *A History*, p. 208.

17. Marina Tsvetayeva, 'The Poem of the End', trans. Elaine Feinstein, in Scott, *Bread and Roses*, pp. 172–5.

18. Kathleen Jamie, 'Mr and Mrs Scotland are Dead', in Armitage and Crawford, *Penguin Book of Poetry*, p. 415.

19. Kathleen Jamie, 'Holding Fast – Truth and Change in Poetry', in Herbert and Hollis, *Strong Words*, pp. 277–81 (pp. 277, 278).

20. Jackie Kay, quoted in Rees-Jones, *Modern*, p. 361.

21. Jackie Kay, *The Adoption Papers* (Newcastle: Bloodaxe, 1991), p. 56.

22. Ibid. p. 20.

23. Ibid. pp. 21, 24.

24. Ibid. p. 29.

25. Grace Nichols, 'The Poetry I Feel Closest To', in Herbert and Hollis, *Strong Words*, pp. 211–12 (p. 211).

26. Grace Nichols, *i is a long memoried woman* (London: Karnak House, 1983).

27. Quoted in Goldensohn, *Elizabeth Bishop*, pp. xvii–iii.
28. Quoted in Leigh Gilmore, *Autobiographics: A Feminist Theory of Women's Self-Representation* (Ithaca, NY and London: Cornell University Press, 1994), p. 7.
29. Moniza Alvi, 'I Would Like to be a Dot in a Painting by Miró' in Rees-Jones, *Modern*, p. 319.
30. Gilmore, *Autobiographics*, p. 6.
31. Quoted in Thom Gunn, *Shelf Life: Essays, Memoirs and an Interview* (London: Faber and Faber, 1996), p. 81.
32. Freud, 'The Uncanny', p. 219, n. 1.
33. Thomas Travisano, *Elizabeth Bishop: Her Artistic Development* (Charlottesville: University Press of Virginia, 1988), p. 63.
34. Lorine Niedecker, 'Paean to Place', in *The Granite Pail: Selected Poems of Lorine Niedecker*, ed. Cid Corman (Frankfort, KY: Gnomon, 1996), p. 79. Alice Oswald's recent book *Dart* (London: Faber and Faber, 2002) would also merit scrutiny in this context.

CHAPTER 7

Experimentation and Form

Here, in the final chapter, we turn to the formal and experimental qualities of poetry by women. There are a number of qualifications to make before proceeding any further. The first is to note that, as this book has already shown, poetry by women is hugely varied in tone, voice, subject matter and form. To look for any peculiarly 'feminine' choice of form might be specious. The second is to remind ourselves that the poetry by women which has received circulation, which has been published or anthologised or admitted into a newly recognised female canon is not necessarily representative of the most innovative of women's work. Although there have been exceptions (the modernist and 'Imagist' interventions of H. D. and Lowell in the twentieth century, for instance), poetry which too radically pushes the parameters of orthodox form or which deviates from the model of the brief lyric mode has struggled to acquire an audience, admission to the canon or into the anthologies from which it might derive recognition. Reading habits and publishing practices change, and innovative or atypical poetry by women of previous generations has not always remained in view. As Emily Stipes Watts remarks of the disappearance from sight of Anne Bradstreet's extensive repertoire of long poems: 'Most recent critics and anthologisers tend to favour her short "domestic" verses, those poems directed to her husband, children, or grand children, or the brief, devotional poems [. . .] The long "nondomestic" poems are generally ignored, even though they form the bulk of the first edition of *The Tenth Muse Lately Sprung Up in America* (1650).'[1] In the introduction to her important 1996 collection *Out of Everywhere: Linguistically Innovative Poetry by Women in North America and the UK*, Maggie O'Sullivan comments, 'much of the most challenging, formally progressive and significant work over recent years [. . .] is being made my women.'[2] Yet as she goes on to show, many of these poets with their non-referential, language-based poetics have been omitted from mainstream anthologies, from critical accounts and thus from a new canon of women's poetry.

This chapter, then, has two main aims. First, it enquires about women poets' appropriation and manipulation of conventional poetic modes and motifs. I will be concentrating here on the use which poets of successive generations have made of the dramatic monologue and of mythological and fairytale frameworks. Second, it investigates modern and contemporary women poets' use of innovative, avant-garde form, drawing in particular on the work of Gertrude Stein in the early part of the twentieth century and Susan Howe in the current period.

A question begged by these issues is raised implicitly by the poet Mina Loy in her 1914 'Feminist Manifesto'. Loy is speaking generally about patriarchal society, but her point is, I think, germane to poetry. Is it possible, she asks, for women effectively to write within conventions largely shaped in and by a patriarchal context? Or is it better to strike free of these traditions? 'There is no half-measure – No scratching on the surface of the rubbish heap of tradition, will bring about **Reform**, the only method is **Absolute Demolition**.'[3] The answer points to the impossibility of thinking and writing outside the structure we are in; the lines (or the geography) of this structure may be precisely what women need to explore, test and redraw.

MYTHOLOGY AND FAIRYTALE

The work of some women poets subverts expectation to comic or sardonic effect, playing with the conventions in a confident, witty or persuasive way. For example, children's fairy and folk tales and nursery rhymes, although ostensibly naive forms (and in some instances regarded as women poets' proper sphere), have been used, developed and subverted to considerable rhetorical effect by a number of poets, from Rossetti with her macabre *Goblin Market* to Stevie Smith with her low-key, sardonic 'The Frog Prince' to Duffy with her polemical *The World's Wife*. The specific points that these particular poems make – about childhood, sexuality, gender, power, authority and so on – are in a very real sense subordinate to the larger point, which is about the way expectations and conventions, or the stories we hear and tell, may be erroneous. Such poems ask the reader to pause for a moment, to rethink their lazy assumptions, to look again at what they think they know. In Sexton's 'Cinderella', for instance, the narrator of the prefatory section runs through a list of fanciful scenarios: 'You always read about it', as the poem begins, 'the plumber with twelve children / who wins the Irish Sweepstakes.'[4] Each of these imaginary flights of collective fantasy is dismissed and dispelled by the controlling narrator's repeated and apparently throwaway comment, 'That story'. Similarly Smith's 'The Frog Prince' sets up the convention in order to knock it down. The poem begins, 'The story is familiar / Everybody knows it well.' The question, as the rest of the poem proceeds to show, is whether the old story, although familiar and collective, is really to be trusted. As Smith's narrator admits, 'the stories do not tell'.[5] H. D.'s 'Helen' exposes the mythology associated with the figure of Helen of Troy, revealing the bitter truth of the hostility which, the poem imagines, underlay her subsequent elevation to the position of silent, culpable beauty.[6]

Duffy's coupling of the dramatic monologue with radically revisionary myths, fairytales and stories from popular culture is displayed to particular effect in *The World's Wife*. Here, in these witty and politically charged satires, she imagines the hidden lives of generations of overlooked women, from 'Medusa' to 'Elvis's Twin Sister', 'Mrs Quasimodo' to 'Penelope', 'Queen Kong' to 'Frau Freud'.[7] Duffy's contemporary, Jo Shapcott, works equally well in the form – as evidenced by her poems 'Tom and Jerry Visit England', 'Mrs Noah: Taken After the Flood' and the sequence of poems based on the lives of Robert and Elizabeth Barrett Browning.[8] Duffy's recent collection, *Rapture*, contains few of these kinds of poems. Nevertheless, the urge to reshape the stories which mythology offers us remains strong. In 'Hour', an immediate moment of love is rendered historically resonant, or made permanent and meaningful, by being yoked with the mythological story of Midas (hence the allusion in lines six and seven) and the fairytale 'Rumpelstiltskin'. The poem closes with a reference to the latter's account of the miller's daughter's terrible task of spinning 'gold, gold, gold from straw'.[9]

MODERNIST EXPERIMENTATION: MARIANNE MOORE

The term 'modernism', rather like 'Romanticism', is a slippery one to handle. There are problems in defining the modernist period: does it run from 1910, as Virginia Woolf famously suggested ('on or about 1910 human nature changed'), or does it have its roots rather earlier, say in the mid-Victorian period?[10] Does it continue up to the Second World War, or is modernism over by the end of the 1920s? What are the characteristics of modernist art forms?[11] Loosely, one might say that modernism is characterised by an interest in experimentation, in novelty, in innovation and, in particular, in the possibilities of melding the issues, technologies and practices of the present with those of the past. The rise of modernism coincided with a number of important cultural changes. In the light of the work of Charles Darwin, Sigmund Freud, Karl Marx and thinkers such as Friedrich Nietzsche, there was a sea change in attitudes towards hitherto sacred truths about self, society, faith, authority, language and meaning. In sum, modernity heralds a number of crises (of identity, governance, representation and so on), and modernist art responds to these challenges in multiple ways. Technological development, mechanisation, urbanisation and the beginnings of what we now recognise as globalisation all led to a rethinking of the nature of artistic representation and reception. Literature reshaped the boundaries between hitherto distinct creative forms – between poetry and painting, poetry and sculpture, literature and jazz. The high modernist period (the immediate post-First World War period through to the mid-1920s) had been regarded as being dominated by a small coterie with Eliot and

Pound as its prime movers. Of late, scholarship has identified and restored to visibility the work of a number of women writers including Mew, Loy and Wickham.

An important thread within modernism was 'imagism'. This was a poetic movement which developed under the auspices of Pound and F. S. Flint between 1908 and 1910 and which fostered the work of a number of the innovative female poets discussed in this book, notably H. D. and Lowell. In an early declaration of intent, Flint described the characteristics of imagism thus:

1. Direct treatment of the 'thing' whether subjective or objective.
2. To use absolutely no word that did not contribute to the presentation.
3. As regarding rhythm: to compose in sequence of the musical phrase not in sequence of the metronome.[12]

Imagism is characterised by the use of *vers libre*, or what Pound called 'straight talk'. It represents a radical rethinking and a radical re-presentation of experience.

At this time, Ezra Pound pronounced what has since been taken as the motto for the modernist movement: 'make it new'.[13] For Mew, H. D., Lowell, Loy, Stein and a number of others, this mantra encapsulated much more than a rethinking of poetic form; it meant, too, a revisioning of gender, sexuality, desire and subjectivity – and perhaps more importantly the language in which to represent these. It has been said of Mew, for example, the earliest of the group of writers listed above, that she 'drew on both turn-of-the-century social concerns and the new modernism's experimental techniques for the expression of subjectivity and emotion'.[14]

This clean sweep (the metaphor is, perhaps, fitting) was seized by some women poets as the opportunity entirely to rethink their world. As H. D. comments in 'Notes on Thought and Vision': 'My signposts are not yours, but if I blaze my own trail, it may help to give you confidence and urge you to get out of the murky, dead, old, thousand-times explored old world, the dead world of overworked emotions and thoughts.'[15] Celeste Schenck has argued that, for H. D., 'the notion of breaking sentence and sequence was a way of rupturing political assumptions of great pertinacity and of making a radical criticism of power and status.'[16] H. D.'s 'Lethe' (1920) illustrates the appropriation and then inversion and transgression of conventional form. 'Lethe' reads as a form of anti-elegy. Its succession of negations (particularly in stanza two with its anaphoric line openings: 'nor sight', 'nor river-yew', 'nor fragrance' and so on) refuses the consolations and thereby the expectations associated with the elegiac form.[17]

Gertrude Stein's work, from prose pieces such as *Three Lives* (1909) or *The Making of Americans* (written between 1906 and 1908 although not published until 1925) through to the poetry of *Tender Buttons* (1914), displays a fluidity, a sensitivity to the nuances of language and an unexpected because subtle precision which render the reader newly alert to the object of the text. Of her own well-known and often misquoted saying, 'Rose is a rose is a rose is a rose' (a line from the poem 'Sacred Emily'), Stein later explained:

> I notice that you all know it; you make fun of it, but you know it. Now listen! I'm no fool. I know that in daily life we don't go around saying 'is a . . . is a . . . is a . . .' Yes, I'm no fool; but I think that in that line the rose is red for the first time in English poetry for a hundred years.[18]

This process of defamiliarisation extended beyond the object of scrutiny and towards all manner of other apparent certainties – certainties of language, reference, subjectivity, gender, genre and even, in the case of *The Autobiography of Alice B. Toklas* (Stein's own life story, written by Stein in the persona of her companion Toklas), of authorship.

The work of the American poet Marianne Moore also merits scrutiny in the context of modernist experimentation. Moore was born in 1887. She was a precocious, eccentric and energetic child and a prolific writer. Her two or three times weekly letters home from college numbered as many as fifty-four pages each, and at her peak as a poet she still wrote up to fifty letters a day.[19] She was an equally prolific reader and a collector of odd snippets of information, many of which would surface (sometimes credited and explained, sometimes not) in her poems. She was a friend and early supporter of Bishop and an astute critic.

One of the many definitions of modernism is that it is a kind of writing which is 'experimental, audience challenging, and language-focused'.[20] This is a perfect description of Moore's work. Like a true modernist magpie, she draws her material from anywhere and everywhere, juxtaposing new ideas, objects and perspectives in a seemingly obscure style, often qualifying earlier thought in a sometimes mystifying way. Fellow poet and critic Randall Jarrell observed:

> She not only can, but must, make poetry out of everything and anything: she is like Midas, or like Mozart choosing unpromising themes for the fun of it, or like one of those princesses whom wizards force to manufacture sheets out of nettles.[21]

Moore, although supremely accomplished with conventional poetic form in all its variety, was unwilling to be restricted by it. In her early work, like many other modernist women such as H. D. and Loy, she developed her own styles of free verse and of syllabic verse (that is, verse which counts syllables not metrical patterns) using long prosy sentences. As Thom Gunn describes it:

> She waived the whole question of distinctions between verse and prose by treating it as simply irrelevant, and her doing so must have been deeply annoying to those who had always considered that poetry, in its rhythms, diction, and subject matter, should be in some way 'elevated'. She was obscure, learned, allusive.[22]

This is not to say that her verse is formless. Rather, she uses daring, complex, experimental forms which are not always familiar but which are nevertheless chosen with some deliberation to make an exact fit with what she wishes to say. For Moore, poetic form of whatever shape or provenance provides the skeletal support for the poem. Without it, the wonders of the imagination would be worthless. To quote Jarrell again: 'Miss Moore's forms have the lacy, mathematical extravagance of snowflakes, seem as arbitrary as the prohibitions in fairy tales; but they work as these work – disregard them and everything goes to pieces.'[23]

The form offers a challenge. The syllabic verse which she made her own relies on a predetermined number of syllables in each line, with indentations to emphasise some of the rhymes. The stanza shape fluctuates to reflect the syllabic length. Once rhyme is added, it has been described as 'one of the most restrictive measures a poet can deploy'.[24] In 'Bird-Witted' (1941) or 'The Mind is an Enchanting Thing' (1944), each stanza is often a continuous sentence; hence the cadenced flow of the language develops naturally throughout the poem, telling a story and leading the reader to a conclusion.[25] In 'The Paper Nautilus' (1941), the stanza instead of the line forms the basic unit. Many of the lines run on; the line breaks fall so as to open up the resonance of each word and phrase. For example, lines in stanza two ('white outside and smooth- / edged inner surface / glossy as the sea, the watchful') suggest that the descriptions may apply equally to the nautilus or its host the sea. This implicitly enforces their connectedness. 'The Paper Nautilus' displays internal rhyme rather than obvious and simple end-rhymes, and this adds to the ebb and flow of the poem – a movement which is entirely appropriate given its subject.

Moore's formal emphasis on syllables rather than stress (metre) allows her to be exact, faithful and detailed in her descriptions. Her close attentiveness to the tiniest, most precise elements of a thing observed have often been noted. Of her own work, Moore commented: 'Precision, economy of statement, logic employed to ends that are disinterested, drawing and identifying, liberate – or at least have some bearing on – the imagination.'[26] However, this is not the same as her contemporary William Carlos Williams's notion of 'No ideas but in things'. Her observations are not there for their own sake, but rather because, in the words of Richard Gray, she felt that 'by observing an object lovingly, she could discover significance *in* it which extended *beyond* it'.[27] Moore's interest in precise, scientific, mathematical detail has re-emerged of late in the poetry of Lavinia Greenlaw, among others.[28]

Like Bishop, Moore makes extensive use of unexpected similes, for example in 'The Mind is an Enchanting Thing'. She uses these to isolate and interrogate the bizarre but ultimately fruitful connections between apparently distinct objects, seeking comfort in proof of some kind of latent relationship or communion. 'Poetry' was first drafted as a thirty-line poem but later condensed to just three, thereby abiding by Moore's own comment in 'To A Snail' (1935) that 'compression is the first grace of style'. It suggests that the seemingly random and certainly non-judgemental assembling of all kinds of equally important and telling elements in a poem is the only way to make a truthful (for her 'genuine') and meaningful commentary on life. Poetry is important because it is concerned with the real, and if the real is made up of tiny, petty details, then this is a suitable subject for poetry. Conversely, if poetry seems to have small-scale preoccupations, this reflects the minutiae of life itself and is thus intrinsically significant. As she insists in the fourth stanza of the original version, all 'phenomena are important'. However, they only become interesting when tempered by the full poet (as distinct from 'half poets') who retains an ability to 'present' (line twenty-three) the 'genuine' with poetic trimmings (' "imaginary gardens with real toads in them" ').

CONTEMPORARY AVANT-GARDE POETICS

Contemporary 'avant-garde', innovative or 'Language'-based poetry by women is radical and disruptive, not only in its engagement with poetic form and convention, but in its rethinking of the nature and representation of gender identity. It has achieved a reputation for abstraction and complexity, and seems, on the surface at least, to have little in common with 'mainstream' poetry by women and little to say about the kinds of issues which a feminist criticism might value. However, this would be a misreading of the political nuances of the work. To quote Linda Kinnahan, such poets 'often see their work in terms of a larger feminist project to reveal relationships between structures of language and power, particularly as these shape constructions of gender and affect the material lives of women'.[29]

Initially, the most striking aspect of this radical and experimental poetry is its apparent impenetrability. To take as just one example Susan Howe's 'A Bibliography of the King's Book or, Eikon Basilike', the first thing we will observe is the material strangeness of the poem on the page.[30] The lines of text criss-cross horizontally and vertically although at oblique angles, none of which are exactly perpendicular with any of the four edges of the page. The space and the words are absolutely indispensable to each other; they define each other's meaning and thus the meaning of the poem as a whole. The first vertical line ('first' if we read as per conventional Western practice from left to right, itself a practice which is put to the challenge by this form) refers to the process of stepping 'between' and to a 'Brazen Wall'. The very structure of the poem with its multiple gaps and in-between spaces, with its own flamboyantly self-imposed barrier to access and comprehension, presents precisely that which it describes – a 'Brazen Wall'. Thereafter, key words ('Court', 'Justice', 'Chair', 'Heroic' and so on) stand out from the text. These are capitalised wherever they appear (medial capitalisation), not only, as has become conventional in poetry set for the page, at the beginnings of lines. Curiously, 'A Bibliography of the King's Book or, Eikon Basilike' seems to set up a succession of binaries ('Language' and 'secrets', 'Justice' and 'Injustice') which it simultaneously confounds. There the 'secrets' speak; 'Justice' is a mere façade (a 'pretended court') while 'Injustice' prevails.

The second section of the poem, headed 'ENGELANTS MEMORIAEL', while more familiar in form on the page, similarly refuses interpretation by any conventional means. It reads like a fragment of description in which what is being described remains elusive or opaque. The patronymic (or bestowal of identity through male-engendered naming) fails; we are told of 'Similar' but 'not identical' portraits, but the names of those described (is it one sitter? Two? More?) are run on typographically and thus incomprehensible to us. Without punctuation or without some system of order on the page, the identity or identities of the object/s remain hidden.

The subsequent parts of the poem, which are printed consecutively at 180 degrees to each other (that is, upside down), repeat sections and phrases from part one ('brazen wall', for instance), albeit this time in lower case letters. Words are printed at multiple and jagged angles, sometimes running across each other such that strange phonemes are engendered (pi, yH) or obliterated. Certain terms do remain and catch the eye, 'blood' at the top of the page; the repeated words 'populacy', 'populacy', 'O make me / of Joy' in the top right-hand side and 'Obligation' in the bottom right-hand corner. The effect of the internal repetitions (that is, the reproduction of the same page twice) is to demonstrate that meaning is contingent on the reading process, on the position of text on page, and on our perception of originality. For a moment, when we realise that this is the same text twice, we are wrong-footed. This so radically challenges our expectations of poetry, of authorial responsibility, of authenticity and value and any number of other cornerstones of cultural life that we are left without any understanding of how we might deal with it. A repetition such as this is, one more typically might assume, a mistake – and thus the poem forces us to rethink our perception of error and intention. This particular 'mistake' (the fact that this section of text is repeated upside down) requires us, too, to re-evaluate our sense of any number of other binary poles – top and bottom, up and down, back and front, right and wrong. The next section of the poem, too, concentrates on error. Densely printed on the page with three lines at 90 degrees to each other and five lines printed in the opposite direction to most, the poem highlights the possibly self-referential terms 'faults', 'Gaol' and 'apology'.

Finally and unexpectedly, in the closing sections of the poem, we see the whole rooted in historical circumstances – the 1648–9 trial and execution of Charles I. In solemn language, the poem introduces us to the scene, although this is disrupted again by the repetition of confused lines from sections three and four. Now, for the first time, we have named speakers or *dramatis personae* (Dr Juxon and the king), and some of the displaced words from earlier sections are restored into what we might once have read as their rightful position, an assumption which we might now wish to rethink.

The last two sections function in two ways. First, as a form of blessing, a strange elegy for the executed king: 'kneeling / Old raggs about him'. Second, as an elegy for language itself, now 'torn among fragments'. Most importantly, though, it functions as a celebration and confirmation of its own poetics: 'this still house', it affirms, in an 'unbeaten way' remains to have the last word. Even – or especially – fragments, as this poem has shown, are ripe with rich meaning, with 'Emblems gold and lead'. The closing three lines register the importance of the speaker's task. The 'I' here takes centre stage. She foregrounds her marginality (she is 'outside' and must transcend 'space') in order to tell this story, to give it voice. Telling stories, the closing line suggests, is to *create*, not simply to reflect, meaning. This is 'poetry as making or praxis rather than poetry as impassioned speech, as self-expression', to quote Marjorie Perloff's observation about contemporary avant-garde poetries in general.[31]

The poem is inextricably – if unexpectedly – political. It enquires about the processes by which meanings are produced and read. It shows a masculine form of authority (hence king, high court and naval militia) literally in pieces, scattered across the page. So too subjectivity (and here Howe draws on a persuasive modern trend in philosophical, psychoanalytical, feminist thought) is to be understood as both diffuse and contingent on language, hence the association of 'my self and words'. For Peter Middleton, Howe's work is 'a paradigm of that kind of formal literary experiment which uses linguistic disruption to challenge the existing symbolic order'.[32] The poem asserts, in the end, the power of language over history, and it demands a new form of reading. Such poetry requires us, in O'Sullivan's terms, to 'critique the meaning of authority, the reading of history, to undertake a radical revision of both meaning and history, and of the hegemonic alliances that have excluded certain groups of actors – women, American Indians – from those histories, those lawbooks'.[33]

Contemporary Californian poet Leslie Scalapino's 'New Time' also problematises chronology, subjectivity, perception and reference in its evocation of an uncanny and indeterminate world which is part desire, part nightmare.[34] The referent of the poem is perpetually deferred or displaced such that from the outset the reader is unclear who or what the poem designates. 'New Time' is interesting in part because – like much experimental poetry – it forces us as readers to recognise our own habitual expectations and practices. As with the Howe poem above, we first attempt and then have to abandon conventional ways of reading. The radical form of the text notwithstanding, we must concede that our first (and arguably our *only*) reading strategy entails an attempt to identify familiar poetic elements and, with these firmly pinned down, to make the poem assimilable to real, recognisable, external reference. As British poet and critic Veronica Forrest-Thomson explained of the problem of trying to naturalise or translate poetry such as this into an easily comprehensible language: 'The attempt to relate the poem to the external world limits our attention to those formal features which can be made to contribute to this extended meaning.' In doing this, we risk a 'blindness to the complexity of those non-meaningful features which differentiate poetry from everyday language and make it something other than an external thematic statement about an already-known world'.[35]

In Scalapino's 'New Time', apprehension, in the sense of understanding, is a synaesthetic phenomenon. We are made to see, hear and touch the object of the text:

> silk black iris that's chest
> thorax lifted off (set down:
> weighing) it doesn't come
> from them – is lifted off breathing.

A deeply sensuous poem, the narrative circles around and around its object, touching it, glancing off it and then moving away – hence the blocks of space on the page. The blanks punctuate moments of communication.

The poem is explicitly and polymorphously sexual; it refuses to identify in conventional binary terms which gender or what kinds of sexuality are being invoked. The 'black oar parting the blue' perhaps signifies a male-dominated heterosexual act; the 'bud-outside-but which is fully open' may connote female and/or male sexuality. Earlier in the poem, allusions to the moon, to buds and to the 'bulb' arguably favour the former reading. Similarly, the 'black silk irises' and 'voluptuous lips' of the closing section might be said to signify a fecund female sexuality – particularly when read alongside Luce Irigaray's invocation of the same:

> A woman touches herself by and within herself directly, without mediation, and before any distinction between activity and passivity is possible. A woman 'touches herself' constantly without anyone being able to forbid her to do so, for her sex is composed of two lips which embrace continually. Thus within herself she is already two – but not divisible into ones – who stimulate each other.[36]

Scalapino's poem exemplifies a poetics of *différance* (in Derrida's sense of both differentiation and deferral). Meaning, identity and gender are all shown to be shifting, elusive and contingent. In the words of 'New Time': 'Why should they dismiss it because it's not the same? / It *exists* because it's not the same.' We might extrapolate from this that masculinity and femininity are mutually constitutive and mutually defining. To accept a hierarchy is to overlook the mutuality of the construction. The poem also obliquely raises questions about identity politics or about the kind of essentialism which would confidently mobilise a homogenous group identity. Here 'people' are seen as other to and separate from 'I':

> what's coming is people attacking as
> sustaining their being in existence.
> the one black oar parting the blue in fact –
> it is conditional on spring.
> I am.

The poem plays with the *cogito ergo sum*; it gives us the *sum* ('I am') but omits the *cogito ergo* ('I think therefore). Subjectivity is a function of existence within a network or structure; it is not a function of an inner essence, intelligence or consciousness. The poem concludes on an appropriately questioning and provisional note: 'the inner isn't contending either . . .?'

Other avant-garde poetries of this period refuse to name the subject 'I', or they experiment with the conventions by refiguring it in various ways. Contemporary Los Angeles poet Wanda Coleman's poetry does this to particular effect, questioning the status and authority of the subject 'I' by the insistent use of the lower case 'i'.[37] Contemporary British poet Denise Riley's poem 'A Note on Sex and the Reclaiming of Language' puzzles out the distinction (if there is one) between 'she' and 'I'. This is a poem, above all, about processes of representation, and it is notable how often that prefix 're' is used throughout the poem, as though to emphasise that there is no original, there are only successive and sometimes misplaced attempts to re-present (re-inhabit, re-possess) it. Such a strategy 'avoids essentialism and remakes these tiny particles [the "I" or "i"] as vehicles that can represent women as subjects'.[38] Similarly, Harriet Tarlo has shown that Ntozake Shange's long poem *for coloured girls who have considered suicide when the rainbow is enuf* (1978) interweaves multiple voices and subjectivities, some fixed, others indeterminate, to create a new 'feminine gender and genre through voice and movement'.[39] Riley is explicit about the strange convention by which the 'I' comes to stand for a whole host of – in fact indeterminate – things. Her poem 'Dark Looks' asks: 'What forces the lyric person to put itself on trial though it must stay rigorously uninteresting'. She is also curious about what happens, in linguistic, representational and interpretative terms, when punctuation is used in unconventional places to draw attention to the distinction between self, gender and context. As the poem 'Affections Must Not' concludes, 'I. neglect. the house'.[40]

CONCLUSION

There has been a long history of experimentation in women's poetry (or what Veronica Forrest-Thompson calls the 'tradition of innovation').[41] To take up the pen at all has been, as this book has shown, a radical and transgressive gesture. From Sappho to Margaret Cavendish, from Anne Bradstreet to Phillis Wheatley, from Ann Yearsley to Jackie Kay, from Emily Dickinson to Susan Howe, from Elizabeth Barrett Browning with her 'sort of novel poem' *Aurora Leigh* to Australian poet/novelist Dorothy Porter with her thriller-in-verse *The Monkey's Mask* (1994), women have unsettled and disrupted poetic conventions and readerly expectations.[42] For some critics, for example Jane Dowson, it is precisely in this contestatory relationship with tradition that the definition of a female poetics might be found.[43]

SUMMARY OF KEY POINTS

- The variety of women's poetic practice should be noted, as should some of the material constraints on its full development and exposure.

- Women have worked in implicit and explicit ways to revise some of the conventions attached to specific forms (such as the fairy-tale, the elegy and the dramatic monologue).
- Women poets have been central to the development of modernist and imagist poetics. More recently, the interests of women's poetry have converged with those of 'Language' and post-modern poetry; all ask questions about subjectivity, language and reference.

NOTES

1. Emily Stipes Watts, 'The posy UNITY: Anne Bradstreet's Search for Order', in *Puritan Influences in American Literature*, ed. Emory Elliott (Champaign, IL: University of Illinois Press, 1979), pp. 23–37 (p. 23).
2. Maggie O'Sullivan, *Out of Everywhere: Linguistically Innovative Poetry by Women in North America and the UK* (London: Reality Street Editions, 1996), p. 9.
3. Loy, *Lost Lunar*, p. 153.
4. Sexton, *Complete*, p. 255.
5. Stevie Smith, 'The Frog Prince', in *Stevie Smith: A Selection*, ed. Hermione Lee (London: Faber and Faber, 1983), p. 158.
6. H. D. *Selected*, p. 48.
7. Carol Ann Duffy, *The World's Wife* (London: Picador, 1999).
8. Shapcott, *Her Book*, pp. 39, 99, 25–33.
9. Duffy, *Rapture*, p. 7.
10. Virginia Woolf, 'Mr. Bennett and Mrs. Brown', in *Collected Essays: Volume One* (London: Hogarth Press, 1971), pp. 319–37.
11. See Peter Brooker (ed.), *Modernism/Postmodernism* (Harlow: Longman, 1992) for an overview of these debates.
12. F. S. Flint, 'Imagisme', quoted in Richard Gray, *American Poetry of the Twentieth Century* (Harlow: Longman, 1990), p. 54.
13. See also T. S. Eliot's 1917 essay, 'Reflections on *Vers Libre*'; accessed 12 December 2006 at: http://www.usask.ca/english/prufrock/reflect.htm. Quoted in *Imagist Poetry*, ed. Peter

Jones (Harmondsworth: Penguin, 1972), p. 17. See also Ezra Pound, 'A Retrospect', reprinted in *Twentieth-Century American Poetics*, ed. Dana Goia, David Mason and Meg Schoerke (Boston, MA: McGraw Hill, 2004), pp. 63–71.

14. Parsons, *Farmer's Bride*, p. ix.

15. H. D., 'Notes on Thoughts and Vision', in *The Gender of Modernism: A Critical Anthology*, ed. Bonnie Kime Scott (Bloomington: Indiana University Press, 1990), pp. 93–109 (p. 96).

16. Celeste Schenck, quoted in Dowson, *Women, Modernism*, p. 139.

17. H. D., 'Lethe', in *Selected Poems of H. D.* (New York: Grove Press, 1957), p. 51.

18. Quoted in Jackson Ford, *Gender*, p. 84.

19. See Marianne Moore, *Selected Letters of Marianne Moore*, ed. Bonnie Costello, Celeste Goodridge and Cristanne Miller (London: Faber and Faber, 1998), pp. ix–xv.

20. Quoted in Kime Scott, *The Gender of Modernism*, p. 4.

21. Randall Jarrell, *Poetry and the Age* (London: Faber and Faber, 1973), p. 162.

22. Gunn, *Shelf Life*, p. 40.

23. Jarrell, *Poetry*, p. 163.

24. Michael Schmidt, *Lives of the Poets* (London: Weidenfeld and Nicolson, 1998), p. 607.

25. Marianne Moore, *Complete Poems* (London: Faber and Faber, 1984).

26. 'Interview with Marianne Moore', in Plimpton, *Women Writers*, pp. 3–31 (p. 9).

27. Gray, *American Poetry*, p. 186.

28. See, for example, *Night Photograph* (London: Faber and Faber, 1993).

29. Linda Kinnahan, 'Looking for the Doing Words', in Acheson and Huk, *Contemporary British Poetry*, p. 247.

30. Susan Howe, 'A Bibliography of the King's Book or, Eikon Basilike', in O'Sullivan, *Out of Everywhere*, pp. 11–18. In c. 1640, Charles I is thought to have written *Eikon basilike* ('On the Divine Right of Kings'). John Milton's *Eikonoklastes* (1649) offers a riposte.

31. Marjorie Perloff, 'The Changing Face of Common Intercourse: Talk Poetry, Talk Show, and the Scene of Writing', in *Artifice and Indeterminacy: An Anthology of New Poetics*, ed. Christopher Beach (Tuscaloosa: University of Alabama Press, 1998), pp. 77–106 (p. 93).

32. Peter Middleton, 'On Ice: Julia Kristeva, Susan Howe and avant garde poetics', in *Contemporary Poetry Meets Modern Theory*, ed. Antony Easthope and John O. Thompson (Hemel Hempstead: Harvester, 1991), pp. 81–95 (pp. 81–2).

33. O'Sullivan, *Out of Everywhere*, p. 240.

34. Leslie Scalapino, 'New Time', in O'Sullivan, *Out of Everywhere*, pp. 232–8.

35. Veronica Forrest-Thomson, *Poetic Artifice: A Theory of Twentieth-Century Poetry* (Manchester: Manchester University Press, 1978), pp. xii, xi.

36. Irigaray, 'This Sex', p. 100.

37. For a selection of Wanda Coleman's poetry, see *Postmodern American Poetry: A Norton Anthology*, ed. Paul Hoover (New York: Norton, 1994), pp. 474–80.

38. Mark and Rees-Jones, *Contemporary*, p. xviii.

39. Harriet Tarlo, ' "A She Even Smaller than a Me": Gender Dramas of the Contemporary Avant-Garde', in Mark and Rees-Jones, *Contemporary*, pp. 247–68 (p. 268).

40. Denise Riley, 'Dark Looks' and 'Affections Must Not', in *Selected Poems* (London: Reality Street Editions, 2000), pp. 74, 20.

41. Quoted in Mark and Rees-Jones, *Contemporary*, p. 64.

42. Barrett Browning, *Aurora Leigh*, pp. 5–6; Dorothy Porter, *Monkey's Mask* (London: Serpent's Tail, 1997).

43. Dowson, *Women, Modernism*, p. viii.

Conclusion

Chapter 1 of this book began by citing Isobel Armstrong's comment about women poets problematising rather than polemicising their situation. I want to close by quoting Harriet Tarlo, who insists on the importance of the sometimes difficult – because unconventional – experimental poetry discussed in the last chapter:

> A woman's poetry which asks 'who am I? what am I? as a woman?' as experimental poetry so often does, should be at least as widely read as one which is based on identity politics and which is more likely to say, 'here I am, listen to me, as a woman!'[1]

It is this self-conscious, deliberate and productive problematisation, rather than any straightforward proselytising, which makes this such a dynamic and fascinating field. And it is this shift from a securely identity-based poetics (characteristic of the second wave feminist movement of the 1960s to the early 1980s) to an aesthetic which is marked by difference, displacement, liminality and elusiveness which perhaps signals the next step for women's poetry.

In order to speculate further about the future of women's poetry, we need to understand something about the changing nature of modern feminism. It is commonplace to define current thinking in the field as belonging either to a 'post-feminist' movement or to a 'third wave' of feminism. Both are difficult to define. The concept of 'post-feminism' provokes strong debate, as evidenced by the reaction which met the publication of the first edition of Carol Rumens's anthology *Making for the Open: Post-Feminist Poetry*. As Rumens explains in the introduction to the revised edition of the book:

> When *Making for the Open* first appeared in 1985, its sub-title excited a great deal of comment, much of it hostile. 'Post-Feminist' was commonly misconstrued as 'anti-feminist'. At best, it was perceived to be the tacit declaration that feminism as a political force was obsolete, either because Utopia had already been achieved or because it had been judged to be unobtainable [. . .] I had tried to anticipate some of these objections in my introduction, and sometimes it was hard not to feel that it had either not been read, or that it had been wilfully misread by the politically motivated.[2]

The term 'post-feminism' tends to be defined in two key (and contradictory) ways. It is often popularly taken to refer to the interests and perspectives of a generation of women for whom feminism no longer has any relevance. It is associated with the 'backlash' against the women's movement so persuasively indicted by Susan Faludi in her 1991 book, *Backlash: The Undeclared War Against Women*.[3] As Gillis et al. explain, 'post-feminism' is a term 'that discursively (and recursively) distances multiple cohorts of young women after 1980 from those who participated in the "feminist" decades of the sixties and seventies'.[4] For Kristyn Gorton it describes a shift from 'a "we" solidarity of the 1960s and 1970s to a "me"-based feminism in the twenty-first century'.[5] Ann Brooks, amongst others, reads the term in an entirely different and wholly more positive way. From this perspective, 'post-feminism' (or more properly 'post-feminisms': the use of the plural form registers diversity within the field) provides 'a useful conceptual frame of reference encompassing the intersection of feminism with a number of other anti-foundationalist movements including postmodernism, post-structuralism and post-colonialism'. It represents, Brooks goes on to say, feminism's 'maturity into a confident body of theory and politics, representing pluralism and difference'. It critically engages with 'patriarchal and imperialist discourses', and it is deeply concerned with exploring contradiction and dislocation.[6]

The term 'third wave feminism' is also contentious. It implies – but does not clearly specify – a relationship to the second wave movement which preceded it. More importantly, perhaps, it implies a changed relationship to many of the categories and certainties that second wave feminism was grounded in and finally – in the work of Judith Butler and others – came to reject. As Gillis et al. explain, ultimately

> the concept 'woman' seemed too *fragile* to bear the weight of all contents and meanings ascribed to it. The elusiveness of this category of 'woman' raised questions about the nature of identity, unity and collectivity. Appearing to undercut the women's movement, fundamental principles of the feminist movement were hotly contested. What we now understand as the 'third wave' emerges from these contestations – and the responses to them.[7]

To this extent, 'third wave' feminism connotes a deeply self-reflexive and self-critical set of debates.

As this indicates, there are crossovers between current forms of feminism – whichever label we choose to use – and the renegotiation or critique of the dominant modes of thinking outlined in this book (particularly the binary logic which sees clearly demarcated boundaries between men and women, good and bad, public and private). The self-reflexivity which I earlier suggested is one of the defining tropes of women's writing thus retains its place as an important aspect of a female poetics and of a feminist politics. If the future of poetry, and the future of feminism, lie in a self-conscious reflection on the various processes by which subjectivity is constructed and meaning is produced and received, then women's poetry is well situated to continue its exploration of what it means to be, in the words of Anne Sexton's 'The Black Art', a 'woman who writes'.[8]

NOTES

1. Harriet Tarlo, 'Provisional Pleasures: The Challenge of Contemporary Experimental Women Poets', *Feminist Review*, 62 (1999), 94–112 (99).
2. Carol Rumens, *Making for the Open: Post-Feminist Poetry*, rev. edn (London: Chatto and Windus, 1987), p. xiv.
3. Susan Faludi, *Backlash: The Undeclared War Against Women* (London: Chatto and Windus, 1992).
4. Stacy Gillis, Gillian Howie and Rebecca Munford (eds), *Third Wave Feminism: A Critical Exploration* (Basingstoke: Macmillan, 2004).
5. Kristyn Gorton, '(Un)fashionable Feminists: The Media and *Ally McBeal*', in Gillis et al., *Third Wave*, pp. 154–63 (p. 156).
6. Ann Brooks, *Postfeminisms: Feminism, Cultural Theory and Cultural Forms* (London: Routledge, 1997), pp. 1, 2, 10.
7. Gillis et al., *Third Wave*, p. 1.
8. Sexton, 'The Black Art', *Complete*, p. 88.

Student Resources

CRITICAL CONTEXTS

Scholars, students and readers of women's poetry in the present day are inevitably indebted to the careful and tenacious researches of a number of earlier commentators. Cora Kaplan's critical anthology *Salt and Bitter and Good: Three Centuries of English and American Women Poets*, first published in 1975, was innovative and influential in its selection of the work of a range of otherwise overlooked women writers from Anne Bradstreet and Katherine Philips through Felicia Hemans and Christina Rossetti to Louise Bogan, Stevie Smith and Sylvia Plath. Appearing at around the same time as Kaplan's book was Louise Bernikow's *The World Split Open: Women Poets 1552–1950* (published in the US in 1974 and the UK in 1979). The book is frank in its aims. As the first sentence of the prefatory 'Editor's Note' explains: 'I have tried in this book to uncover a lost tradition in English and American poetry.' In this respect both Bernikow's book and Kaplan's belong alongside the simultaneous work of Ellen Moers, Sandra M. Gilbert and Susan Gubar, Elaine Showalter and numerous others in bringing to light hitherto silenced and unknown women writers.

In the decade which followed these pioneering collections of primary sources came a number of books whose aim was to explicate their significance, specifically from a feminist perspective. In the United States, Sandra M. Gilbert and Susan Gubar supplemented the influential work of *The Madwoman in the Attic* with their 1979 collection of essays *Shakespeare's Sisters*. In the United Kingdom, Jan Montefiore published *Feminism and Poetry: Language, Experience, Identity in Women's Writing*. This first appeared in 1987 and attempted to marry new ideas arising in feminist criticism (particularly ideas about language, subjectivity and the body emerging from the French feminist tradition) with a study of hitherto overlooked poetry by women. A revised and enlarged edition, now extending its initial debates to the study of postcolonial women's poetry, appeared in 2004. These early studies have been supplemented by a number of others (particularly influential interventions in the field are noted below) and by a wealth of period and/or author-specific studies, collections and anthologies.

Primary among my own debts in writing this book have been Robyn Bolam's comprehensive, accessible and informed *Eliza's Babes: Four Centuries of Women's Poetry in English c. 1500–1900* (2005) and Marion Wynne-Davies's *Women Poets of the Renaissance* (1998), which performs a similar service for a more specific period. It is important also to mention Paula R. Feldman's indispensable 1997 anthology *British Women Poets of the Romantic Era* and two books by Isobel Armstrong – *Victorian Poetry: Poetry, Poetics and Politics* and the co-edited (with Joseph Bristow and Cath Sharrock) anthology *Nineteenth-Century Women Poets* (1996). Deryn Rees-Jones's *Consorting with Angels: Essays on Modern Women Poets* with its companion anthology *Modern Women Poets* (both 2005) and Vicki Bertram's scholarship, first in the special edition of *Feminist Review* which she edited in 1999 and more recently in her book *Gendering Poetry: Contemporary Women and Men Poets* (2005), have helped to reshape perceptions of the field of women's poetry in the twenty-first century. The last commences a timely move beyond what Isobel Armstrong elsewhere calls 'the trap of a narrow identity politics' and towards a broader sense of gender and poetry.[1] Rees-Jones's work, in both of the volumes mentioned above and in her co-edited collection

---

1 Armstrong, 'Preface', in Mark and Rees-Jones, *Contemporary*, pp. xv–xx (p. xvii).

Contemporary Women's Poetry: Reading/Writing/Practice (2000), shows the huge potential of new poststructuralist and cultural materialist theories to an understanding of the field. As Mark and Rees-Jones explain, their interest in editing *Contemporary Women's Poetry* is in presenting work which challenges the orthodox perceptual distinction 'between the expressive and the discursive constructions of the poetic subject, articulating the fictionality of the poetic "I", even at its most biographical, while closely examining contextual material which attests to the historical, social, and political specificity of that "I"'.[2] Also important has been Jane Dowson and Alice Entwistle's major study *A History of Twentieth-Century British Women's Poetry* (2005), which restores to view and offers nuanced readings of a wealth of poets whose work has otherwise been eclipsed.

STUDYING POETRY

Writing an essay on poetry can seem daunting to some students. It may be that the language and techniques of poetry seem so alien, so disconnected from the 'ordinary' language of everyday speech or of the prose essay, that it is difficult to see how to reconcile the two forms. It may be that the powerful or unfamiliar ideas and experiences which poetry projects are not easily assimilable into the focused argument that the academic essay often requires. For some students, an anxiety about the terminology of poetry criticism acts as a stumbling block. For others, it is the fear of losing the pleasure of poetry in any attempt to unpick its secrets – or 'unweave' its 'rainbow' as John Keats's *Lamia* put it – that stifles their own work.

We might think of all of these as problems of translation – of language and interpretation – and thus as repetitions of the poetic process itself. How does the poet synthesise ideas, experiences, perceptions, arguments and conventions and translate them into the language of poetry? Thereafter, how do readers, students and critics synthesise their own ideas, experiences, perceptions, arguments and conventions into the alternative form of the essay? If readers

2 Mark and Rees-Jones, *Contemporary*, p. xxiii.

and poets share a problem (that of translation) then it is possible that they share a solution, and it is a solution which might comes from the same source – from language. The starting point of any good essay on poetry must be in the language of the text itself. This is particularly germane when one is studying poetry, as in this book, in the context of a larger set of cultural or ideological frameworks. It would be a mistake – and a disservice to the poetic text – to concentrate exclusively on the broader frameworks or, by a similar token, to treat the poetry as documentary evidence for some larger argument (about oppression, say, or maternity).

The task for the student of poetry in contexts such as these is, first, to read and comprehend the poetry – drawing where necessary to an understanding of the primary source on a range of conventions, traditions, historical and, where appropriate, biographical contexts. I suggest 'biographical contexts' with caution because, as has already been made clear, it is a temptation, but nevertheless a mistake, to unthinkingly conflate poet with speaker, biographical experience with text. Studies of the work of Plath offer a classic example of some of the limitations of such an approach. If one studies Plath's work with what is known of her biographical circumstances at the forefront of one's mind – biographical circumstances which, themselves, come to us in textual form and are as constructed and as mediated as the poetry itself – one will end up in a ceaseless circular argument about causes and consequences. This will almost entirely obliterate the poetry itself. Where it is helpful to draw on extraneous material (interviews, journals and so on), it is necessary to apply as judicious and critical a mind as it is with the poetry itself; one must read this material just as one would read the poetry – with an eye to its structures, strategies, conventions, contexts and modes of meaning generation. Nevertheless, as for example in the case of Bishop, it is helpful to know something of her peripatetic life to fully appreciate the images of travel, cartography and location in her work. For Rossetti, it is valuable to know a little of her experience in visiting Victorian homes for fallen women to fully appreciate the complex morality of *Goblin Market*. It is the task of the student to decipher, assess and synthesise material from this diverse range of sources – with the poetry itself assuming primacy.

CLOSE READING

The starting point of a good essay, then, is a close reading of the poem. There are, of course, as many ways of reading a poem as there are readers, but below are some techniques which students might find helpful both for 'unseen' critical analyses (the kinds of assessment paper which ask the student to comment on a poem or section of a poem previously unknown to them) and for assessed essays or 'term papers' which ask them to comment on – and often compare – a number of poems studied during the course. In every case, it is useful to read the poem aloud before beginning to prepare a commentary on it; in this way elements which are not visible on the page will become clear to the ear.[3]

Reaction

1. Record your first, instant, personal reaction to the text. Jot down your first ideas and responses, making quick and informal notes.
2. Use your notes as a way into a more detailed appraisal, drawing together related points and signalling further areas of enquiry, especially as regards the formal properties of the poem or its cultural context.
3. Produce a fuller, more considered, written analysis of the text exploring in full all the areas identified above.

Paraphrase

1. Paraphrase the text in prose. This is not a brief summary of its meaning, but a translation from poetry into prose of the body of the poem. Pay particular attention to ambivalent parts.
2. What do we lose (or gain) in the prose version?
3. What does this tell us about the 'poetic' techniques at play? About the impact of imagery, rhythm, rhyme, form and so

---

3 I am indebted to B. A. Phythian's *Considering Poetry: An Approach to Criticism* (London: Hodder and Stoughton, 1970), pp. 3–12 where the 'reaction' and 'paraphrase' techniques outlined here are first delineated.

on? Use the insights from this exercise as a starting point towards an understanding of the way in which the poem works.

Question

1. Approach the poem by placing it under interrogation. Ask questions of every element, particularly the parts which seem most challenging or obtuse.
2. Questions might include: What does the poem convey? (Who, what, where, why?) What is the significance of the title? How does the text work? (Metaphor, rhyme, imagery, dialogue, drama, rhythm?)
3. Does the poem succeed? How? Why (not)? Again, use the insights of this approach to draft a fuller reading of the poem.

Of all of the above tactics (and there are many more), of particular note is the importance of reading every element of the text – from the significance of the title to the sequences of images, from the use of alliteration or anaphora to the variation in the rhythm. In every case, it is necessary not just to identify a particular metre or rhyme scheme or style of punctuation, but to say what effect that device has on the meaning of the poem. In Bishop's 'The Fish', for example, one might notice the use of similes, but one needs also to comment on their effectiveness or interpret their significance. In every case, it is necessary to have to hand a good guide to the technical conventions – or poetics – of the text. Over time and with practice many of these (the difference between the iambic and spondaic foot, for example) will become easily recognisable. As a student, it is helpful to remain alert to the appearance and effect of these conventions, and to know where and how to identify and name them. It is important, too, to read the poem's distinctive elements and then to reread the text as a whole; how do effects achieved in one line, stanza or section anticipate, develop or contradict effects achieved elsewhere? Where individual poems are taught within the context of the collections in which they were originally published, it is useful to consider the relationship of the individual text to the sequence as a whole.

Finally, a very productive way into an apparently difficult poem, as I indicate in the 'questioning' approach above, is to start with the most difficult word, phrase or section. It is often in the most opaque part of the poetry that its most interesting elements lie.

Helpful Resources

Boland, Eavan and Mark Strand (eds), *The Making of a Poem: A Norton Anthology of Poetic Forms* (New York: Norton, 2001).

Deutsch, Babette, *Poetry Handbook* (London: Cape, 1965).

Furniss, Tom and Michael Bath (eds), *Reading Poetry: An Introduction* (Harlow: Longman, 1996).

Lennard, John, *The Poetry Handbook*, 2nd edn (Oxford: Oxford University Press, 2005).

Phythian, B. A. (ed.), *Considering Poetry: An Approach to Criticism* (London: Hodder and Stoughton, 1970).

Strachan, John and Richard Terry, *Poetry* (Edinburgh: Edinburgh University Press, 2000).

WRITING ABOUT POETRY

When preparing an assessed essay on women's poetry, begin by thinking carefully through the questions that have been set, selecting a 'short list' of possible choices, and brainstorming some initial responses to each of these. From this possible short list, choose the question that most interests you and that stimulates ideas and arguments which you wish to pursue. Take the time to familiarise yourself with the aims, outcomes and assessment criteria for your course; this will give you a clear idea of what is expected of each piece of assessed work. When you have chosen your question, spend some time analysing the terms of the question, ensuring that you have a full understanding of what is being asked, and that you have defined its key concepts and ideas. It is useful to take the time to refamiliarise yourself with all of the course material; only when you have done this should you select the primary sources which you will be writing about. Reread the primary material several times over, taking notes in relation to the issues suggested by your chosen question. Select your secondary material carefully. Some useful websites are suggested below, but as always it is important to be judicious in your use of internet material; there is no substitute for your own reading of the poetry itself, and there is a wealth of reputable scholarly material available in print. If you read around the subject throughout the course, you will be better prepared at assessment time and you will have an enriched understanding of the texts and issues.

Plan your essay carefully and allow sufficient time to revise, edit and rewrite your material. It is helpful sometimes to write the essay title on a 'post-it' note and to keep reattaching that to the top of each page of your draft as you proceed. This helps to ensure that you remain focused on your chosen question. Check the referencing conventions required by your school or department (often MLA, MHRA or Harvard style), and ensure that you use these correctly and consistently. Also check the guidance issued by your department on plagiarism, and ensure that you are confident about the guidelines in this area. Seek advice from your tutor or study support services if any of the above is unclear. Finally, read your final draft of the essay carefully, checking for spelling, grammar, fluency and clarity of argument. Build in time for printing off the final copy and ensure that you do not miss the set deadline!

Helpful Resources

Amigoni, David and Julie Sander, *Get Set for English Literature* (Edinburgh: Edinburgh University Press, 2003).
Creme, Phyllis and Mary R. Lea, *Writing at University: A Guide for Students* (Buckingham: Open University Press, 1997).
Stott, Rebecca, Anna Snaith and Rick Rylance (eds), *Making your Case: A Practical Guide to Essay Writing* (Harlow: Longman, 2001).

WEB RESOURCES

The Poetry Society – site of the UK Poetry Society; useful links and material on contemporary poets and events: http://www.poetrysociety.org.uk/

The Poetry Archive – online archive of spoken poetry: http://
www.poetryarchive.org/poetryarchive/home.do

The Poetry Foundation – well-resourced site, hosted by *Poetry*
magazine: http://www.poetryfoundation.org/

Poetry International Web – features the work of a range of
international writers: http://international.poetryinternational
web.org/piw_cms/cms/cms_module/index.php?obj_name=
international

Poets.org – wide-ranging site run by the Academy of American
Poets; includes biographical information, full texts of some
poems and useful links: http://www.poets.org/

Voices from the Gaps – resources relating to the artistic work of
American and Canadian women of colour. Includes material on
Lorna Dee Cervantes, Gwendolyn Brooks, Rita Dove and many
others: http://voices.cla.umn.edu/

GLOSSARY

Ballad

A poetic form which typically uses four-line stanzas with the metre
alternating between iambic tetrameter (four feet) and trimeter (three
feet). It usually uses an *abcb* or *abab* rhyme scheme. Sometimes fea-
tures repetitions or a refrain. Derives from oral and folk tradition.

Cultural materialism

A critical theory which proposes reading the literary text in relation to
its many historical and cultural contexts. It is only by situating the
text among a tissue of other texts and discourses, and by reading it in
the light of economic conflicts and contradictions, that we might
understand its cultural place and its ideological meanings.

Dramatic monologue

A poem which assumes the voice and persona of a speaker other
than the actual poet.

Elegy

A poem which commemorates and laments a death. It sometimes uses *abab* iambic pentameter quatrains, although elegies are also found in other and free verse forms.

Free verse

Poetry without any formal regularity of rhythm, rhyme or form. Nevertheless, other techniques are sometimes employed in order to structure and shape the poem.

Gender studies

A theoretical approach which examines and critiques the multiple ways in which gender is constructed, assigned, presented and interpreted.

Language poetry

Experimental poetry emerging in the US and UK since the 1960s. It is interested in the materiality of language and in particular in disrupting the conventions (of production and of reception) which characterise the orthodox lyric form. By radically altering the form of the poetry, Language poets foster a new awareness in the reader of their own involvement in the creation of meaning.

L'écriture féminine

This term describes to a set of ideas emerging from French feminist, psychoanalytic and poststructuralist theories of the 1970s and 1980s. L'écriture féminine refers to the practice by which women writers (and indeed some men) are said to challenge the patriarchal 'symbolic order' of language by re-engaging with their own bodily experience – a connection which has been lost to them at the Oedipal moment.

Lyric poetry

The term derives from the Greek word for 'lyre' and originally connoted a poem sung to music. The form has dominated the Western tradition. It is typically fairly short and meditative in tone. It uses an apparently intimate and immediate poetic voice which gives the impression of conveying the speaker's experience of or meditation on a particular subject.

Performative

Theories of gender performativity derive, in the main, from the work of contemporary American theorist Judith Butler, who defines gender as a 'stylised repetition of acts'. Gender, from this point of view, has no essence or point of origin. It is constantly under construction and constantly on display.

Poststructuralism

A late twentieth-century theoretical perspective which develops and implicitly critiques the work of earlier structuralist theories. It attempts to rethink or dismantle the binary oppositions which structuralism works with and to expose the hierarchies implicit in their operation. Poststructuralism is interested in the instability of language and thus of subjectivity, truth and reference. It explores the contradictions and aporia (moments where meaning entirely breaks down) of the text and demonstrates the multiplicity of meanings produced in the process of reading.

Queer theory

Queer theory questions fixed categories of sexuality or sexual orientation. It explores the foundations, limitations and crossovers which define these terms. It shows an interest in literary texts which, like these categories, are provisional and mutable. It rethinks binaries and the hierarchies which accompany them.

Semiotic order

The semiotic order is the pre-symbolic (and pre-Oedipal) order of language. For one of its major proponents, Julia Kristeva, it is associated with the free play of unrepressed desire, and it emerges in a fluid, uncontrolled, free, heterogeneous and entirely pleasurable form of speech.

Slam poetry

A modern form of spoken or performed poetry. It is characterised by dramatic qualities and a political edge. It has strong associations with popular music (from where it borrows some of its rhythmic and metrical devices) and other contemporary popular cultural forms. It is often performed in a competitive environment.

Symbolic order

The symbolic order of language describes the post-Oedipal form of language. For Jacques Lacan, entry into the symbolic order is also entry into a world constructed on difference and on lack. The symbolic order is associated with patriarchal power and is characterised by order, form, homogeneity and control.

Helpful Resources

Belsey, Catherine, *Critical Practice* (London: Methuen, 1980).

Belsey, Catherine and Jane Moore (eds), *The Feminist Reader: Essays in Gender and the Politics of Literary Criticism* (Basingstoke: Macmillan, 1989).

Eagleton, Terry, *Literary Theory: An Introduction* (Oxford: Blackwell, 1983).

Moi, Toril, *Sexual/Textual Politics: Feminist Literary Theory* (London: Routledge, 1985).

Selden, Raman, *A Reader's Guide to Contemporary Literary Theory* (Brighton: Harvester, 1985).

Widdowson, Peter, *Literature* (London: Routledge, 1999).

GUIDE TO FURTHER READING

Anthologies

Adcock, Fleur (ed.), *The Faber Book of 20th Century Women's Poetry* (London: Faber and Faber, 1987).

Armstrong, Isobel, Joseph Bristow and Cath Sharrock (eds), *Nineteenth-Century Women Poets: An Oxford Anthology* (Oxford: Clarendon Press, 1996).

Bernikow, Louise (ed.), *The World Split Open: Women Poets 1552–1950* (London: Women's Press, 1979).

Bolam, Robyn (ed.), *Eliza's Babes: Four Centuries of Women's Poetry in English, c. 1500–1900* (Newcastle: Bloodaxe, 2005).

Couzyn, Jeni (ed.), *The Bloodaxe Book of Contemporary Women Poets: Eleven British Writers* (Newcastle: Bloodaxe, 1985).

Feldman, Paula R. (ed.), *British Women Poets of the Romantic Era* (Baltimore: Johns Hopkins University Press, 1997).

Hulse, Michael, David Kennedy and David Morley (eds), *The New Poetry* (Newcastle: Bloodaxe, 1993).

Kaplan, Cora (ed.), *Salt and Bitter and Good: Three Centuries of English and American Women Poets* (London: Paddington Press, 1975).

O'Sullivan, Maggie (ed.), *Out of Everywhere: Linguistically Innovative Poetry by Women in North America and the UK* (London: Reality Street Editions, 1996).

Rees-Jones, Deryn (ed.), *Modern Women Poets* (Newcastle: Bloodaxe, 2005).

Reilly, Catherine (ed.), *Chaos of the Night: Women's Poetry and Verse of the Second World War* (London: Virago, 1984).

Reilly, Catherine (ed.), *Scars Upon My Heart: Women's Poetry and Verse of the First World War* (London: Virago, 1981).

Rumens, Carol (ed.), *Making for the Open: Post-Feminist Poetry*, rev. edn (London: Chatto and Windus, 1987).

Scott, Diana (ed.), *Bread and Roses: Women's Poetry of the 19th and 20th Centuries* (London: Virago, 1982).

Stevenson, Jane and Peter Davidson (eds), *Early Modern Women Poets: An Anthology* (Oxford: Oxford University Press, 2001).

Wynne-Davies, Marion (ed.), *Women Poets of the Renaissance* (London: Dent, 1998).

Critical Works

Acheson, James and Romana Huk (eds), *Contemporary British Poetry: Essays in Theory and Criticism* (New York: State University of New York Press, 1996).

Armstrong, Isobel, *Victorian Poetry: Poetry, Poetics and Politics* (London: Routledge, 1996).

Bertram, Vicki, *Gendering Poetry: Contemporary Women and Men Poets* (London: Pandora, 2005).

Bristow, Joseph (ed.), *Victorian Women Poets: Contemporary Critical Essays* (Basingstoke: Macmillan, 1995).

Dowson, Jane, *Women, Modernism and British Poetry, 1910–1930: Resisting Femininity* (Aldershot: Ashgate, 2002).

Dowson, Jane and Alice Entwistle, *A History of Twentieth-Century British Women's Poetry* (Cambridge: Cambridge University Press, 2005).

Ford, Karen Jackson, *Gender and the Poetics of Excess: Moments of Brocade* (Jackson: University Press of Mississippi, 1997).

Greer, Germaine, *Slip-Shod Sibyls: Recognition, Rejection and the Woman Poet* (Harmondsworth: Penguin, 1996).

Herbert, W. N. and Matthew Hollis (eds), *Strong Words: Modern Poets on Modern Poetry* (Newcastle: Bloodaxe, 2000).

Gilbert, Sandra M. and Susan Gubar, *The Madwoman in the Attic: The Woman Writer and the Nineteenth-Century Literary Imagination* (New Haven: Yale University Press, 1984).

Gilbert, Sandra M. and Susan Gubas (eds), *Shakespeare's Sisters: Feminist Essays on Women Poets* (Bloomington: Indiana University Press, 1979).

Homans, Margaret, *Bearing the Word: Language and Female Experience in Nineteenth-Century Women's Writing* (Chicago and London: University of Chicago Press, 1986).

Landry, Donna, *The Muses of Resistance: Laboring-Class Women's Poetry in Britain, 1739–1796* (Cambridge: Cambridge University Press, 1990).

Mark, Alison and Deryn Rees-Jones (eds), *Contemporary Women's Poetry: Reading/Writing/Practice* (Basingstoke: Macmillan, 2000).

Marks, Elaine and Isabelle de Courtivron (eds), *New French Feminisms: An Anthology* (Brighton: Harvester, 1981).

Montefiore, Jan, *Feminism and Poetry: Language, Experience, Identity in Women's Writing*, 3rd edn (London: Pandora, 2004).

Ostriker, Alicia, *Stealing the Language: The Emergence of Women's Poetry in America* (London: Women's Press, 1987).

Parini, Jay and Brett C. Millier (eds), *The Columbia History of American Poetry: From the Puritans to our Time* (New York: MJF Books, 1993).

Rees-Jones, Deryn, *Consorting with Angels: Essays on Modern Women Poets* (Newcastle: Bloodaxe, 2005).

Roberts, Neil (ed.), *A Companion to Twentieth-Century Poetry* (Oxford: Blackwell, 2001).

Scott, Bonnie Kime (ed.), *The Gender of Modernism: A Critical Anthology* (Bloomington: Indiana University Press, 1990).

Severin, Laura, *Poetry off the Page: Twentieth-Century British Women Poets in Performance* (Aldershot: Ashgate, 2004).

Index